FINDING MY RADICAL SOUL

FRANCES CROWE
FINDING
MY RADICAL
SOUL

A MEMOIR
with
MARY-ANN DEVITA PALMIERI
& MARCIA GAGLIARDI

FOREWORD by AMY GOODMAN

Haley's
Athol, Massachusetts

With thanks to generous organizational sponsors

AMERICAN FRIENDS SERVICE COMMITTEE of
WESTERN MASSACHUSETTS

CITIZENS AWARENESS NETWORK

FIRST CHURCHES of NORTHAMPTON
PEACE and JUSTICE COMMITTEE

HAYDENVILLE CONGREGATIONAL CHURCH
PEACE and JUSTICE STEERING COMMITTEE

HOUSE of PEACE

IRAQI CHILDREN'S ART EXCHANGE

JONAH HOUSE COMMUNITY

KARUNA CENTER for PEACEBUILDING

MEDIA EDUCATION FOUNDATION

MERRIMACK VALLEY PEOPLE for PEACE

MOUNT TOBY FRIENDS MEETING

MOUNT TOBY FRIENDS MEETING
PEACE and SOCIAL CONCERNS COMMITTEE

NATIONAL PRIORITIES PROJECT

NEW ENGLAND PEACE PAGODA

NORTHAMPTON COMMITTEE to STOP the WARS

NORTHAMPTON FRIENDS MEETING

NORTH SHORE COALITION for PEACE and JUSTICE

NUCLEAR and CARBON FREE FUTURE COALITION of
WESTERN MASSACHUSETTS

PEACE DEVELOPMENT FUND

PEDAL PEOPLE COOPERATIVE

RAGING GRANNIES of WESTERN MASSACHUSETTS

SHUT IT DOWN AFFINITY GROUP

SMITH COLLEGE CENTER for RELIGIOUS and SPIRITUAL LIFE

TRAPROCK CENTER for PEACE and JUSTICE

UMASS DEPARTMENT of AFRO-AMERICAN STUDIES

UMASS HISTORY DEPARTMENT

UMASS SOCIAL THOUGHT and POLITICAL ECONOMY
DEPARTMENT

UMASS WOMEN, GENDER, SEXUALITY STUDIES
DEPARTMENT

WESTERN MASS CODE PINK

WILPF Boston Branch

BROADSIDE BOOKSHOP
ODYSSEY BOOKSHOP
THE SOLAR STORE of Greenfield

Individual donors are listed on Page 283

Haley's
488 South Main Street
Athol, MA 01331
haley.antique@verizon.net
800.215.8805

International Standard Book Number
hardcover: 978-0-9897667-8-4

International Standard Book Number
trade paperback: 978-0-9897667-7-7

International Standard Book Number
eBook: 978-0-9897667-9-1

With special thanks to Caltha Crowe and Connie Harvard.

Photographs and posters from the author's collection unless otherwise credited. Front cover photo of Linda Pon Owen and Frances at Vermont Yankee in 2012 by Marcia Gagliardi. Back cover photo of Frances climbing the Seneca Falls Army Depot fence in 1983 by Nancy Clover.

Haley's gratefully acknowledges use of Frances's words with permission from a book by Tom Weiner, *Called to Serve Vietnam*; from a series of video interviews by Robbie Leppzer of Turning Tide Productions; and from a student thesis by Sarah Hunter.

Library of Congress Control Number: 2014958619
Cataloguing in Publishing data:
Crowe, Frances, 1919-
         Finding my radical soul : a memoir / Frances Crowe ; with Mary-Ann DeVita Palmieri & Marcia Gagliardi ; foreword by Amy Goodman.
         pages cm
ISBN 9780989766784 (cloth)
ISBN 9780989766777 (paperback)
ISBN 9780989766791 (ebook)
1.   Crowe, Frances, 1919- 2. Women pacifist--United States--Biography. 3. Political activists--United States--Biography. 4. Pacifists--United States. I. Palmieri, Mary-Ann DeVita. II. Gagliardi, Marcia. III. Title.
JZ5540.2.C76 A3 2015

for my husband
Tom

and our children
Caltha, Jarlath, and Tom

and our grandchildren
Patrick, Rosa,
Sean, Simone, and Tomas

the Crowe family about 1996
from left, front, granddaughters Rosa and Simone,
Tom and Frances, grandsons Patrick and Sean;
back, Jarlath and Becca, Jerry and Caltha, Tom and Nancy with Tomas

Be aware.
Reflect.
Resist with compassion.
Build community.
Be the change you visualize.
                    —with appreciation to
                    Mahatma Gandhi

Resist with Compassion.
You are great. Thank you,

Frances Crowe
Sept. 16

Contents

Illustrations

Read On, Be Inspired, and Get Active

a foreword by Amy Goodman

What better cause is there to devote one's life to than to the cause of peace?

In your hands is a written record of a life devoted to just this. Frances Crowe is a remarkable woman, and her memoir stands as a tribute to her ongoing activism and also as a lesson to us all about how we might direct our energies to the pursuit of social justice, how to organize, how to weave together the disparate and often conflicting strands of ideals, work, family, and community into a coherent whole.

I first met Frances Crowe through her activism. I wonder how many people can say that? Thousands, no doubt. Frances is a tireless, courageous activist as the stories so personally and colorfully told in these pages clearly demonstrate.

Western Massachusetts has a well-earned reputation—and a hard-earned reputation—as being a center of grassroots peace activism. This didn't emerge out of a vacuum. It's not because there is something special in the water. It is because of focused, dedicated hard work on the part of many, across issues, and across generations. And it is due to the work of Frances Crowe (she writes herein, "I still have trouble receiving gifts and attention," which I choose to ignore).

When we founded the *Democracy Now!* news hour in 1996, we knew that only fifty percent of eligible voters were likely to vote that November. We wanted to know not only why were people not going to the polls but what else were people doing to effect change in their communities? How were people organizing—how were they participating in our democracy, conducting the work of a democratic society on a daily basis, beyond the act of voting on election day? We traveled the country and reported on these issues, domestically and globally, from February through November. After the election, when our show was supposed to end, people called and asked that it continue. They were hungry for alternative perspectives, to hear those who weren't invited into the corporate news studios. So we continued, broadcasting every weekday, now for almost twenty years. From the dozen or so community radio stations that originally carried *Democracy Now!*, the program is now broadcast on more than thirteen hundred stations globally.

Much of that increase in broadcast carriage comes from the efforts of activists in their communities working to bring the show to their local airwaves. Paramount among those activists, without question, is Frances Crowe.

Anyone who knows Frances is familiar with that sparkle in her eye, that impish smile, as she marches into the next organizing battle against seemingly impossible odds. As she details in the book, she spearheaded the campaign to bring *Democracy Now!* to the public airwaves of the Pioneer Valley. "Who was this woman?" we wondered as we sat in our studios in the garret of a hundred-year-old firehouse in New York City's Chinatown.

It was after September 11, 2001, the US was at war, and Frances knew that people needed information in order to organize. But in the lead-up to the invasion of Iraq, the US media system was simply parroting the talking points of the Bush administration. From the US media system, we had endless front-page stories about weapons of mass destruction. When people challenged that official line, they almost never got air time. We regularly had the full debate on *Democracy Now!*, however, and Frances felt that these were the voices that would empower people to actively oppose war. Remember, this was at a time when roughly fifty percent of the American people opposed the war in Iraq. But you never heard their voices in the media. From her perch in Northampton, Frances fought to change that. She tells the story in her chapter on the media in this volume, but she can't know how deeply we appreciate the efforts she made to bring *Democracy Now!* to her commnunity.

As she writes, her activism spans a century from denial of access to athletic facilities as a young girl in Carthage, Missouri to opposition to nuclear arms, the war in Vietnam, South African apartheid, the US's dirty wars in Central America, and onward into the invasions and occupations of Afghanistan and Iraq, our current, seemingly endless wars. She weaves into the tale deeply personal accounts of her family life and the struggle throughout for equality for women.

Frances Crowe is marching still, ever closer to one hundred years of age and smiling as she continues the struggle. She is often found at demonstrations, but her life itself is a demonstration, a demonstration of the joy of resistance.

Read on, be inspired, and get active.

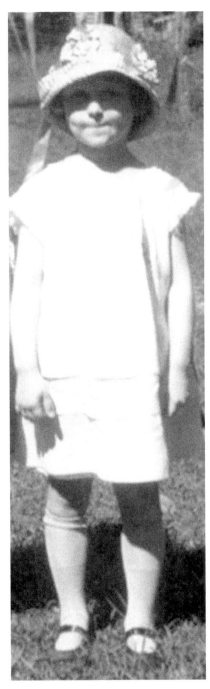

Frances Hyde, 1923

Most of the ministers in town opposed the program and demonstrated in front of the high school against it. I thought about it. Something stirred within me against war and killing. I can remember talking at the dinner table about war and saying emphatically, "I will never go into the army. I'm opposed to training to kill. I admire anyone who refuses to go to war and kill."

Beginnings

Nineteen-nineteen, the year I was born, ushered in a decade of prosperity and optimism. The last shots of World War I, called the "war to end all wars," exploded only months before my birth, and the League of Nations began its challenged existence. My small town of Carthage, Missouri embodied the nationwide climate of hope for a productive, peaceful future.

The fact that I grew up in a small Midwestern town at the end of World War I shaped me in ways that continue to this day. The atmosphere surrounding my childhood fostered a strong antiwar feeling. I remember my mother telling me she took me to my first march when the soldiers from Carthage came home. I was only a baby, but I have always had the feeling that war has defined my life.

When I was little, growing up in a solid Midwestern family, our parents impressed on my three sisters and me the importance of social awareness. Our active, spirited, stay-at-home mother and conscientious father raised us with love and plenty of family time in an observant Roman Catholic home. Looking back, I can see the influence of my early years in the person I would become.

Our parents were good wholesome people struggling to bring up a family. My father, William Chauncey Hyde, a small town businessman, ran his own plumbing and heating business. Our genealogy shows him as Chauncey William Hyde, but he identified himself as William Chauncey Hyde. When his brother started a greenhouse business, my father added a florist shop as part of his store. Plumbing and heating occupied one side of the store; cut flowers and plants occupied the other. At the beginning of highway advertising, he also ran an outdoor advertising business. Large companies, like Coca-Cola and Pepsi, but mostly tobacco companies, advertised along roadways. My father belonged to the local building and loan association, the Rotary Club, and the park board. He saw himself as—and was—a conscientious young businessman.

My father's father, Stephen Hyde, a physician, came from an old English New England family and like many of the men in his family, he had his degree from Williams College. Also, many men in the family were New England Protestant ministers. My father's great-great-uncle Alvan Hyde, the 1790s Presbyterian revivalist, went to Yale Divinity School. We think he taught in Northampton, Massachusetts when he got out of Yale and eventually became a minister in a church in Lee, Massachusetts. I can picture him in his church delivering a two-hour sermon written out in little notebooks filled with his version of a prescription for the moral life.

page from the 1783 notebook of Frances's great-great-uncle, the Presbyterian minister Alvan Hyde: toward the bottom of the page, he writes "Unholy lies and wicked practices are certain evidence to you that you are out of the right way and traveling in the broad road to destruction."

In the 1930s, I made a detour on a trip to a summer camp job to meet one of my New England uncles, another Alvan Hyde, president of a Ware, Massachusetts, bank.

My grandfather Stephen, a physician, didn't follow the path to ministry. His family had moved to Palmyra, New York, where he married Katie Higgins, from Sligo, Ireland. She came to Palmyra during the potato famine and worked in my grandfather's house as a domestic. When he came home from Columbia University School of Medicine in New York City, they fell in love and married. I don't know why they decided to settle in Missouri outside of Carthage. Perhaps there were a lot of people leaving the Northeast because of the flu. Or perhaps it was that my grandmother's background was so obviously different from his family's. He never practiced medicine but taught school and farmed. My grandmother was Catholic and Irish. There's a family story that tells of how my grandmother saved an egg every day when she collected from the hens and then took them to the priest when she went to Carthage.

Life was hard for my grandparents. The land was poor, and my grandfather broke his hip on the farm. In those years, not much could be done for him, and he was on a crutch for the rest of life. The Catholic priest went to visit him once a month, and I suppose they talked. So eventually my grandfather joined the Catholic Church. Then all the children, including my father, became Catholic.

Of my grandparents, my father's father was the only one I knew. He was a pleasant man with a white beard that fell to his chest. He still kept ties with the family in New England. They sent him the Sunday *New York Times, Atlantic Monthly,* and *Harper's Magazine* when they finished with them. He read prodigiously, and when the priest came out, they traded things to read.

My grandparents brought up five boys, including my father, and one girl. All of them prospered. Two succeeded in the greenhouse business when that type of business was emerging. My Uncle Steve always said he had the largest greenhouse west of the Mississippi. He grew tomatoes that he sent to Chicago twice a week when the trains went through. Then he got into growing roses. Another uncle had a greenhouse in Parsons, Kansas.

My father's New England intellectual Protestant background probably had a strong influence on his own outlook on life. I think he had a feeling of being special, from a New England family, the product of ministers and educators. In some ways he felt a little superior, perhaps, to some people on surrounding farms. He enjoyed classical music, learned to play the clarinet, and had a great respect for reading and education. He always

three years before Frances was born, her Hyde family included, from left, front, Lawrence Trudell, Katherine Hyde, Paul Hyde, an unidentified cousin, Margaret Trudell, and Eddie Trudell; second row, Pliney Hyde, Harriette Hyde holding Katie, Frances's grandfather Stephen Hyde, and her grandmother Katherine Higgins Hyde; third row, Stephen Hyde, Sue Hyde, Ed Trudell, Hattie Hyde, Frances's father William Chauncey Hyde, and her mother, Anna Heidlage Hyde had a subscription to *National Geographic* magazine. He also kept in touch with the outdoor life and was an avid fisherman into his old age.

As a Catholic and relative newcomer, my father seemed to walk a very fine line in Carthage. When he was just a boy and walked to town to high school, he said the children would gang up on him and try to beat him up in the beginning of the year. He had a leather book bag, and one day, he filled it with stones. When the young bullies approached him, he started swinging this leather book bag around his head. He told them he was willing to hit them, but he never did. After that, they never bothered him.

Even as a respected businessman he had to negotiate the class structure of Carthage. I remember one time when he picked me up at school to go home for lunch. Everybody went home for lunch in those years. The editor of the newspaper stopped him, berating him and scolding him because the building and loan board had not granted a loan to someone the editor felt should have had the loan. My father just didn't respond. I realized he was humiliated by having someone speak to him like that in front of me. Young as I was, I got the feeling he had to be quiet in order to survive as a businessman and Catholic in Carthage. I suppose my father's response was nonviolent. But I was really angry that anyone would speak to him that way.

My mother, Anna Heidlage Hyde, was a full time homemaker. She was the youngest of a large farm family of German Catholic immigrants. Her parents first lived around Washington, Missouri, not far from Saint Louis, and then they moved to Sarcoxie about twenty miles from Carthage where the land was more fertile. Like other immigrants of the time, they came to the US for new opportunities. They could get land cheaply and have their own farms and large families. That was their dream, and in my mother's family it actually happened.

All of my mother's brothers stayed. They had good land and built productive farms. My Uncle Hugo had a difficult time, however. When he was young, he broke his hip like my father's father and had to manage on one crutch. Their land in Monett wasn't quite as good, but I loved to visit them and have great memories of the fun we had together. They had two boys and a girl. We played down in the valley at an old cabin that they said dated to the Civil War. It was beautiful and remote, and we brought the cows in. They were very poor, but before we went home they always offered us some supper. They popped corn and poured clabbered milk on it for the children. I loved it—like yogurt on popcorn, a really filling meal. His wife was pleasant and hardworking, and their children all turned out well. I felt very close to them.

My mother's older brother Henry had a farm on the prairie in Sarcoxie. I remember Uncle Henry telling my father, "Did you know that they're giving subsidies now? If you don't grow something, they will give you money! It doesn't seem quite right to me, but I think I will put in for some." That must have been the beginning of the farm subsidy program. They had two sons, Norvil and Grover. Grover was my age. He taught me to drive when I was about thirteen. He let me drive an old jalopy down through the fields to bring the cows back. He was a pilot in World War II and unfortunately was killed.

One of my mother's sisters married someone from Germany. When they opened up land in Oklahoma, he went on horseback to find the best land and claimed a piece of bottom land in Chickasha. They, too, succeeded as farmers and had a large family. And like everyone else in my parents' families, even when the parents didn't go to college, the children did.

When my mother was only fifteen, she went to Saint Louis to work as a governess for a family. From that experience, she got a job in Chicago working for the Palmers, one of the families building railroads. There she picked up a lot of what good living could mean—embroidery, silver, fine linen. I have no memory of her looking disordered or unkempt. She dressed very well and liked to shop for nice things, especially for us girls. She had good taste in clothing and decorating. Her hope chest was filled with beautifully embroidered linen hand towels, pillow cases, sheets, and tablecloths. She made many of our clothes when we were young and hand smocked our dresses. My daughter Caltha remembers hand-smocked dresses and Halloween costumes my mother made for her when she was little.

I don't know how my mother ended up in Carthage, but it wasn't far from Sarcoxie where she grew up. She met my father when they were both in their middle twenties. I assume they met through the Catholic Church. Although she left the farm to go to the city, I think she really missed farm life. She told me about how much fun they had at threshing season when everybody came and helped them bring in the hay. Before they put hay in the barn, they had a square dance in the hayloft. Farmers helped one another harvest, coming together for a day. Each farm got help from perhaps five or six other farmers to harvest. Women planned and prepared the meals and set up tables in the yard under the trees. At the end of the day, they had a barn dance. She really missed things about that life when she ended up in Carthage. She didn't find the sense of community that she had on the farm.

My mother and father married in 1914 in Colorado Springs, Colorado. My mother was in Colorado for the summer with her employer, the Palmer family. My father traveled to Colorado for the wedding. His family had a long history in Colorado, as the Hydes had made important contributions to the creation of the YMCA of the Rockies in Estes Park, where people can camp in tents or cabins or hostels and hike the Rockies.

I have an iconic photo of my parents on their wedding day, proudly posed on one of the rock formations in the Garden of the Gods park in Colorado Springs. My mother stands on the dramatic rock in her impeccable white dress, my father in his suit, their first day as a married couple.

Frances's parents William Chauncey Hyde and
Anna Heidlage Hyde on September 29, 1914, their wedding day, in
Colorado's Garden of the Gods park

My parents returned to Missouri by train and settled in a small house in Carthage. There they planned to contribute to their community and have a family of well-educated, successful children whom they could be proud of. That was the image that was held up for us all to aspire to.

My mother was hard working, always cleaning, moving us children through a routine: dressing, meals, out to play, naps, preparation for meals, bed. One of my sister Mary's friends remembered how my mother pushed out all the furniture in a room so she could "really clean." I remember helping her with the laundry, hearing the old washing machine sloshing, sloshing, sloshing, as we fetched out the larger pieces, like cotton throw rugs and quilted coverlets, and bent over stationary laundry tubs in the basement to rinse them by hand before putting them through the wringer. This was when we would talk often about where I was going, what I wanted to do. She strongly urged me to get out of Carthage.

She talked to me a lot about what life was like for her growing up on the prairie around Sarcoxie. She seemed to have been very secure in the farming, small-town community. She never felt poverty, but instead a condition of everyone working the land, together building Middle America—with lots of fun. Our parents wanted us to have everything—the nicest doll carriages in the neighborhood and our own playhouse. I didn't want a playhouse. I wanted a trapeze, so my father built us a trapeze, too. Mother watched carefully whom we played with. She didn't like our neighbors on Clinton Street. She felt they were not good enough for us and wanted us to move to another neighborhood. In fact, I can't remember her feeling that anyone was good enough for me except perhaps one or two of my friends. My mother herself probably felt lonely. Such changes went on in our society then. Because she had high standards for us, Mother often seemed tense.

I definitely put her through a lot. I must have been a very difficult child. When I was seven years old, she planned a surprise birthday party for me. We still napped, and I woke up when the children arrived. I was furious that she planned the party without my having a part in it. In about the fourth grade, I wanted to have lunch at school, just once to take my lunch. My mother agreed, but I didn't get to carry it like everyone else. My father delivered it to me in a large roses box filled with baked potato, creamed beef, and a piece of pie. That made me furious. I just wanted a sandwich in a brown bag like the other children who brought their lunch. I think she thought we were too good for that.

I still have trouble receiving gifts and attention that others plan for me. When I wonder if there is an ulterior motive, I feel self-conscious. I feel embarrassed. Of course, many times, people give gifts or attention with no ulterior motive, and then it makes me feel good. I didn't always dislike positive attention when I was little. But sometimes, because I rebelled, my mother did what she could to keep me in line. Sometimes she punished me. I think she felt she had to so that I would grow up properly. She used

10

Frances, left, with her older sister Harriette, younger sister Marybelle, and her parents Anna and William, about 1924

a soft, flexible branch from the tree usually on my legs or arms. It hurt. I also remember being put to bed for several hours in my youngest sister's crib. I felt insulted and humiliated.

Sundays were always special in our family. They started on Saturday when we cleaned the car and house, polished the silverware, killed one of our chickens, and made noodles and ice cream. Then on Sunday we got dressed up, had homemade cinnamon rolls for breakfast, went to mass and then home for chicken dinner, ice cream, and cake. In the summer, we got our bathing suits together and went off to Sagamount Pools or to the river for an afternoon swim and picnic. I'm exhausted thinking about it, but she loved it. And it wasn't just our family at these Sunday meals. Our next-door neighbor Tom Taylor, closest in age to my youngest sister, remembers being invited to Sunday dinner, always promptly at 12:30. A favorite of my mother, he remembers her fondly. He gave his daughter the middle name Anne in honor of her.

Sometimes Sunday dinner itself became an outdoor picnic. Then we'd have fried chicken, potato salad, and layer cake. We piled into Un-

11

cle Steve's Cadillac. Aunt Sue, Cousin Catherine, and Mother—always dressed in hose, hat, and a clean dress even on a picnic—sat on the back seat. My two sisters sat on jump seats that popped up in front of the back seat, and I sat in the front between Uncle Steve and Father with my youngest sister on Father's lap.

My mother always wanted to learn to swim. As we grew up, I think each of us tried to teach her out at the river. She always wanted to drive too, but unlike swimming, she learned and had a great time driving to the grocery store and doing errands on her own.

Mother loved holidays—making costumes for Halloween and really going all out for Christmas, Easter, May Day, Fourth of July, and the Hyde family reunion. We had such fun going to Joplin to shop for clothes, prom dresses, college outfits, and Christmas presents. We took the trolley car, had lunch, and shopped for shoes, always at Rosenbergs where we got to use the X-ray machine that showed you the bones of your toes in the shoes so you could tell if they fit right.

Mother loved our monthly family outings with Aunt Sue and Uncle Steve. She liked to cook and was a very good cook. She and Aunt Sue had something of a rivalry about who fried chicken the right way. Aunt Sue fried it light, and Mother fried it dark. Mother didn't like it if Father ate more of Aunt Sue's than hers. Mother's special layer cake with white icing and a bitter chocolate drizzle was legendary in the neighborhood.

Frances's Aunt Sue, left, with, from left, Frances's sister Marybelle, Frances, Frances's mother Anna, and Frances's sister Harriette on a Sunday outing at Spring River, Carthage, Missouri

During the Depression, I remember Mother often feeding people who came to the door looking for food. She gave them a broom and told them to sweep the walk in front of the house while she made them two huge sandwiches and a pot of coffee. Then she invited them in to sit at the kitchen table to eat. She often sat with them and asked about their lives while they ate.

Our parents shared deep similar moral and ethical values. They differed in cultural ways: my father's quiet, assumed New England values versus the more outgoing, demonstrative, social, joyful German farm family. Both were quite religious, especially later in life when Catholicism was their base of belief and a great support at difficult times. When we grew up in Carthage, there were no Catholic schools, and our Catholic education came through a class in the Baltimore Catechism.

My mother loved the radio. She listened to Amos and Andy, the popular radio show—what we would now call a sitcom—about residents of Harlem, and Father Charles Coughlin, a controversial Irish Catholic priest, one of the first to use the airwaves to sermonize. Later she became a baseball fan and listened to games. Of course, she never just sat and listened. Rather, she scrubbed the kitchen—the walls, the floor, the woodwork—while she listened. When Carthage got a Pittsburg Pirates farm team, she and my father had a box and went to every game. They loved it.

I think my mother had a good sense about people—who could be trusted and who couldn't be, who was headed for trouble and who was going to be successful. She was a good storyteller and could laugh. I don't ever remember her saying untrue things about people or gossiping. She wasn't a goody, goody; she just had her eye on the prize and plugged away. She gave me a real purpose in life, and I feel extremely fortunate to have been her daughter. She was very proud of all of us and had high expectations for us. I think I am like her in many ways. Later when I returned home after being away, she always showed interest in every detail of my life. She listened, seldom criticized, and just eagerly heard everything. We stayed up late into the night to talk. She shared all the news with me and often wrote to my sisters and me, giving us the news. She trusted me and my adventures. She loved children, especially her grandchildren. My father was interested in what we were doing but not the way Mother was. Her life was our lives.

We were four girls. My older sister, Harriette, was always the obedient one who offered to do the chores. I think my father really wanted me to be the boy. He gave me a carpenter's set with a hammer and saw when I was little. And that must have rubbed off on me somewhat. I

13

Frances's sisters Margie and Marybelle, from left, and Harriette, right, with Frances about 1926

never offered to do housework and, unlike my sisters, wanted a bicycle and to go to summer camp. I was a bit of a rebel from the beginning. I remember once Harriette, who had beautiful curls, decided that she didn't like those curls and wanted me to cut them off. I know I had already cut two on one side when my mother discovered us. She was very unhappy with me, and I was punished. My younger sister, Marybelle, was very social. She had lots of friends and took an interest in music. The youngest, Marjorie, was closest to my father. By that time, he had given up the idea of having a boy.

The first house I lived in, on Clinton Street, was a small bungalow with two bedrooms, one bedroom for my parents and one for the four of us girls. We had a big back yard with a barn, and my father had a playhouse made for us so we could play at housekeeping in the yard. In the beginning, we had a cow and later we had chickens.

When I started at Carthage High School, my father bought a parcel of land in an established neighborhood on Main Street almost across the street from the Mark Twain Elementary School. My parents planned the house. It had an upstairs with four bedrooms, twice as many as the house on Clinton Street, as well as a front porch and a sleeping porch, a formal dining room, a living room, and a kitchen with an eating area.

We walked every place that we needed to go in Carthage and usually at least once a week I walked downtown with my mother when she did the shopping. I learned to ride a bike in the alleyway behind the house. I rode my bike to school every day past large old homes and churches on every corner, imposing Protestant churches, built of limestone quarried in Carthage and polished to look like marble. Carthage had lots of churches. We were not far from the Carthage town square. An apartment building and small commercial college stood nearby, and a few blocks further on, the overall factory. Carthage had two main industries: stone-quarrying and overalls.

Carthage was a small city of about ten thousand people at the intersection of then Route 66 and Route 71 just north of the line that divided North from South during the Civil War. Two major battles took place nearby, and the city almost completely burned down at the hands of pro-Confederates late in the war. I remember people thinking they treated blacks well. I was never conscious of racism as I grew up, but vestiges remained of Missouri's position as a border state during the Civil War. A school for blacks only and a park for blacks only in the southern part of town existed as part of de facto segregation. We attended schools for whites, only, and went to parks for whites. As I look back, I realize that we called a black woman who worked for my mother Lillian, her first name, and probably I never knew her last name. I certainly don't remember it. On the other hand, we called a white woman who worked for my mother Mrs. Pratzman, and I probably never knew her first name.

For a while, Lillian worked for my mother to help out cleaning and ironing. She had two daughters in college. I remember sitting in the kitchen talking with Lillian, who sometimes joined our whole family for lunch. Also Robert, a black man, came and did outdoor work for us. He did the shoveling and raking and the heavy lifting, moving the summer furniture inside or outside depending on the season. My father brought home used billboard paper from the side of the road when advertising signs came down, and Robert helped my mother line the entrance to the cellar with it to keep down mud and dust. Robert and Lillian both lived in the southern part of town where the railroad tracks came through. I don't think my parents were racist, but they did accept the status quo.

Mrs. Pratzman sometimes took care of us. She baby-sat us but also did some chores around the house. If my mother went out in the afternoon to shopping or church meetings, we went down to Mrs. Pratzman's house. Those were memorable occasions for me. Although she was white, she lived in the black community. When she was at our house, Mrs. Pratzman let me put on the record player and turn the Victrola crank for music—

waltzes, Sousa's marches. When we went to her house, we walked there, the forbidden area of town, to her small snug house. She had no electricity or indoor plumbing, just an outhouse with a hand pump at the sink, and a wonderful garden. We stayed with her until my father picked us up. I loved it there because she had a garden and chickens that were running free and a well, the kind of simple life that appealed to me even then. My sister later told me that we probably called her Mrs. Pratzman rather than by her first name because she didn't have a husband and did have a son and the title added respectability. I wonder now if it had something to do with her being white as well.

Classism made itself evident in Carthage. I was more conscious of that than I was of racism. If you came from the farm or from a working class background, people not from a farm or the working class looked down on you. A society column in the local newspaper presented people the paper thought deserved admiration, and people emulated them. The column reported on so-called "society"—who had lunch where, parties, engagements, and weddings, almost as if Carthage had débutantes. It was crazy, but I later realized that Carthage had no monopoly on small-town newspaper society pages in the early and mid twentieth century. The so-called society people evidently tried to imitate Saint Louis society. If you didn't run with that crowd, then to them you didn't matter. The working class had no place in so-called Carthage society during those years.

Churches had importance in town, too. My impression was that the wealthy of Carthage were mostly Episcopalian. My parents attended a very small Catholic church with maybe just two dozen families. The small parish did not have enough resources to have a school. Also the Ku Klux Klan was very active in our area at the time. They even targeted me one time as a Catholic. When someone threw stones at me on my way to school, I felt certain they were children of Klan members.

One of my friends brought home to me one day just where Catholics stood in the scheme of things in Carthage. We walked home from school as I first got to know her, and she told me, "I always cross the street when I pass the Catholic church. They have guns in the basement. That side door that goes to the basement—that's where they store the guns."

I was incredulous. I knew what she said didn't have an ounce of truth. "What?" I asked. "That's the coal bin."

"No," she insisted. "They are putting weapons in there." When I asked why, she answered, "They're going to rise up against the people of Carthage."

When I asked my parents about it, they just looked at each other and said, "That's interesting." They knew there were no guns, and they may

Frances, second row, right, with her sisters and cousins, about 1925

have read prejudice against Catholics between the lines. My friend's parents were part of the up and coming culture of Carthage. Her father had his own business, and they were on the rise.

Classism, racism, and religious intolerance all percolated there in Carthage under the surface. I remember when I was about five years old, my mother and I walked by the jail as we always did on the way downtown, and I saw a fence going up around the jail yard. When I asked my mother about that fence, she said that she didn't know. But that night as my father watered the garden, I heard him talking to the next-door neighbor also watering his garden. The neighbor asked my father if he was getting tickets for the hanging. My father said, "No, of course not."

When I asked my father to tell me more, he didn't want to talk to me about it. I kept after him until he told me the authorities planned to hang someone in the jail yard and were giving out free tickets to the execution. It made me angry that people would celebrate someone's death as if it were a show. My father didn't want tickets. He opposed capital punishment and thought it inhumane to make a public spectacle of a hanging. But a quiet, obedient businessman, he wouldn't speak out because he knew the climate of the community. It made me angry that his business interests kept him from being more honest and open about his feelings. But I'm sure he felt that he had to keep quiet if he expected to be successful. I think my questioning of a lot of things that were going on began then.

In the fifth grade, some girlfriends and I formed an International World Peace Friendship Club that met at a teacher's home. We made fudge and wrote to people all over the world. We took ourselves very seriously, all these little children working to make peace.

One of my mother's nieces, Rebecca Frye had a strong influence on me as I grew up. She taught physical education at the University of Oklahoma. Every summer she went to New York and taught phys ed at the New York University summer camp on the Hudson River. When she visited, she took the bus to our house and spent the weekend. Then we put her on a bus to New York. We always went swimming with Rebecca. She helped me develop my stroke and taught us children the wonderful songs that she sang at camp. I loved her visits and decided I wanted to be a physical education teacher like her. My mother admired her. She represented freedom, independence, and getting on with your life through taking advantage of opportunities. She nurtured in me a pattern that shaped my summers for most of my school years. From high school through college, I never spent a summer at home and went always to one camp or another.

My father influenced me to start swimming and going to summer camp. It all started when a woman from the local YMCA came to see my father about his annual contribution. One of my father's relatives, Albert Alexander Hyde who invented Mentholatum Deep Heat Rub, actively supported the national YMCA and established the Estes Park YMCA in Colorado.

My father always gave to the local Y. A family man with four daughters, my father said to that woman raising funds, "I know you have a nice swimming pool, but it is not open to women, and I'm going to withhold my contribution until you have swimming for women. I want my girls to learn to swim." I was so proud of him. The Y decided that girls could have swimming lessons from seven to nine in the morning. I think it was three mornings a week. My mother got us up very early, because we had to walk to the Y and, of course, we could not eat later than an hour before swimming class. In those days, we believed our food had to be digested or we would get cramps while we swam.

Swimming at the Y led to my first summer at camp and the first time I felt I had a chance to get out of Carthage. I was about eleven years old when the head of the YMCA came to see my father to talk to him about sending Harriette to a new summer camp the Y sponsored in the Ozarks. I guess he figured if my father wanted us to learn to swim, he would want to send us to camp. Harriette wasn't sure about the whole thing and said she wouldn't go unless I did. I didn't hesitate and said, "I'd love to go!" And so off we went to camp for two weeks.

Harriette got homesick the second day. She called our parents and said, "I want to come home."

When they came down to get her, I asked, "Since Harriette's not using her time, can I stay another two weeks?" I ended up staying for the rest of the month that summer.

So began my understanding of a world outside of Carthage I could move into. In following summers, I ended up being a camp counselor first in the nearby Camp Fire Girls camp, then in the Girl Scout camp in Joplin where I was a junior counselor in a cabin. Later in other camps, I worked on the waterfront and had responsibility for a unit, which included several cabins. I worked at a camp near Saint Louis and when I was in college, I worked every summer at a different camp. One year I went to Wisconsin, and another year, I went to Plymouth, Massachusetts. I so loved the camp life, the out of doors, community, camaraderie, and camp songs.

One of my first demonstrations involved physical education. The city undertook construction of a new gym for boys at the high school, and my

Frances, back row left, on a swimming excursion, with her sisters and cousins

friends and I wanted a gym for girls. We decided to mobilize. We drafted a petition asking why the school planned no gym for girls. The father of one of my friends was the principal of the high school. We went to him, and he commended us. "I support you," he said succinctly. So we got a lot of signatures and presented our petition to our friend's father. He took it to the school committee. He thanked us and said we had done a good job, expressed our needs, and gotten signatures. But we did not succeed. The school committee told us it was a very good idea but the budget didn't have enough money. Eventually the town built a big gym for the boys next to the high school. The gym did not include girls, and the school committee didn't even put us in the old gym in the Elks Lodge.

In our high school in 1935, the administration discussed the possibility of introducing the Junior Reserve Officer's Training Corps (JROTC). Common in high schools at the time, this program offers military training to high school students. Most of the ministers in town opposed the program and demonstrated in front of the high school against it. I thought about it. Something stirred within me against war and killing. I can remember talking at the dinner table about war and saying emphatically, "I will never go into the army. I'm opposed to training to kill. I admire anyone who refuses to go to war and kill."

"You wouldn't say that if you had lived through World War I and had to use brown sugar and brown bread instead of white sugar and white flour," my father said. He remembered the rationing his family experienced during the war when Americans accepted hardships to demonstrate their support for the war against the Axis. But even at a young age, I understood that, while he had experienced great inconvenience in order to support the war effort, no cause justified war's sanctioned killing or risk of dying. My questioning of war began then.

Although my father and mother always encouraged my independence and standing up for what needed to be done, my father thought I should stay in Carthage, go to the local business college, and get an office job working at the factory that made overalls. But my mother had a different idea. One day as I helped her with the wash, she urged me to leave.

"Frances, you've got to get out of Carthage," she said. "You've got to make your own life. Don't do what so many of the girls do and go to work at one of the factories. Don't go to commercial college. You can do more with your life." So when my father encouraged me to stay in Carthage, my mother was adamant, "No, Frances will get a college degree and then she will figure out what she wants to do with the rest of her life."

I think she always felt that Carthage was very class structured with a power elite that one could not overcome. On one level she was very ambitious for us to be part of it, although the power elite really did not do much that I might consider useful or ethical. Money was their chief value. My mother knew I was too rebellious and would never adjust nor fit in, so I should find my place elsewhere.

Despite my father's wishes, all of us left Carthage except for my oldest sister Harriette. Marybelle went to the University of New Mexico after spending time at Stephens College in Columbia, Missouri. In New Mexico, she met her husband Halim El Dabh, a Fulbright scholar from Egypt who specialized in musicology, provided choreography for Martha Graham, and became a professor at Kent State University in Ohio. Marybelle worked as a social worker in Boston where she ran a settlement house program to serve the immigrant population of the South End and, when she moved to Kent, she continued her career in social work. Many years later, after graduating from Stephens, my youngest sister Margie went to the University of Colorado and studied geology. She married Russell McLellan, a mining engineer. Margie taught junior high science in Boulder, Colorado.

Harriette also went to Stephens College, then to Pittsburg State University in Pittsburg, Kansas, where she got a degree in education. Harriette married Jack Murray, a designer and commercial artist. They lived

Frances's sisters Harriette and Margie, from left, and Marybelle, right, with Frances about 1954

22

in Kansas City for some years. When my mother died, Harriette, Jack, and their children John and Sarah moved back to Carthage to help my father at home and in the floral business. When my father retired, Harriette and Jack took over the business. Before her marriage, Harriette taught elementary school.

All my sisters have died, but we all had children, and many of the cousins keep up their family ties. My daughter Caltha, with help from her cousins, organized a reunion five years ago in Estes Park, Colorado. Caltha, with her brothers pitching in, got another reunion together three years ago at Mount Desert Island in Maine. She also planned a gathering for her daughter Rosa's wedding in Colorado in 2013. Nearly all of my sisters' children, all of my children, and nearly all of my grandchildren attended. Family members traveled from the east coast, the west coast, and as far away as Nicaragua. I am so happy that all of us Hyde girls have produced these children and grandchildren who enjoy life, pursue varied and fulfilling interests, and want to stay in touch.

Carthage, a close-knit family, growing up in the aftermath of World War I, and some awareness of the social turmoil of the time set me on a path for life that required social responsibility. A certain amount of travel, camp, athletics, and my parents' tolerance of my rebellious spirit fostered curiosity, adventure, and perhaps above all a feeling that encouraged me to live my life and be useful in the world.

Frances and Tom Crowe on VJ Day 1945
on an island in the Gulf of Mexico near New Orleans

The US had dropped an atomic bomb on Hiroshima, Japan. Almost instantaneously I was against war. "There has to be some way to stop this madness," I thought. I unplugged the iron and went out on the streets of the New Orleans French Quarter looking for some way to confront the insanity of war. I had to find somebody interested in nonviolence.

Beyond Carthage

I left Carthage as America became more prosperous after World War I and industrialization matured. Then, as World War II loomed, I could not escape the issues of the day. No one could, and like many other Americans, I wanted to be involved. By the time World War II ended, however, I harbored no doubt that war, weapons, and the nuclear bomb have no use. On the way to that conclusion, I got my college degree, moved to New York City, and worked in the war industry. And met and married my husband Tom.

Like my sisters I went to Stephens College, a two-year women's college in Columbia, Missouri, in the center of the state. The college had innovative courses and encouraged women to develop roles and skills for the modern world. When I went to Stephens, I wanted to major in physical education because I wanted to be a gym teacher like my cousin Rebecca. In high school, we didn't have many sports activities open to girls. One teacher in the sixth or seventh grade thought women should get more exercise. She asked us girls each to bring an old broom handle to school. Then she lined us up outside at recess to do exercises. I loved the feeling of swinging the wooden stick and stretching my body, which never did get taller than five feet, two inches. It was good exercise, but it wasn't exactly formal physical education.

When I got to Stephens, I tried out for the swimming team. I thought I swam pretty well. I had swum at the Y for years, had gone to summer camp every summer, and did stroke training with my cousin Rebecca. But my competition at Stephens had trained on swim teams in big city high schools, so I didn't have much of a chance. I played on the soccer and field hockey teams at different times, but I really stressed myself out trying to keep up with young women who seemed like pros to me. After two years of that, I thought, "I don't think I want to spend the rest of my life pursuing a career in physical education."

I became a dorm counselor at Stephens as a way to help pay my tuition. Working with students, I took an interest in psychology. The psychology courses I took at Stephens centered on studying personality, motivation, and interrelationships. We took courses that exposed us to a range of subjects and work opportunities. The college considered itself progressive and provided a good transition for my sisters and me. Stephens gave us a chance to gain independence and learn to be comfortable with college life so when we went on to a university, we had confidence in our possibilities for success.

After my two years at Stephens, I considered where I wanted to continue my education. One of my friends talked about going to Bryn Mawr. She wanted to go to an eastern women's college. I liked that idea, because I had a vision of getting back to my Hyde roots in New England. I wanted to understand that part of my background. But my friend and I also talked about going to France for a year. We thought about traveling in the French countryside and going to a French university. It was a crazy idea at the time, because neither of us spoke French and Germany seemed ready to begin its occupation of France. With the war in Europe threatening, we crossed studying in France off our list of possibilities. Also, I wanted to go to a school where the weather would sometimes be cold.

In the Stephens Library, I found that Syracuse University in New York had a strong psychology major and also a resident assistants' program for dorm counselors similar to the Stephens program. Syracuse also had a strong reputation for media and propaganda studies, always intriguing to me. Even in elementary school when my father's business included putting advertising billboards up on the highway, I told him, "I don't believe in advertising that forces opinions on people." Syracuse looked like a college that my parents could afford. And I qualified for admission. From the beginning, Syracuse suited me well. I started out as a resident assistant in a small house, and in my second year—my fourth in college, because of Stephens—I was a counselor in the same house.

It was a big trip from Carthage to Syracuse, more than eleven hundred miles. I took the train, and the ride took more than a day. In those days, when people attended school far away from home, they weren't able to go back and forth for holidays and breaks. Phone calls were a luxury, and when we communicated with people back home, it was most likely by letter.

At Syracuse, I took a class in industrial psychology that focused on time and motion studies, and I see evidence of it to this day in my approach to housekeeping. I also took a philosophy course taught by someone opposed to war. Young men in the class talked about the Catholic Worker movement founded in 1933 by Dorothy Day. During the Depression, Catholic Workers set up shelters and soup kitchens for the poor and embraced the cause of peace in the world. I didn't get to know the young Catholic Workers very well then and regret that I didn't follow up and question them about their beliefs, which I probably would have endorsed. I often wish I had acted on those leanings earlier. I guess I just wasn't ready. I wasn't aware. But even then I read a lot—not escapist reading. I read to learn about how the world worked and what was going on in the world.

Also during my years at Syracuse, I tried to figure out how I stood in relation to religion. I applied to the Catholic sorority. The sorority sisters turned out to be young women I admired and whose company I enjoyed. I lived at the sorority for one semester during my second year. At the same time, I began seriously to question Catholicism and its beliefs, particularly its policies about women. It wasn't the first time I'd chafed about something I associated with Catholicism. I remember once having an encounter with the priest when I was about seven or eight or maybe a little younger. He scolded me for something about the catechism, and I said, "It's just questions and answers you have to memorize that no one really explains, and I don't really understand."

"When you grow up you will," he told me. That answer didn't satisfy me then nor does it now.

Even though not more than fifty people participated in our Carthage Catholic parish, my mother and father whole-heartedly lived their Catholic faith with us. When I told my mother after college I no longer practiced Catholicism, she said, "I will pray for you because you are missing something. It is the center of my life. I worry for you that you won't have the comfort from this belief that I have."

In 1940 and 1941, the women in the Catholic sorority raised questions about the attitude of the Catholic church toward women and ministry. We also questioned the church's attitude toward family planning. Through the Catholic sorority, I found out about a discernment group at Syracuse's Saint Thomas More House Catholic Student Foundation. People met on Friday nights to talk about doubts about their faith and goals in their lives. At the first meeting I attended, the priest leading the group appealed to other students and me. He opened himself to the group's questioning. I found the give and take discussion a perfect way to examine my beliefs and doubts.

Not long after, I sat in mass one Sunday and felt the questions of the discernment group touching my conscience. I thought, "This isn't me. This isn't right," and I got up and walked out.

I met my husband Tom at Saint Thomas More House while he was in medical school. He went to undergraduate school at Syracuse and when I got there he was a poor struggling medical student.

Tom graduated from Crosby High School in Waterbury, Connecticut in the early 1930s. He received a classical education and earned top honors. His parents wanted him to receive an appointment to Annapolis for a tuition-free education. He qualified and went, but it turned out not to be a good place for him, and he left. His older brother Tim came to the rescue. Tim worked in the insurance business in upstate New York. He said, "Don't stop now. Go to Syracuse." Tim went to Syracuse himself and knew its programs. Tom paid attention to his brother who, along with their sister, a teacher, assisted Tom financially to attend Syracuse. He also received a scholarship and worked in a fraternity for his food and in Saint Thomas More House for his room. He did well academically and got into medical school there without any trouble.

One of Tom's jobs at Saint Thomas More House involved setting up chairs for group meetings. He joined some groups, including the discernment group. I got to know him there and found him the most interesting person in the room. He seemed to know so much more than I did and had great insight. Tom and I had interesting discussions at the tea breaks. He, too, had doubts about his Catholic faith, so we talked about the church and our own beliefs.

That first Christmas at Syracuse, the sorority had a Christmas dance. They wanted me to go, but I said that I didn't know anyone. One of the women said, "Ask Tom. He doesn't go to anything social." So I got up my courage and asked him. It amazed him that someone would invite him to a dance, but he accepted. He wasn't the greatest dancer, but neither was I. We nevertheless had some good discussions on the dance floor.

We saw each other during the rest of our time at Syracuse. He had no money to go on a conventional date (and in those days, the man always paid), so we took long walks on and off the Syracuse campus, and that's the way we got better acquainted. Tom came from an Irish Catholic family in Waterbury. Both his parents emigrated from Ireland. His father was a fireman, and his parents had brought up six children, five of whom went to college. I felt his values equaled mine. His family stressed education and making a success of oneself just as my family did. From the beginning, our values were in sync, and we found it easy to talk to each other about what we thought and struggled with.

Our families met for the first time when we graduated from Syracuse, me as an undergraduate with a bachelor's degree and Tom as a doctor with an MD. I introduced Tom to the rest of my family, and I met his parents, brother, and sister-in-law. The only thing I remember from that first visit was my youngest sister saying, "His socks don't even match." I found out later that he told his mother, "That's the woman I'm going to marry."

Then Tom went to Hartford to intern at Saint Francis Hospital, and I went back to Missouri to work as a dormitory counselor at Stephens. Former students often returned to Stephens to live as counselors in the dorms for room and board and a small stipend.

When I graduated from Syracuse, that fall back at Stephens, my younger sister Marybelle was in her second year at the college. During that year, she became very ill. She coughed a lot, but no one could find out what caused her illness. One morning when I went to visit her, I found her asleep in her dormitory. I took her to the infirmary and asked them take an X-ray of her lungs. I went back to work where they called me from the health center and said I should get right over there. The X-rays showed she had an advanced case of tuberculosis. I was devastated. I had to get her out of class and tell her the diagnosis. She was the fifth girl from our high school who had come down with TB.

In retrospect, someone should have realized something was seriously wrong with Marybelle. She had fainting spells in high school and weighed as little as eighty pounds, but our local doctor concluded that she was "going through normal teen years." When she rode to Syracuse with the family the summer before for my graduation, she spent the entire trip stretched across the back seat on her sisters' laps.

Because our local sanitariums had an unpleasant reputation, my parents decided Marybelle should stay at home and the family would take care of her. Marybelle spent five years in bed on her back, particularly difficult for the most social among us sisters. She had a hard time. TB carried a stigma, and her friends feared they would catch it from her. Marybelle recalled that my father told her when he saw the local doctor who failed to diagnose the TB, the doctor said, "But you were such a nice family!"

Poor Marybelle thought it was somehow her fault, and in some ways, my parents seemed to think so, too. Mother kept house meticulously, but people erroneously thought unwholesome living conditions caused the disease. Mother often scrubbed down Marybelle's bedroom from top to bottom. She gave her a hot toddy each evening before supper to stimulate her appetite and struggled to get extra rations for Marybelle, as all this occurred during World War II and food rationing. Some of her friends, however, remained loyal, especially our young next door neighbor Tom who crossed the yard to play games with her every afternoon after school. My youngest sister, Margie, still lived at home and gave her some company, but Margie too complained about how lonely she was during that time because other people thought she carried tuberculosis and they might come down with it.

For more than two years, Marybelle had to undergo twice weekly procedures with air inserted between the wall of her chest and the outside of her lungs to compress the lungs and close the cavities that held the tuberculosis bacillus. A few years later as Marybelle emerged from her illness, Tom and I helped get her into a program at Saranac Lake in New York. The town was well known for its "Cure Cottages," and they had a reentry program that helped TB victims return to work and school after their long convalescence. She went for a year, and then the administration asked her and a friend to leave. Because they often went to town or didn't always follow the strict rules, the administration considered them a bad influence on other patients. My parents gave her three hundred dollars a month and money for a train ticket. She and her friend headed for Arizona where the climate would be good for her, but instead they stopped in Albuquerque, New Mexico where she entered the University of New Mexico.

I was still working at Stephens in December 1941 when the Japanese bombed Pearl Harbor. The war in Europe had raged since 1939, but this act drew the US into the conflict. Some of the girls in the dormitory I supervised had fathers in Pearl Harbor. It was such a big event, and I began thinking, "What am I doing here? I need to get involved in the war effort." Like so many others, I was swept up in war hysteria.

Tom decided to go into the army as a physician. The whole ethos of the time was commitment to the war. He volunteered and signed up to be in the infantry as the unit physician.

Captain Tom Crowe, unit physician

32

I tried to think of a way to get involved. I thought about the WACs (Women's Army Corps), the WAVES (Women Accepted for Volunteer Emergency Service/US Naval Reserve[Women's Reserve]), and the American Red Cross. None of those appealed to me. I couldn't accept the authority of the armed services, and the Red Cross didn't seem to offer the kind of involvement I wanted.

Then I saw in *The New York Times* that Mount Holyoke College in South Hadley, Massachusetts offered a summer institute in industrial supervision called Engineering, Science, Management, and Defense Training for Women. It was designed to help women go into industry to replace men going off to fight. I thought that sounded interesting and decided to explore it. I applied, got into the program, and in the summer of 1942 went to Mount Holyoke.

The program provided its graduates with an entrée into wartime industries where they might find a job. With thousands of men joining the armed forces, manufacturing companies wanted to find and train women to take over for them. Factories geared up to build the planes, vehicles, ships, armaments, ordnance, and supplies for war. The course at Mount Holyoke trained me to help women make the transition to war work. The US Office of Education sponsored the course in cooperation with Northeastern University, Boston.

Twenty-five of us took the course. Almost half had recently graduated in 1942. I was just slightly older than they but considerably younger than some of the women who got their degrees in the 1920s and 1930s. The course emphasized "personnel administration, special problems of supervision, labor relations, and shop practice." The "shop practice" meant going to Holyoke, an industrial city south of South Hadley, to learn about life in a factory. We operated machines and worked under conditions of actual production. We lived in Porter Hall at Mount Holyoke. Courses in the syllabus included Women in the Production Program of Great Britain; Organization of a Personnel Department; Problems of Women Workers in Aircraft Production; What Supervisors Should Know about Organized Labor. Meanwhile, planes from Westover Air Force Base in nearby Chicopee kept flying over us headed to the war in Europe while we attended class. The war effort took place all around me, in the classroom and in the air.

I got a job right away. And a lot of program graduates did. A survey of women who finished the course found them working at Western Electric as invoice checker; at Chase Brass and Copper Company as production line inspector; at Bendix as radio tester and calibrator; at Squibb and Company as trainer and interviewer; at Morey Machinery

Company as assistant to the president; at Liberty Mutual Insurance as claims adjuster.

I found work at Sperry Gyroscope on Long Island. The company made gyroscopes for submarines and ships. I decided to live in Manhattan, where I found a room at International House at 500 Riverside Drive near Columbia University where I planned to do graduate work in psychology. I had a fine room for seventy-five dollars a month. I shared a bath and lived on the fourth floor, an all women's floor in the front looking out over the Hudson River. Every morning when I got up, I counted ships that had come into the river that night.

Unfortunately, at Sperry everything seemed disorganized. After taking the long commute out to Long Island on two or three subways and the commuter rail, I had a desk and nothing to do. "Don't worry," my boss said. "The work will start. For now sit at your desk and read *The New York Times.*" Sitting around and waiting did not appeal to me. So I took it upon myself to go out and talk to people working in the factory, particularly women, and ended up writing an employees' handbook for women.

Management and women employees didn't know what it meant to have women on the job in a previously nearly all-male environment any more than I did. So I thought, "I'll try to find out what they're supposed to do." And that became the handbook. I talked with employees about what they needed to know and went to supervisors to find out rules regarding situations like lunch hours, conditions for the job, emergencies, and bathroom breaks. People had been assembled rapidly, and it mattered to workers and supervisors to define conditions.

After a while, I decided to change jobs. Commuting so far took a lot of time, and Sperry remained disorganized. However, because I took the course at Mount Holyoke with government funding, I couldn't accept just any job. The training obligated me to work with a war-related industry. I looked around and got a job at the Bell Telephone Laboratories in Greenwich Village. A well-established firm, Bell developed radar and communications systems for the war. The company had a cafeteria and medical system for the workers. It had a women's division with its own personnel department with women in charge, and that's where I worked. I found it refreshing to be working with women.

Bell Labs wanted to find women to take the place of former male employees then off at war. Like other war industries, Bell guaranteed military war veterans their jobs when the war ended. Women would step aside to honor the commitment, but at the time in 1942, the end of the war seemed a long way off. One of my duties was to recruit young high school women graduates with a background in science or math for engineering firms developing radar for the war. After a brief stint as recruiter, most of my work took place at the plant. I helped set up day and night care to accommodate children of women workers. I also helped organize an escort service to and from the subway for women at night and, building on my experience at Sperry, wrote an employee handbook.

It's interesting, though, how you do things at a given time without considering the implications. My responsibilities involved signing people up to work at the firm. They had to sign an inventor's contract saying that they would not claim credit for any invention they worked on and that they released all rights to any invention. For giving up all their rights to their work, Bell gave them a dollar, and they willingly signed. I didn't think too much about it. I just went along. It astonishes me now that I did not question this unfair practice. In hindsight, I realize that the corporate war culture had grabbed my mind.

I got to Bell Labs by a much easier commute than I had going to Sperry. At a station not far from International House, I got on the A Train, the Seventh Avenue subway. The A Train still goes straight down to Twelfth Street, where I got off and walked a few short blocks to work. It often took less than half an hour versus the hour and a half or two I spent going to Long Island.

I had no problem living in the city. I liked it. Only once when I had been out on Long Island, I came back and got on the wrong subway and ended up in East Harlem, then not considered a safe place by many white people. I had a map and realized International House was not very far across the park. "I'll just walk," I thought.

A mounted policeman approached. "I don't think that's a good idea," he told me. "You should get back on the subway." That was the only time anyone warned me to be careful. I had a great sense of freedom in New York, and I got to know the city well.

With the job at Bell Labs, I could more easily do graduate work. So besides working forty-eight or fifty-two hours a week six days a week, I took classes at Columbia at night, including with Seymour Melman who would become well known for his theories of industrial psychology. Classes in psychology seemed more and more irrelevant to me, however, and they didn't hold my interest. I wanted to understand more about why we were at war, and the courses I took at Columbia didn't serve. I heard about the New School for Social Research offering courses on world politics, and I decided to leave Columbia. The New School was close to my work. From 1934, its University in Exile provided refuge for scholars fleeing anti-Semitic persecution in Germany. Refugees from Russia and Germany brought fresh perspective, and I took their courses for insight into circumstances surrounding the war in Europe.

I also took an adult education class in industrial psychology at the Jefferson School of Social Science operated by the Communist Party on Sixth Avenue and Twelfth Street. The Jefferson School opened its adult education program in 1943, and not long after, I took a class in Soviet propaganda. During the Red Scare and Joseph McCarthy's pursuit of American Communists, the Jefferson School experienced persecution. The Jefferson School closed in 1956 as part of the upheavals in the American Communist Party resulting from revelations about violence in the Josef Stalin regime.

During those days, I regularly read *PM*, a progressive small-format daily newspaper. The Chicago millionaire Marshall Field III financed *PM*, and among its writers were I. F. Stone and Theodore Geisel, later known as Dr. Seuss. Influenced by studies and reading, my thoughts more and more questioned the war and our government. New York provided a great environment for experiencing progressive ideas.

New York not only provided challenging ideas. I found opportunities to keep up with the physical activity I loved. At the New Dance Group in Greenwich Village, I took a dance class with Pearl Primus, an ethnographer and talented interpreter of African dance. She helped us perform unusual exercises in modern dance that stretched the body and lifted the soul. After class I once felt so energized that I walked home all the way to the International House, a distance of more than a hundred blocks or about eight miles.

Living at International House gave me added perspective, and I very much enjoyed it. Founded by a YMCA official, it intentionally gave people from around the world a place to live and learn from each other while they attended Columbia University. I met people from all over the US and other countries. One woman, a Jew who had escaped Germany, helped me understand wartime Germany. She couldn't afford to eat in the cafeteria downstairs, and I sometimes saw her boiling an egg or fixing toast in one of the kitchenettes on each floor. For the first time, I became conscious of the long history of Israel several years before recognition of the State of Israel.

Living at International House and working in New York exposed me to ideas and perspectives I had not encountered in Missouri or Syracuse. I learned about the suffering of war victims and inequities causing war and resulting from it. By the end of my three-and-a-half-year stay in New York, I was ready to say, "War is not the answer."

When I first lived in New York City, Tom trained with the army infantry in Pennsylvania, where he acted as physician to the unit. He went on long marches to get toughened up. He said mostly he took care of blisters. He came to see me in the city a few times, and I managed to visit him once in Pennsylvania. After training, he received orders to ship out and, as was the practice of the wartime military, he could not reveal where his duties would take him. The future became very uncertain, and through an unspoken understanding, our correspondence slowly ended. He disappeared from my life for three years, a not unusual circumstance for couples during the war.

He got in touch with me late in 1944 when he was transferred to a troop ship bringing men home from Panama. First he contacted a couple of people in New York who knew me and asked them where I lived and how he could reach me. The first person he called wouldn't tell him, but someone else said, "I think she's at International House."

"Are you still there?" he asked when he telephoned. "I'm in town and I want to see you." So we got together.

Tom came into port at New Orleans once a month and, compliments of the military, flew to New York each month to visit me for a few days. We renewed our relationship and pretty much picked up where we left off. I still worked at Bell Labs, though, and could not easily take off time during the day. After maintaining our relationship for about seven months with Tom's trips to New York, we decided that I would move to New Orleans, and we would get married and live there. So, in May of 1945, we got married.

In New Orleans, I worked at a few jobs—as a proofreader at Jackson Barracks that ended in disaster because I was a terrible proofreader and as a personnel officer at Godchaux's, a long time department store in downtown New Orleans. It didn't much bother me that I didn't find work I wanted to do. I was ready to make the transition to being married and having a family, which in the 1940s pretty much meant not having a job. After the war, women expected to go home and back to the ironing board after the men returned. I didn't think much about it, because I was ready to do just that—leave my job at Bell Labs and become a homemaker. Many years later, I saw the film *Rosie the Riveter* in Greenfield in the United Radio, Electrical, and Machine Workers Union hall. Everyone laughed, but tears rolled down my face. I hadn't thought about myself as one of those women who worked like a man and then obediently gave it all up when the men returned. But that's just what women then, including me, did.

Mr. and Mrs. William Chauncey Hyde

announce the marriage of their daughter

Frances Lorena
to

Doctor Thomas Joseph Crowe
Captain, United States Army

on Wednesday, the sixteenth of May

Nineteen hundred and forty-five

Jackson Barracks

New Orleans, Louisiana

the announcement of Frances and Tom's wedding

My life turned around in the summer of 1945. When I woke up the morning of August 6, 1945, the main thing on my mind was getting ready for Tom's arrival back in port that day. We had been married only a few months, and much of that time Tom was on a homebound troop ship. Soon after getting up and dressed, I plugged in the iron to get place mats ready for dinner. A new bride, I wanted everything perfect. I wanted to welcome Tom home after his month away.

I had the radio on, and that's when I heard the news. The US had dropped a bomb on Hiroshima, Japan. And not just any bomb. Tom had told me that he heard rumors aboard ship that the US planned to drop a mega bomb on Japan. I figured this was it. News reports didn't have many details, say how many had been killed, or detail the extent of damage, but somehow I knew it was bad. For years, I had seen no value in war, and the violence of the act shook me to my core. Almost instantaneously I was against war. "There has to be some way to stop this madness," I thought.

I unplugged the iron and went out on the streets of the New Orleans French Quarter looking for some way to confront the insanity of war. I had to find somebody interested in nonviolence. I didn't know many people in New Orleans nor did I know my way around the city. I found no peace center, but I did find a used bookstore. "How do I learn about peace and alternatives to war?" I asked the owner as he talked with me about the war.

"Start with Leo Tolstoy," he answered. "He is the father of nonviolence. His essays on war are so important."

I don't exactly remember the books I read then, but in 2012, I read Joseph Lelyveld's book *Great Soul: Mahatma Gandhi and His Struggle with India* and learned that when Gandhi started moving toward nonviolence, he didn't know much about it. Someone sent him a packet of information including John Ruskin's essays and Tolstoy's writings and told Gandhi that he should start by reading them. Which Gandhi did. And that's what I did, too.

So I read about Tolstoy's concepts of "nonresistance to evil" and acceptance of our finite presence on this earth. Tolstoy writes of a good god, which he capitalizes as God, and encourages his readers to tend toward what he conceives as each individual's own essence—the goodness of God. I saw that war, bombing, and destruction cannot count as good. Tom, a physician who had taken the Hippocratic Oath to do no harm, emerged from World War II equally certain that war serves no good. As our life together unfolded sometimes in unexpected ways, our mutual understanding became increasingly clear that each of us might embrace nonviolence in order, we hoped, to make a difference.

the Crowe home on Round Hill Road, Northampton
where Tom and Frances raised
Caltha, Jarlath, and Tom

We shared deep concern that the US had opened Pandora's box by splitting the atom to develop nuclear weapons. But our plans and dreams focused on starting a family for ourselves and a career for Tom. Tom did his residency at Strong Memorial Hospital in Rochester, New York.

Raising a Family

After Hiroshima I realized that war and peace defy simple approaches, but I did not focus exclusively on that dilemma. Tom and I found happiness together after three years apart. We looked forward to beginning our family. He had his career to establish, and I had a household to organize. And in almost no time, it seemed, I had children to raise while Tom did his residency in radiology at Strong Memorial Hospital at the University of Rochester.

Tom decided to go into radiology, a specialization ironically fostered by recent exploration of the potentials of nuclear activity. The American Board of Radiology originated in 1934, the same year Frédéric and Irène Joliot-Curie discovered induced radioactivity. Five years later, Frédéric Joliot-Curie confirmed other scientists' work concerning sustained chain reactions like the one developed to produce the devastating bombs the United States dropped on Hiroshima and Nagasaki.

Because of Tom's specialized interest, he was very conscious of the dangers of radiation. We spent many hours talking about the science and ethics of nuclear weapons. We shared deep concern that the US had opened Pandora's box by splitting the atom to develop nuclear weapons. But our plans and dreams focused on starting a family for ourselves and a career for Tom.

Tom did his residency at Strong Memorial Hospital in Rochester, New York. His older brother, one of his siblings who had helped him go to college, said, "Strong is the place you should go."

By then, both Tom and I had figured out that we opposed war. "Well," I thought, "in Rochester we'll find people who feel the same way and will want to organize a peace center." But that didn't happen. We decided Rochester probably wasn't going to be the place to do political work.

We didn't find a group in Rochester that shared our growing beliefs in the immorality of war and nuclear weapons. I did, however, meet Nevin Scrimshaw during his final years of medical school at Rochester when he interviewed me for a study on the diet of pregnant women. He had done an internship in a nutrition program situated in Central America. By 1946 when Dr. Scrimshaw set up his study in Rochester, I was pregnant. He also helped organize a food coop that unfortunately operated way across town. We didn't have a car, and I just couldn't manage to get over to it. But Nevin had a great spirit. He founded the department of food science and nutrition at Massachusetts Institute of Technology and later was associated with the International Nutrition Foundation. He spent his life improving nutrition for children.

We also met Dane and Ann Prugh. Dane was a resident in psychiatry, and he and Ann were Quakers.

In the spring of 1946, I got a job teaching a course in personnel administration at Rochester Community College. Tom's brother Tim was a vice president of New York Life Insurance, and he knew the head of the college. Tim told him I had experience working for Bell Labs, and so I was hired to teach a course on personnel work. Mostly I talked about what I had done, including writing employee handbooks and helping women in the workplace. I think I was there to encourage women that there was something besides typing for them and that they could be useful in industry. I taught one semester. At the end of the semester, I was four or five months pregnant and never returned.

We lived in a small apartment. When I became pregnant, we moved to housing built for students who had gone back to school on the GI Bill, a program that paid World War II veterans' college tuition and also a stipend while they attended college. Tom's brother called them "tar paper shacks." Students called them "Splinter Village." They were right across the street from the hospital and really cheap. We moved a month before the baby was due. I helped with the move, went up and down stairs, and assisted with lugging our furniture. I guess all the activity had an effect. The day after we moved, I went into labor, and Caltha was born a month early in December of 1946.

Tom always said that if he had a son he wanted him to be called Jarlath, the name of an Irish saint. I thought if we had a girl, I needed to have an equally interesting name. I looked through all the books trying to find a name that sounded good with Crowe—Cara Crowe, Karen Crowe. Then, when I looked through a book of flowers, I found the name Caltha, the name of the marsh marigold. That seemed perfect, Caltha Crowe. And Caltha loves it. She says she's never met another Caltha.

So my life in Rochester became defined by taking care of Caltha, walking to the grocery store, checking out books at the library, and tending our garden. We didn't have a car and lived on a hundred dollars a month. We paid twenty-seven dollars a month for housing. In February of 1948, our son Jarlath was born.

After Tom did his residency in radiology in Rochester, he accepted a job in Hartford, Connecticut at Saint Francis Hospital to be assistant radiologist for a year. While we were in Hartford, we socialized with people who had the popular new thing, a television set. We didn't want one, because we thought it was crazy: chairs lined up in a living room so people could watch a little black-and-white screen. When we finally got a television, we kept it in a locked room until 1962. Tom never watched it.

He thought it was silly. Sometimes the children watched it right before dinner while I prepared dinner.

More seriously in Hartford, we realized that Jarlath was profoundly deaf. There had been indications, but doctors kept telling us that Jarlath had enlarged adenoids or an infection or both. First he had his adenoids out; then he received radiation treatment.

"It has not improved," I said.

Then the doctor said, "It's middle ear infection." I don't think any of them had the courage to tell us. Or, since they were our friends, they couldn't face the fact that we had a deaf child.

In retrospect I realize that even the first day he was home it crossed my mind that he might be deaf. He was sleeping so well even though there was a lot of noise around him. I really walled off the thought, however, and chalked it up to a young mother's natural worry for her child. But as time went by, I continued to notice that when Jarlath stood in the crib looking out the window, he saw the light change when I entered his room and then he turned toward me. I realized that he reacted to visual clues, not aural clues. He didn't hear me. Also he sometimes got frustrated and banged his head when he didn't understand. Finally, after everybody kept assuring us he would grow out of it, I said, "We need to take him to see someone who doesn't know us."

Tom called Dane Prugh, our old friend from Rochester, then a psychiatrist at Children's Hospital in Boston. Dane said we must see Dr. Carlisle Flake, head of the Department of Otolaryngology and Communications Disorders at Children's. So we made an appointment and took Jarlath into Boston, about a two-hour drive from Hartford. As I tried to describe the way Jarlath responded to stimuli and Jarlath ran around his office, Dr. Flake said, "I will examine him, but I could have diagnosed him on the telephone. Your stories are so typical of a child with hearing loss."

Dr. Flake helped very much. "I just read an excellent article on oral education in *Volta Review*," he told me. He gave me a copy and added, "I want you to read it." I had not heard much about oral education. Most state institutions at the time taught sign language and were residential. I thought both those conditions made the deaf very isolated, and it disheartened me to think that Jarlath would grow up with strangers using a language different from his family's.

Oral education, a method for teaching the deaf since the time of Aristotle, relies on facial expressions, body language, residual hearing, speech reading, and learned speech to provide communication. It does not depend on signs. American Sign Language, a visual language with its own grammar, uses signs as well as finger spelling and body gestures. ASL is a relatively more recent method brought to the US in the nineteenth century by Thomas Gallaudet and Laurent Clerc.

In Dr. Flake I finally found someone who gave us something we could do to help Jarlath. It was the beginning of a whole new way of working with him, and that was very reassuring. Dr. Flake pointed to a window of opportunity when children are very young and you have to get language into them. You don't use signs, but you really communicate and get them to watch you. And then you can take advantage of the child's potential to learn. Jarlath was about eight months old, a perfect age for the approach.

Back home, Tom went to visit the American School for the Deaf in West Hartford. I didn't go. I was determined that Jarlath would live at home and have an as-normal-as-possible family life. We would educate him orally.

At the American School, Tom learned about a woman who had taught at the Clarke School for the Deaf in Northampton, Massachusetts. Clarke School emphasized oral education. We contacted the woman, and she came to our house in Hartford to help me with early training. She came once a week and taught me techniques to help Jarlath focus his attention. I put an old bedspread over a card table and got underneath to play with him. I told him we were camping to get him to look at my face. I showed him a ball, then held his face as I said ball, and then I held his hands on my face as I said ball again.

Because I spent a lot of time working with Jarlath, we decided to send Caltha to a preschool program. That gave me uninterrupted time to work with him while Caltha could get the stimulation she needed. We read in the paper that the Quakers (officially the Religious Society of Friends) planned to open a new preschool program in Hartford not far from where we lived. Caltha went there three mornings a week, and I spent those mornings getting Jarlath to focus and to speak, and life wasn't quite so frustrating for him. Right from the beginning, I felt that oralism was the way to go. And I just knew innately that I wanted to keep Jarlath at home. We wanted to give him all that a family could, and we weren't going to send him off to a state institution.

In the summer of 1950 when he was two, I went with Jarlath to the John Tracy Clinic in Los Angeles, California. Spencer Tracy had a deaf son, and the child's mother, Louise Treadwell Tracy, took an active interest in deaf education. She felt it essential to train parents to work on oral education with their deaf children. So at the Tracy summer institute at least one parent had to accompany the deaf child. Caltha, Jarlath, and I went to California. Since I was to be with Jarlath all day, my mother came with us to care for Caltha, who was three by then. My cousin

Caltha and Jarlath about 1948, top, and 1950

Martha Anne lived nearby, and she found a house for us and helped us negotiate Los Angeles.

Every day Jarlath and I took the bus to the Tracy Clinic. There I met other parents, mostly mothers, of deaf children. The institute lasted a month or six weeks. We received many ideas and techniques for working with our children. More important, we got to meet other parents of deaf children. We had time to share concerns and stories while we pushed our children on swings in the playground or watched as they played games with each other.

I desperately wanted to get Jarlath the help he needed. We looked all over the country for oral programs. The Boston Catholic diocese ran one, and we found others in Saint Louis, Missouri, Portland, Oregon, and New York City. We visited them all. But we also had to think of what would be a good place for Tom to set up a practice and where would be a good place for the children and me to live. We liked the Clarke School in Northampton best. Unfortunately, even though it emphasized oral education, Clarke insisted that all students should live there.

While I was at the Tracy Clinic, I heard that Clarke had a new headmaster, George Pratt, whose deaf daughter attended the school. I called Tom in Hartford and asked if he would go up to Northampton and talk to the headmaster. I wanted us to see if they would take Jarlath as a day student if we moved to Northampton.

When Tom got there, the headmaster was on a ladder painting a wall to get his house ready before moving in. Tom introduced himself and asked him if we could enroll Jarlath as a day student. "If you move here," Dr. Pratt said, "you can enroll him and he can live at home." We found out later that he had not shared this decision with his staff. For us it was the best news.

The idea of moving to Northampton was appealing. It is in a college area that at the time made a home for four colleges. Since then Hampshire College opened its doors to make it the Five College Area. Dr. Connor, the radiologist in town, did not have board certification and wanted to sell his practice and house on Center Street. So Tom bought the practice, and we moved to Northampton in 1951.

It was difficult to get started. Tom borrowed money from his sister and brother to go to medical school, and we needed to pay that back as well as get a bank loan for Dr. Connor's house and practice. Then, as the first board-certified radiologist in Northampton, Tom's practice took off, and he became very busy. He started the radiology department at Cooley Dickinson Hospital and went once a week to the state hospital and once

Tom with Caltha and Jarlath about 1952 on Center Street

a week to the Veterans Hospital. He even went to the UMass Health center. He ran all over the place.

For the first year, we lived over the office. That was not too successful because it seemed Jarlath often had a temper tantrum when Tom had an office full of patients. I always said Jarlath was a ten-acre child. He needed to get out and run and not be confined to that house. Because Jarlath was too young to start school, we decided that the Smith College campus preschool program where Caltha went would be good for him. In the beginning, they were hesitant to take a deaf child, but then they said yes. Priscilla Deane (later Priscilla Deane Freund), a Smith College student of education, said she would like to work with Jarlath, and he started at the Smith preschool with hearing children. In the early twenty-first century, it would not be unusual for a teacher's aide to work closely with a deaf student in a mainstream classroom, but Priscilla's work was quite unusual at the time.

After we lived on Center Street above the office for a year, we decided it was not working out. We moved to a house on Prospect Avenue, a small house with three bedrooms and a yard that was all brick-walled in. We thought that would be an ideal place for Jarlath where he could run and play outside safely.

Regrettably, the house turned out not to be the safe haven for Jarlath as we had hoped. I contracted pneumonia our first winter there with orders to stay in bed. I had a sitter take care of four-year-old Jarlath. She was an older woman and, I thought, very responsible. Somehow he got out of the yard and followed—or was lured by—some older children in the neighborhood. I think they probably made fun of him. They got him to go up to a house under construction. In the building the workers had left a vat of unslaked lime, a highly caustic substance used in making mortar among other things. One of the children picked up a brush sitting in the lime and threw the lime at Jarlath. He came walking home, crying and rubbing his eye. Somehow he found his way up to my bedside. When he told me what happened, I called Tom right away. Tom told me to get water into his eye, but by the time we got him to the hospital, his eye was chiefly gone.

That unnerved me. All I could think was, "Can I handle him?" It was certainly the most difficult time of my life. It really shook my confidence. I felt, "I can't do this. What if he loses the other eye?" So, as I recovered from pneumonia with the extended bed rest that was advised in those days, for one year he lived at Clarke School in Yale House. I think it reassured me that he could adjust. But the next year we felt it was better for him to live at home, and he very much wanted to live at home.

Jarlath has mixed memories of his year as a boarder. One of the teachers, Miss Mary Frances Ragin, positively influenced Jarlath's life. Many of the pupils from that year became his lifelong friends. Some of the children, who were after all very young and in an unfamiliar situation, missed their parents desperately. Jarlath said he was lucky to live not far from his own home when he was a boarder at Clarke and then was very glad that he was able to live at home and still attend the school.

With the birth of young Tom in 1952 our family was complete. A League of Women Voters meeting was scheduled the day I went into labor. I had to ask my husband Tom to let everyone know I couldn't attend.

Because I had read a small book about natural childbirth, we decided to explore that possibility. Tom and I worked on breathing and relaxing with contractions, and I discussed the possibility with my obstetrician. He agreed to permit Tom to be in the delivery room in spite of the prevalent custom not to permit a father to be present. Thus Tom was born. The ob-gyn was pleased because he had been convinced it could be done.

I went to Carthage for my mother's funeral in 1954. While I was there, Tom called and said that George Pratt from Clarke told him a house on Round Hill Road right across from the school was for sale. Someone had bequeathed it to the school. Tom said, "They're asking fourteen thousand dollars for it." I knew it was a big house and wanted to wait to think it

Frances's mother Anna Hyde with Caltha, about 1953

over, but Tom said that it might sell to someone else. So I agreed. We had a little trouble getting a loan for that house. The first bank we went to said we were overextending ourselves, but Tom persevered and found another bank. With his practice expanding, we were able to handle it easily. We ended up living there for fourteen years.

The house on Round Hill Road had three stories with fourteen rooms. So the house proved ideal for children to play and live in. When Caltha decided to return to Northampton in 1964 to go to Smith College after high

GREETINGS 1958

Tommy   Jarlath   Caltha

Tam & Frances

1958 Crowe family holiday card with
Tommy, Jarlath, and Caltha from left

school in Pennsylvania, she lived at home in her third-floor lair for the first year before moving to campus.

The house I live in on Langworthy Road came on the market in the late 1960s. When I looked at it, it was summer and the windows were open and the sunshine was coming in. The living area was all on one floor, and it reminded me of a Midwestern house. I thought, "This is the house for us to live in the rest of our lives." One of its main features was a large finished basement. Tom always teased me that I had already made up my mind that the downstairs would be a wonderful place for a peace center when we decided to buy the house, which looked more like a house in Missouri than any other house I'd seen around.

Much of my early-married life involved pursuing education for my children. Caltha went to The George School, a Quaker prep school in Pennsylvania, and then to Smith College. The Vietnam War escalated during Caltha's four years at Smith College, and she took part in the student movement to oppose US involvement in Vietnam. She was a founding member of Smith-Amherst Students for a Democratic Society (SDS). That's how she got to know her first husband, Kirk Mellor, another founding member of Smith-Amherst SDS. Caltha and Kirk married after Kirk's graduation from Amherst while Caltha was still a student at Smith.

Smith-Amherst SDS took on a project of envisioning what a more progressive college education would look like in the Pioneer Valley. A 1965 six-million-dollar donation from Harold Johnson encouraged implementation of a late 1950s idea to enact collective, progressive philosophies from the existing Valley colleges. In 1958, the Pioneer Valley college presidents of Smith, Amherst, Mount Holyoke, and UMass fostered The New College Plan for a model that became Hampshire College. As part of their progressive college project, Caltha and Kirk with other members of Smith-Amherst SDS organized a meeting of a hundred or so students at our house on Round Hill Road to brainstorm and produce reports for Hampshire College planners. They divided into small groups all over the house, and I cooked Julia Childs's boeuf bourguignon for them all.

Although many parents, even progressive parents, did not care much for their college children's radical activities in that era of a much publicized Generation Gap, Tom and I supported Caltha's work and took pride in it.

After her graduation, Caltha and Kirk moved to New Haven, Connecticut where she managed the draft resistance office, joined an early feminist group, and participated in organizing a labor union among Yale workers. She traveled to China as part of a United States China People's Friendship Association national activist tour in 1976 and then to Cuba in 1979 with the New York *Guardian* newspaper, a left-wing publication without relationship to the London *Guardian* and no longer in print. She also both volunteered and worked in parents' cooperative schools and childcare centers. These experiences with young children ultimately led to her career as an educator.

Caltha and Kirk divorced after eleven years of marriage. She remarried after a few years. She and her husband, Jerry Allison, an artist, have been married for more than thirty years and have a daughter Rosa born in 1984, a writer and psychologist who works in the social media field.

While working in childcare, Caltha discovered her deep interest in the growth and development of young children. She studied for a master's degree in early childhood education at Goddard College in order to obtain teacher certification and subsequently earned a masters degree in Educational Leadership from Bank Street College of Education. Caltha taught in Illinois and Connecticut public schools for more than thirty years.

Caltha learned about Responsive Classroom, a cooperative, non-competitive approach to teaching that creates safe, joyful, and engaging classrooms for all children, while teaching in Westport, Connecticut. Caltha took a number of workshops at Northeast Foundation, home of the Responsive Classroom, then located in Greenfield, Massachusetts, and later Turners Falls, Massachusetts. She brought some teachers from Westport with her. They stayed here while they did their training. Eventually she got all of Westport involved in Responsive Classroom. The organization kept asking her to do more training and to do writing for them. Eventually, she worked exclusively for them doing workshops all over the country. She has written three books for them, *Solving Thorny Behavior Problems*, *Sammy and his Behavior Problem*, and recently she wrote a book on bullying, *How to Bullyproof Your Classroom*, published in 2012. Although she is retired from classroom teaching, she continues to be very involved with Northeast Foundation.

I think the Responsive Classroom curriculum is peace education at the elementary school level. The Collaboration for Academic, Social and Emotional Learning recognized it as one of twenty-three school-based programs that promote students' self control, relationship building and problem solving. About thirty people work for them in Turners Falls, and another two hundred educators work around the country as consulting teachers for Responsive Classroom. Caltha is on the board now and when she comes north to Turners Falls, she visits me.

We very much wanted to find the right education for Jarlath. Northampton's Clarke School for the Deaf attracted us with its worldwide reputation for excellence in oral education. The school didn't offer parent training, so I took the teacher training. Clarke bases its approach to oral education on students in residence each bonded in close relationship with a teacher. In our atypical case, I had served my son as teacher, sometimes with methods different from the Clarke approach. Furthermore, also groundbreaking for Clarke, Jarlath attended school during the day but lived at home where I continued as his primary speech and language mentor. Clarke provided an at-school mentor for him and allowed me to be the at-home mentor, so he had two mentors, a situation new to both Clarke and our family. As soon as he was old enough, we enrolled Jarlath as a day student, one of the first non-residential pupils at Clarke. Jarlath's attendance at Clarke surely was the right thing for our family.

Jarlath's wife Rebecca Wathen-Dunn, whom we call Becca, also has hearing loss. She was educated in the traditional Clarke residential setting where a child's primary adult connection is to the teacher. She lived

Jarlath, about 1960

at Clarke, where they met. We knew her parents and invited them to lunch when they came out to visit from the Boston area. However, there wasn't any parent organizing. The staff really didn't believe in it. Becca feels she missed a lot when her parents turned her over to Clarke. Becca remembers being lonely and scared when her parents out of necessity left her at Clarke. She couldn't communicate yet and didn't know why her family left her there.

The oral method really worked for Jarlath. Eventually, he received cochlear implants and can communicate with all of us very well. His speech is good, and because we demanded speech from him, he did not learn signs. He didn't know a sign until he went to college because we had kept him totally away from that. When he pointed at something he wanted, we insisted that he ask for it by name and precede his request with, "Please may I have . . . " Sometimes I took him downtown and sent him into Woolworth's to get something like a spool of thread. I'd give him the money and say, "You go in and get it."

Except for his year as a resident, Jarlath went to Clarke as a day student until fourth grade. Then one day one of the teachers called me and said, "Jarlath ran over to the gym from Hubbard Hall with his raincoat over his head. He didn't want to bother putting on his raincoat and so just ran ahead with it over his head."

As far as I know, Jarlath was not punished at school that day for running with his raincoat over his head. On other occasions, however, Jarlath remembers misbehaving and being punished for it, sometimes by being sent to a dark closet. Eventually because of a set-to with a teacher, Jarlath refused to return to Clarke. I believe it centered on Zorro, a late 1950s TV program about a swashbuckling Spanish nobleman seeking justice. Jarlath and his classmates acted out some fight scenes during an afternoon walk to woodworking class. I got a call around five to send Jarlath back to Gawith Hall at Clarke.

Jarlath told me he walked into a schoolroom full of crying residential classmates who had been punished for horsing around. The disciplinarian teacher accused Jarlath of instigating Zorro reenactments, and from the expressions of his classmates, Jarlath knew they had been punished more severely than usual. He came home and refused to return to Clarke. His father and I accepted his decision and looked for alternatives for his education. He was about nine years old.

Years later, Jarlath told me that he had become bored at Clarke and acted out in order to attract the attention that would eventually make it possible for him to leave.

After Clarke, the public school wouldn't take him and neither would the Smith Campus School where Caltha and young Tom went. Jarlath would have been the only student who could not hear, and it would not have been part of the school staff's expertise to teach a deaf child. Some years later in 1972, Chapter 766, the Massachusetts Special Education Law mandated an appropriate education for every child regardless of disability. Massachusetts did offer Clarke as special education for the state's deaf children even before Chapter 766.

Finding a school other than Clarke that he could attend was quite a challenge. Finally we found a small private school in Shelburne on the Mohawk Trail, the Roberts School, where Jarlath went for fifth grade. It was mostly a residential school for hearing children, many of whose parents worked in the theater in New York City. They said they would take Jarlath as a day student. It was very hard because I had to drive him up there. We advertised in the paper, and I found a woman who taught in Greenfield and lived in Northampton. She took him up in the morning and dropped him off in Greenfield where the school had a bus picking up children to take them to Roberts. In the afternoons, I took our son Tom in the car with me to pick him up.

Things went well through the winter. Jarlath loved it at Roberts. If he finished all of his work in the morning, he could go out and clear trails they had behind the school and prepare them for skiing. He loved skiing, so that did the trick for him along with caring attention from several teachers who took time to help him learn. Jarlath liked to read, and teachers encouraged him to keep up with class work. However, we discovered in the spring that one of the young teachers had given him answer sheets for notebooks he was assigned to finish. When I found that out, we asked the teachers, "What is going on?" He finished out the year, but we watched very carefully and made sure he was doing his own work.

After the Roberts School, we explored public schools. A teacher at the Vernon Street School in Northampton said she was willing to try to work closely with Jarlath. He attended Vernon Street School for sixth grade. Again in a class of students who could hear, mainly what he did there was read books. He read something like sixty-four books on school time. All the reading was fine for his language and developed his good reading and writing skills. But after a year at the public school, he decided he really wanted to be with Caltha and Tom at the Campus School, so we enrolled him for seventh grade. He told me he loved it there, and teachers spent extra time with him, again the only deaf student among a classroom full of children who could hear.

We hired a retired schoolteacher in town, John Tewinkle, a Quaker. He had taught in Africa for many years. He tutored Jarlath every evening after supper. He sat with him and went over what he had done in school that day. It was before children with special needs were assigned aides in public schools. The teachers sent their outlines home, and John reviewed them with Jarlath. He did that for several years while Jarlath was in the public school and then at the Campus School. Jarlath made many friends at the Campus School, including boys and girls who would grow up to be friends of his for life.

When he was ready for eighth grade, he went to Williston Academy, then a college preparatory boys school in Easthampton. It became co-educational after merging with the Northampton School for Girls in the seventies. He went as a day student, again a deaf student among the hearing, and graduated from Williston. He then did a postgraduate year.

While Jarlath was at Williston, we took him to see a college counselor who himself was deaf. He tested Jarlath and felt he was very bright and could do college work, a revolutionary thought for a deaf child in those days. That was the first year of the National Technical Institute for the Deaf in Rochester, New York, a program organized by Rochester Institute of Technology, kind of RIT for the deaf. Jarlath applied and was accepted for the first class.

After Rochester he came back to Northampton. Living at home didn't work for him. A couple of years earlier my sister in Carthage called to say that her daughter had left the university and things weren't working out for her at home in Carthage. Sarah came here to Northampton with her cat and slowly found her way. She has had a long career with the US Postal Service in personnel and is now postmistress for the Town of Hampden. Since this worked so well for Sarah, I suggested to Jarlath that he go to Carthage, a new environment, and get a job.

Jarlath saved money from his job in Carthage and decided to travel in the West. He loved the West and the outdoors. He often went to summer camp—which sometimes worked out and sometimes didn't, depending on how well organized the camp was. One summer when he was still in high school, we sent him to the National Outdoor Leadership School (NOLS) in Lander, Wyoming. I felt that he needed to get out into the wilderness. I talked on the telephone to Paul Petzoldt, founder of NOLS, and he said, "Send him out, and I will train him."

We put Jarlath on a plane, and when he came back six weeks later, he looked so much taller. He had done a "solo," an experience similar to Outward Bound where a person is dropped into the wilderness and has to depend on himself and his wits to survive. He thrived in the outdoors. He participated in the 1971 Deaf Olympics at Adelboden, Switzerland and the 1973 European Ski competition at Les Aires, France even though he didn't have depth perception because he had only one eye.

After Carthage, Jarlath traveled for a while and ended up in Montana working for a fish hatchery. After that job he took the federal civil service exam and worked for the Fish and Wildlife Service in Warren, Pennsylvania. In Warren he married Belinda Greenwood, whom he had met at NTID in Rochester. Patrick was born a year later, but that marriage ended in divorce. Jarlath was left with Patrick and eventually received custody. Then Jarlath transferred with the Fish and Wildlife Service to the fish hatchery near Sheffield, Massachusetts in the Berkshires so that, as a single parent, he could be closer to extended family. That was such a good move for both of them. Jarlath eventually married Becca, whom he reconnected with at a school reunion.

After Jarlath retired from Fish and Wildlife, he served as a research subject for studies about deafness conducted by students at MIT. His life experience is so unique, and he had useful information. He also provides a great support for me, showing up once when I was on trial for civil disobedience.

Our son Tom started at the Smith Campus School like Caltha. Then he decided he wanted to go to public school, and he did for one year of junior high. His father thought he wasn't getting challenged as much as he should have been. So he enrolled in Williston Academy in Easthampton during the sixties when private schools underwent considerable upheaval. The boys chafed under rules requiring them to wear ties and jackets and cut their hair, and so did Tom. One year, a national fast took place for four days to stop the Vietnam War. Tom fasted quietly but didn't tell anyone at Williston. It seemed to me that he was more and more alienated from the school.

Then I ran into someone at a party who said she had found a school in Vermont, the East Hill Farm School. A small school where children ran the farm with lessons organized around farm chores and real life situations, it sounded ideal. I called the school and made arrangements to visit the school and talk with the headmaster, Dick Bliss.

I went up to Andover, Vermont and looked around. The school had an enrollment of ten boys and ten girls. The children slept in cabins in the woods, and with supervision, they did all the cooking and ran the farm.

I drove Tom up there on a Friday in a snowstorm. He loved it from the start. He learned self-sufficiency through cooking, plumbing, carpentry, auto mechanics, farming, and beekeeping. His classmates included grandchildren of Dorothy Day, founder of the Catholic Worker movement; children of Alexander Solzhenitzyn, the Soviet dissident, and Robert Frank, photographer of *The Americans*. Students ate what they grew and butchered a cow once or twice a year. Tom once told me, "East Hill was an important part of my life."

After graduating from East Hill, Tom came back to Northampton. He didn't feel ready to go to college. He lived in a little cabin in Hatfield with Pablo Frank who had also just finished at East Hill. They raised tomatoes to sell, and Tom did carpentry work. He took courses at UMass. He did well in the courses and decided to apply to college.

Tom applied to Antioch College in Yellow Springs, Ohio, a good fit for him because of its requirement for practical work experience along with classes. Before setting off to college, he worked on a farm in Ireland owned by one of my husband's relatives. Then he traveled around Europe.

When Tom was in high school, we traveled to Haiti in August 1967 to Albert Schweitzer Hospital where my husband Tom set up the X-ray department. Jarlath and Caltha already lived on their own and didn't join us on the trip. Young Tom and I worked in the hospital. I mostly fed the babies in the nursery and did clerical work. Young Tom worked with Dr. William Larimer Mellon Jr., who started Albert Schweitzer Hospital in 1956 in Deschapelles, an impoverished part of Haiti. The Mellon fortune financed the hospital. Often in the operating room, the surgeon would let Tom hold the retractors. So it was a very good experience. The fact they let him, a young teenage boy, help with surgery made a big impression on Tom and encouraged his life's work.

When Tom went to Antioch, one of his first work experiences was to go back to Haiti and work in a hospital. He said that it was not nearly so interesting because they had him setting up the pharmacy where he was working with drugs and not people. At that point he wasn't even talking about going into medicine. But about a year after he graduated from Antioch, he called from Portland, Oregon, where he was doing carpentry, and said that he was thinking about medical school. He asked if we would pay for the pre med course at the University of Portland. My husband and I were both very happy that he had decided on his own to study medicine.

After pre med, Tom applied to the medical school in Cincinnati and then did his residency in orthopedics in Cincinnati. In the meantime he met his wife, Nancy Shope, an Oregon nurse who had traveled in Africa. They got married the summer before medical school. After residency, Tom held a position at Ellsworth Hospital in Maine for many years but recently transferred to the Machias Hospital, a small community hospital.

He drives up to Machias Sunday night and Thursday evenings he drives home to Blue Hill where he and Nancy have a big house where they raised their three children—Sean, who during medical school has with others supported, fundraised for, and staffed a student-run free clinic; Simone, a non-profit administrator working to address food insecurity and hunger; and Tomas, who during college volunteered with organizations dedicated to providing health care in the under-developed world.

During all our time in Northampton, my husband Tom's practice increased, and he worked hard. A year hadn't passed after moving to Northampton before he took a partner. Eventually the practice included five doctors. In those years, the radiologist did both diagnostic and therapeutic work. About three years into the practice, Tom decided the

Frances's grandchildren, clockwise from top left,
Rosa, Patrick, Simone, Tomas, and Sean
in the early 2000s

two should be separate. He was more interested in therapeutic radiology than other doctors in the practice, so he went off to Roswell Park in Buffalo, New York for special training. Rosalie Bertell, a doctor and a sister of the Gray Nuns of the Sacred Heart, had worked there. She wrote *No Immediate Danger: Prognosis for a Radioactive Earth* on the dangers of radiation exposure from nuclear weapons and nuclear reactors. After his experience there, Tom became very interested in cancer, its causes, its care, and its cure. He set up and ran the first radiation therapy program in the Valley.

In the early seventies Tom retired from his practice because he developed blepharospasms, a neurological disability where you can't keep your eyes open. He decided to get involved in cancer education. Sydney Farber Institute in Boston asked Tom to set up a cancer education center in Springfield. With others, Tom established Cancer Cooperative funded by the Sydney Farber Institute. It was close to the bus station, so Tom could take the bus to Springfield and walk to the center without having to drive a car.

For a while Tom was the director and had five or six people working there who went all over the Valley doing cancer education programs. He somehow managed despite the limitations and then discovered that with Botox injections he could keep his eyes open. At that time, however, Botox had not been approved for use in the US. So a doctor in Boston at Mass Eye and Ear ordered the Botox from Canada, and Tom went into Boston to get injections there. One day he got a call about nine in the morning from his doctor in Boston asking if Tom could go in that day to be interviewed for a national television program highlighting the importance of Botox. I was downstairs working in the office when Tom asked if I could drive to Boston. I closed the office, and we drove into Boston. Eventually Botox was approved.

The Springfield Cancer Cooperative did very well until Ronald Reagan was elected president. Then many federal health programs were cut, and almost overnight the center was forced to rely on volunteers before it shut down.

Tom died on May 2, 1997. He had his first heart attack in 1985 and open heart surgery in 1996. He told us that aftereffects of surgery might cause a stroke, but he was willing to take that risk. A devastating stroke not long after surgery knocked out a central part of his brain. After the stroke, it was hard for him to maneuver around the house. He tried to help me know how to help him. He suggested that I make cardboard models of the rooms in our house so he could visualize where the furniture was, but that didn't work. We tried rearranging the furniture, but that was no use either.

Massachusetts General Hospital in Boston had a helpful program, so we took Tom there for whatever expertise in stroke treatment there might be. Tom stayed for a week, but they had no cure. For a while, he went up the road from our home for outpatient care to Cooley Dickinson Hospital where he had founded the radiology therapy department. But eventually, he had to go to an extended care facility. Both a physical therapist and psychiatrist instructed me that nothing more could be done. They made it clear that I could not care for him at home. So he went to the Overlook rehabilitation center a few miles away, and I went there every day. That is where he died a few weeks later.

While Tom was in Overlook, our children came often and were supportive. They came in from their jobs and commitments to be here at this very important time. It was an emotional, difficult time of leave taking, but we did as a family what every family has to do.

Tom practiced the art of medicine with great compassion. He was dedicated to his patients, and he was a dedicated husband and father. We enjoyed each other and our children. He was determined to spend good time with them. He did all kinds of things with the children. We hiked and skied. He taught the children to ski and took them to places they chose, including Tuckerman's Ravine, the challenging head wall of Mount Washington. We got a canoe and all enjoyed it when the kids were around. We canoed the Connecticut River from Deerfield to Northampton one spring.

Once, we hosted two East German men in Northampton before the Berlin Wall came down. The experience gave us an opportunity to see one another as human beings and not as enemies. We visited Russia with the organization Enduring Peace when our children were young and in summer camps. And we had a fine family trip to Europe in the summer of 1964 when Tom took two months off. We bought a car in France and then drove to Italy and put the car on a boat to drive through Yugoslavia and Greece. In Greece, we met my sister Mary and her husband Halim.

I belonged to the Cooley Dickinson Hospital Auxiliary and served for a time on the board. We also went to dinner parties with friends and hosted them at our home on Round Hill Road.

Tom was very interested in his Great Books club and spent time reading and preparing for the monthly meetings. He took courses with Learning in Retirement, a Five-Colleges peer-led program. He wrote poetry. He had a one-man scull he rowed on the Connecticut River, and he learned how to ride a horse.

COOLEY DICKINSON
HEALTH CARE
MASSACHUSETTS GENERAL HOSPITAL AFFILIATE

30 Locust St.
Northampton, MA 01061

Tel: 413-582-2000
cooley-dickinson.org

Dr. Thomas J. Crowe founded the Radiology Department at Cooley Dickinson Hospital and served as our first full-time radiation oncologist.

In June 1976, Cooley Dickinson Hospital broke ground for the new Radiation Therapy Department. At that point the new facility was constructed underground in the courtyard adjacent to the hospital's front entrance. In August 1977 when the Radiation Oncology Unit opened, it was named in honor of Dr. Thomas J. Crowe, who was instrumental in establishing the hospital's original radiotherapy department in the 1960s. It is located 22 feet below ground; it is reached by elevator from the lobby.

The Dr. Thomas J. Crowe Radiation Oncology Unit Dedication: "In tribute to the man who has been largely responsible for the important accomplishment, the hospital's Board of Trustees has announced that the new cancer center will be known as The Dr. Thomas J. Crowe Radiation Oncology Unit."

Dr. Crowe was associated with the hospital from 1951. He was instrumental in establishing the hospital's original Radiotherapy Department in 1960 with the installation of the Cobalt 60 unit for cancer therapy. In 1971, he became the hospital's first full-time Radiotherapist and while serving in this capacity, established a weekly Tumor Board Conference and Tumor Registry. Dr. Crowe was responsible for planning the professional aspects of the new Radiation Oncology Unit including the Varian Clinac IV linear accelerator."

By naming the area The Vitkauskas Crowe Radiation Oncology Suite in 2010, the Board of Trustees recognized husband and wife Ernest and Margaret Vitkauskas for advancing the hospital's ability to serve cancer patients with a $1.7 million bequest that permitted purchase of a second linear accelerator, an Elekta Synergy machine.

Cooley Dickinson acknowledgement of Dr. Tom Crowe's role in founding the radiology department at the hospital

Tom was very engaged in life and looked on life with a sense of humor. He always said he was trying to understand the world and I was trying to change it. Now I'm trying to understand the world. After Tom died, I was invited to spend two weeks at a peace retreat center, Windcall, in Bozeman, Montana. Time reading the works of Gandhi and Martin Luther King, Jr. and walking in the mountains helped restore my perspective and prepare me for moving ahead with my life.

Tom's gravestone at Mount Toby Friends' Meeting bears this inscription: "Scholar, Healer, Friend to All Whose Humor and Compassion Enriched Our Lives."

Some people think that Tom existed as Mr. Frances Crowe, but nothing could be farther from the truth. He was living his life and I was living mine in a good, loving marriage that is the most important thing in my life.

Frances and Tom take their place as puppeteers for a 1990s fund raiser

Gazette Friday Jan. 19., 1962

WOMEN

We enter the New Year resolved to
raise our voices for life and sanity;
for schools, for medical research,
for patient and unremitting
international negotiation;
against the shelter program, against
nuclear testing, against the whole
arms race which imperils our hope
for the future.

1962 WILPF Northampton New Year ad

The speaker said the US encouraged the war instead of pushing for peace. It became quiet. The students sat in the bleachers and some on the floor, and I remember thinking, "Everybody is listening." I noticed the janitor at the door of the gym, mop in hand, very attentive to the speaker. I thought, "This is it. This is what we have to do. People need to know what is going on, and we can help that to happen."

Branching Out in Northampton

Early in our marriage, I worked with Tom to establish a well-educated and compassionate, responsible family. It was the 1950s, after all, and I hoped to emulate the secure, traditional family life my mother and father had provided.

When we first moved to Northampton in the early 1950s, I felt I should get to know the medical community in town. We women wore hose and heels in those days before the pantsuit liberated everyone. I went to meetings of the women's auxiliary of the Cooley Dickinson Hospital, but I found they weren't talking about anything very meaningful to me. I was looking for more.

As the children grew, I was a Brownie leader and Cub Scout den mother. I volunteered with the Parent-Teacher Organization. Tom and I were very hands-on in orchestrating our children's education.

For some years, Tom and I went square dancing every week. We went to theatre, attended concerts, and went to museums. A friend from the Round Hill Road years reminded me recently that I had decorated that home with art and attractive curiosities. I audited courses in art history at Smith College. Museums and opportunities to appreciate art emerged in the area, and whenever Tom and I traveled alone or with our family, we visited museums. I particularly enjoy a copy of a detail of Henri Rousseau's *The Dream* on my study wall. Don Grant, whom I draft-counseled years later during the Vietnam War, painted it for me.

The house on Round Hill Road was a great place for meetings, and slowly I found my work and friends—mostly people deeply involved in the peace movement. I became more comfortable living in Northampton. I was an active member in the League of Women Voters almost from the beginning of our time in town.

As the children grew, we had a Chihuahua named Juno we gave young Tom for his birthday. One of young Tom's classmates bred Chihuahuas, and that's where we got Juno. Tom often studied with Juno in his lap. When Caltha, Jarlath, and Tom went away to school, Juno missed them. She ran to the window often to look for them. In those days, we allowed the dog to run free because there was no leash law.

Northampton was a quieter, more rural place when we first moved there. Although Smith College gave it the charm of a college town, the downtown area seemed sleepy by comparison with what it became by the late 1980s when it took on its more urban character. We enjoyed the community, and with Tom, I became involved in a number of community projects.

Through Tom, I worked with the National Committee for a SANE Nuclear Policy, a national organization founded in the late fifties to work to stop testing nuclear weapons in the atmosphere. Concerned physicists and doctors like Tom founded SANE because they worried deeply about dangerous effects of radioactive isotopes in the atmosphere from testing. Scientists monitored fallout on the New York side of the Hudson River near New York City. They felt that tests sponsored by the United States caused radioactive isotopes to collect in clouds and then show up as radioactivity when it rained on agricultural fields.

The possibility of Strontium 90 in milk concerned Tom and me. We canceled our delivery of fresh milk because we didn't want our children drinking milk from cows grazing on pastures where contaminated rain might fall. I tried to get the children to drink powdered milk produced before testing in the atmosphere became commonplace. I mixed milk powder with strawberry or chocolate flavoring or anything I could think of that might make it taste better, but they wouldn't drink it.

Finally I realized that addressing the problem meant more than limiting activity to my own family. I had to work for a political solution. Tom and I discussed it and then helped start a local SANE committee. Typical of similar male-dominated organizations in the early fifties, women did all the telephoning and organizing and found appropriate places for men to speak. Even when SANE organized a big demonstration in New York in the early sixties, men including Benjamin Spock and William Sloane Coffin spoke while women organized. Few women at the time were physicians, psychiatrists, or ministers, so it was understandable that men took featured roles. Our tasks included creating car pools, one of them centered in Northampton to drive to the demonstration. Eventually, national SANE wanted each of its members to sign a loyalty oath affirming never having been a Communist nor planning to be one in the future. Our Hampshire-Franklin County SANE chapter discussed the loyalty oath and decided we wouldn't sign such a statement. That was the end of SANE in the Connecticut Valley.

At about the same time Tom became active in Physicians for Social Responsibility (PSR). Tom and I went to their first conference in Boston in the early 1960s. Information they circulated about threats of nuclear testing and nuclear weapons astonished and troubled us. The thought of the dangers made us numb. As a radiologist, Tom always understood problems associated with radioactivity, but the conference brought it all home with new clarity. Together, we decided we could no longer be bystanders but must take action.

Back in Northampton, Tom decided with Carl Saviano, a psychiatrist, and a few others that they should have a PSR chapter here. The organization focused clearly on nuclear weapons and weapons testing, and PSR sponsors vibrant national and international initiatives. Tom usually ended up serving as secretary, preparing mailings and agendas.

Tom and I organized with SANE and PSR, and I also worked in Northampton with the Women's International League for Peace and Freedom (WILPF) in the sixties. We attended an American Friends Service Committee (AFSC) institute week at Lake Winnepesaukee in New Hampshire for people interested in peace and justice in New England. It led to my being asked to provide a regional AFSC office in Northampton and organize events with speakers about peace and justice.

Sometimes, too, others and I organized events independent of AFSC. Pete Seeger performed in Northampton for one of the events I helped put together, probably in 1960. My friend Teddy Milne heard Pete, the well-known folk singer, and thought he should come to Northampton to perform. She contacted him, and I set about finding a hall and filling it. I remember that Pete did not charge us much for his appearance, so we didn't sell tickets. We opened the hall up for free-will donations and got enough money to give Pete. Smith College donated the use of John M. Greene Hall, and we found a campus group to co-sponsor. We filled the hall, and I was energized by the great success of the event.

Gertrude "Trudy" Huntington, a Quaker and well known scholar of the pacifist Amish, introduced me to WILPF. A widely published author about the Amish, Trudy moved to Northampton in the late 1950s when her husband accepted a position teaching American art history at Smith College. She came from the Philadelphia area, got her undergraduate degree from Swarthmore, and earned her PhD at Yale. Our close friendship bonded around our children and motherhood, and Trudy introduced me to the peace movement. She told me about WILPF, an international organization founded in the Netherlands in 1915 in response to the violence of the First World War.

Trudy and I endorsed WILPF's goals of nonviolence, world disarmament, peace, justice, and freedom for all. We also admired WILPF's history including not only women at The Hague but other WILPFers like Quaker economist Emily Greene Balch, settlement worker Jane Addams, and early women pioneers in issues of peace and justice. We decided to see if women in Northampton had any interest in a chapter of WILPF. We put together a list of women to invite to a tea at my home on Round Hill Road. I remember that I wrote the invitations on Crane stationery note cards embossed with Mrs. Thomas J. Crowe. To our

Trudy Huntington and her sons Daniel, left, and Caleb, 1967

surprise, about seventy women showed up. My big living room could accommodate everyone. Many were faculty wives, and there were also a few Quakers and mothers of people I met through the children's' schools. We put the chairs in circles facing the center and talked about goals of national WILPF. We discussed what we might work on. We decided to take on nonviolence in the family and work out from there. We started from where we were as young parents.

Trudy and I worked hard with our local WILPF chapter. We met mornings and had what might now be called working groups. We took an interest in childhood play and had a group called "Give them a paintbrush instead of a gun." We rotated our monthly meetings to different homes and talked about possible nonviolent children's play. We collected cardboard boxes of all sizes and experimented with children to see what creative things they could make with fruit and vegetable boxes.

In January 1962 we put an ad in the newspaper signed by 125 area women. It said: "We enter the New Year resolved to raise our voices for life and sanity; for schools, for medical research, for patient and unremitting international negotiation; against the shelter program, against nuclear testing, against the whole arms race which imperils our hope for the future." We sought better ways for people to live together in the Cold War era. The shelter program referred to the federal government's establishment of public fallout shelters.

We sponsored an essay contest in cooperation with schools. The topic was "Reflection on War and Peace," and the prize was a trip to New York including a visit to the UN. Also in cooperation with schools, we organized high school institutes, all-day conferences often scheduled at UMass with titles like "In a World We Never Made," "Racial Crisis," and "Human Rights Day." Local high school students attended the conferences and considered issues of war and racism. Ruth Hawkins worked hard to continue the institutes in Chicopee and Springfield even after WILPF grew inactive.

In the six or seven years of its existence, our chapter kept quite busy. We campaigned for the Equal Rights Amendment, and WILPF cooperated with an effort to bring students from Harlem to Northampton for a summer session. We sponsored a panel on chemical and biological weapons, a symposium on the draft, and a course in black history at Northampton High School. We also brought impressive people to the area to speak, including Dorothy Hutchinson, president of the US section of WILPF from 1961 to 1964 and chairman of International WILPF from 1965-1968; Carmelita Hinton, progressive educator and founder of Vermont's Putney School; Barbara Deming, noted feminist; Bill Hinton, Carmelita's son, a China expert; Russell Johnson, peace education secretary of the Amer-

1965 notice of a League of Women Voters talk by Carmelita Hinton

ican Friends Service Committee; and Mildred Scott Olmstead, national administrative secretary of WILPF from 1946 to 1956. Olmstead encouraged us to work on national legislation. It wasn't my first interest. I don't think I have ever had a lot of faith in legislation. It seems to tie us up, and nothing ever seems to happen. Nevertheless, I found it energizing to work through WILPF with women from around the world.

WILPF has headquarters in Geneva, Switzerland and maintains an office near the UN in New York City. With its birth from frustration with World War I, WILPF mobilized women newly empowered to vote. Born as I was in 1919 at the war's end, I earnestly hoped that the First World War would be the last world war. With WILPF, I had confirmation that I was not alone and had a community of experienced, well-educated women from all over the world saying no to war.

We named our WILPF chapter for Jane Addams, and for a while we were the fastest growing chapter in the country. In 1966, some of us attended a national meeting in Philadelphia where Staughton Lynd, a Quaker dedicated to peace and justice work, and Martin Luther King, Jr. spoke against the war in Vietnam. Coretta Scott King participated for a while with WILPF. WILPF officers invited me several times to be on the national board, but I always said, "No, my work is right here. There is plenty to do."

As a chapter of WILPF, we received reports every month about war, peace, and related issues. The WILPF newsletter provided information about the Vietnam War emerging in Southeast Asia. WILPF endeavored to educate people about the situation in Vietnam. We read articles written by Asian women about their region. WILPF pays attention to women and their concerns.

Even these days, WILPF continues. It has an impressive website and many regional, state, and national committees working to end drone warfare, nuclear weapons, nuclear power, and US involvement in war. Every summer, Robin Lloyd invites New England WILPFers to her family summer home in Rochester, Vermont for a weekend conference. Twice, when I could carpool, I attended. I enjoyed it, but it did not have sufficient focus to make me a regular attendee. Robin participates with our Shut It Down Affinity Group dedicated to closing the Vermont Yankee nuclear reactor in Vernon and encouraging cleanup of the reactor site. Hattie Nestel, also of our Shut It Down Affinity Group, presented her PowerPoint program about nuclear power at Robin's encampment one summer.

As the 1960s progressed, Vietnam emerged as a big issue. As early as November, 1966, we met with Vietnam as a major topic and began to

WILPF Seattle reprint of a 1965 article by Dr. Benjamin Spock about wrong and brutal United States policies in Vietnam; the article was originally published in Sane World

figure out what to do to oppose the war. I remember reading in *The New York Times* in 1968 that a group of young men working for the International Volunteer Service in Vietnam had resigned. They advised Vietnamese farmers about how to grow better sweet potatoes but stopped as they experienced the war build-up. Don Luce directed a group of volunteers. He asked himself why he and his group worried about sweet potatoes when they should be trying to stop the war. All the volunteers resigned and returned to the US. I read that Don lived in Calais, Vermont, so I called and invited him to speak.

Our local WILPF chapter sponsored his speaking tour. I took him to Easthampton High School, where he addressed the audience from under the basketball hoop. Many people supported the war early on, and very few people opposed it. Don spoke very quietly about Vietnamese people and his work with them. He said the US encouraged the war instead of pushing for peace. It became quiet. The students sat in the bleachers and some on the floor, and I remember thinking, "Everybody is listening." I noticed the janitor at the door of the gym, mop in hand, very attentive to Don. I thought, "This is it. This is what we have to do. People need to know what is going on, and we can help that to happen."

I took Don around during several tours. He was on the radio. He spoke at Williams College. Alice Scheffey, whose husband taught at UMass and Williams, had a dinner for him and invited friends. I was developing a whole network.

Don put together a slide show called "Hearts and Minds in Vietnam: An Inside View." If Don wasn't available, I took the slide show wherever I could and showed it to people. I tried to get into churches, especially, as the issues were ethical and moral. Without realizing it, I laid the groundwork for outreach we did later for AFSC, for referendum campaigns like the nuclear weapons freeze initiative, for opposition to the draft, and for the drive against apartheid in South Africa. I kept notebooks with information on all the towns and the people in them that I could work with.

As the war heated up, the women's movement developed. With fresh aspirations encouraged by the women's movement, many in our group wanted to write their own books or go back to graduate school or get jobs. Membership in our WILPF chapter dwindled, and in 1969 we closed it. However, in large measure through WILPF, I found my work: peace education, stopping war, and eliminating nuclear power and nuclear weapons.

Not long after we moved to Northampton, Tom and I became interested in the Religious Society of Friends, the Quakers. Dane Prugh and his wife, our friends from Tom's residency, introduced us to Quakerism, and in Hartford, Caltha went to a Quaker-run nursery school in the basement of the meetinghouse. We liked their philosophy. But we didn't start attending the meeting until we moved to Northampton. As a member of the Leonard Club for Men, Tom attended a lecture about Quakers by Bill Scott, who taught at Smith.

Tom reported to me what he had heard, and we talked about it. We liked that the Quakers have no hierarchy and believe that God exists in every person. Quakers also carry a clear message of peace and justice. John Woolman, an early Friend, declared that war is not the answer. Woolman said we need to look at the seeds of war in our possessions. He dedicated himself also to abolishing slavery, and he brought his commitment to England in the 1830s. When Quakers acquired farmland on a Deerfield, Massachusetts hilltop, they named it Woolman Hill.

We started going to Quaker meetings, and although Tom officially joined the Society of Friends in 1958, I waited until 1978 to join. I decided I had been acting to the best of my ability in the Quaker way, and it was then that I formalized my relationship with the Friends.

Early in our Pioneer Valley days, the Quakers then met in Northampton just once a month. Meetings rotated to Greenfield, South Hadley, and Amherst. In addition to meetings, Tom and I felt we wanted to have something more for the children, like a first day school. Quakers call the days of the week first day, second day, third day, and so on to avoid implications suggested by more traditional names. The first day is analogous to Sunday, and in a first day school, children receive religious education based on Quaker principles while their parents participate in Quaker meeting. In order to have a first day school, conducted by Gladys Meyers, we started having a meeting at our house up on Round Hill Road. Gladys was a social worker and came with lots of things for the children to do. When the Huntingtons arrived in Northampton, they attended Friends meetings.

I went to the Northampton meeting for the first time at Smith College in the basement of a house on Elm Street and Paradise Road, where Smith religious community activities occurred. We took the children. I was out at the playground with them, and I asked the person working with the children, "Does this meeting really act on their beliefs?" I was looking for a group interested in acting to change society. I guess I still am looking. I very much admire what Quakers say, but New England Quakers are slow in doing. Quakers sit in silence waiting for the spirit to speak to them, and then they stand and share. It tends to make action very deliberate, considered, and slow. Still, Quakers dependably do what they say they will do.

When working for social change, it's easy enough to run ahead of the spirit and get out of tune with the other people. In the silent meeting for worship, you have a chance to get back in touch with important values. Winning the battle has less importance than remaining faithful and honest while carrying on ethical work. How you accomplish work matters to Quakers and not whether you achieve victory.

Through the Quakers, I searched for something the family could do in the summertime so we could all work on peace and justice issues together. The American Friends Service Committee (AFSC) sponsored week-long summer peace institutes patterned along the lines of Chatauqua institutes about literature, arts, philosophy, and current events. We went as a family and lived together as did other families in a cabin with bunk beds. Our friends the Huntingtons attended, too. Everyone ate meals together in a central dining room.

We started each morning with assigned workshops to talk about current issues facing us. In the afternoon, interest groups met. At about three-thirty, everybody stopped and went swimming. After the evening meal, we attended more programs. The children had separate leaders. We met people from throughout New England who worked for social change.

The first institute we went to was at Avon Old Farms School in Connecticut. Presenters included A. J. Muste, a founder of the Committee for Non Violent Action; Staughton Lynd, a Quaker teaching at Yale who tirelessly worked for peace; and Bayard Rustin, a leader in the nonviolent civil rights movement. Milton Mayer, a Quaker progressive who wrote about Germans in pre-World-War-II Germany, came and talked about issues of war and peace. Of course they were all men in those years, but it was exhilarating to hear significant speakers describing their positions.

I was really riveted. I had been looking for this. I remember about the second day there when Milton Mayer spoke. I asked questions and engaged in a lively dialogue with him. Russell Johnson, one of the organizers and a former minister from Petersham about an hour's drive from where I lived in Northampton, approached me. "Frances," Russell said, "how would you like to be on the outreach committee of the New England AFSC Peace Committee?"

"I would love to," I answered. Russell didn't exactly specify what being on the outreach committee meant or what my responsibilities would entail, but I wanted to get involved. I have found through my life that when you work on the issues, opportunities open up before you and encourage you to follow where they lead.

As it turned out, the AFSC Outreach committee never met, and I never had to go to Cambridge for meetings. But if AFSC sponsored a speaker, I arranged for food, lodging, and speaking engagements in the Northampton area. I drove people around to their appointments and set up radio and newspaper interviews for them. Often, we met with the publication or broadcast agency editorial board. In the doing, I learned. I learned who to contact and how to approach them. I learned how to convince people to give speakers an opportunity to offer their information. And, incidentally, I learned a lot about driving in Western Massachusetts.

Of course, things got crazy sometimes. When a speaker stayed in our home as a guest, I got up and made breakfast for the family and our guest, got the children off to school, and then went off with the speaker to drive to Williamstown or wherever. I tried to be back home in time for the children's arrival after school and to prepare dinner. I remember one particularly challenging episode involving Reginald Reynolds from England, a Quaker who served as Secretary of the No More War Movement in the 1930s. He declared conscientious objection during World War II. I took him around, and we got home about three-thirty or four in the afternoon. I had to prepare dinner and get him to an evening meeting. "It would be so nice to have a fire in your fireplace and a cup of tea," he announced.

"Yes," I thought. "That would be nice." I'm sure I did it. I remember collecting wood and building a fire. But after that I decided, "No more Reginald Reynolds for me. I need someone who will help me a little bit." He wanted me to sit down by the fire and have a cup of tea. I hadn't even made the beds or washed the breakfast dishes, and I still had to get dinner.

I worked to balance everything because it was good for me to reach out, listen to the stories, and work to have the stories heard by others. My work with the outreach committee also meant that I made contacts in local communities and with supportive teachers. For example, I met Arthur Serota, a radio commentator and lawyer in Springfield who always welcomed the speakers AFSC and I provided.

Carmel Budiardjo, a British woman from Indonesia, arrived in Western Massachusetts in 1973 thanks to Russell. Carmel's husband was an Indonesian government official, Suwondo Budiardjo. The Suharto regime imprisoned Budiardjo soon after the 1967 takeover from Sukarno. For seven years, the Suharto regime also detained Carmel Budiardjo in Java as a political prisoner. She came to speak about her experiences as a

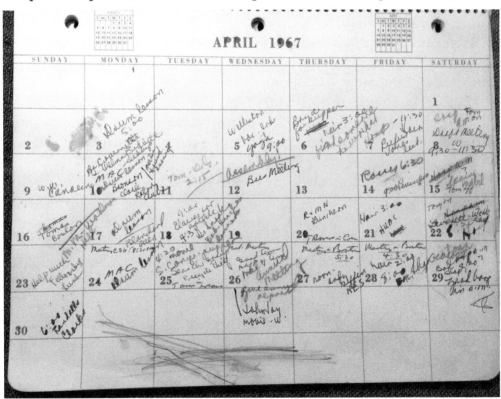

page from Frances's 1967 appointment calendar

79

*Frances and Tom's home on Langworthy Road, Northampton, where Frances set up her American Friends Service Committee (AFSC) office in the basement in the mid/late 1960s after the
Crowe children grew up*

political detainee. She stayed with us, and as always with speakers we hosted, I found inspiration.

Then AFSC changed focus. Instead of sponsoring speakers, the organization wanted multicultural emphasis with people organizing locally around issues. I began to rethink my goals. One summer I worked with students at UMass trying to influence the budgeting and use of Housing and Urban Development (HUD) money in the city of Springfield. The city wanted HUD to subsidize hotels and high-rise buildings like the Monarch Life Insurance building on Main Street near the highway instead of low-income housing. Students protested the city's plans and opened a storefront headquarters in Springfield.

I tried to help the students and got some money from AFSC to hire Tom Bell, a young man recently graduated from UMass. About the second week after the office opened, someone threw a brick through the front plate glass window. Tom came up to Northampton from Springfield and told me, "I can't take this, Frances. There's too much hostility down there. It's all loaded against us. And I'm pulling out. I'm going to go to a Buddhist meditation center in Colorado. I'm sorry but I'm just too angry to deal with this." I understood. People need to provide for their own and their family's well being before they can change things for the better in the world.

AFSC organized each summer institute around a theme and perhaps in 1964 or 1965, the institute focused on racism. Leadership of

African-Americans evolved across the country as civil rights legislation passed. Muhammad Kenyatta led a movement challenging large churches in Philadelphia to give money and stocks to black groups with no strings attached.

As similar movements emerged elsewhere in the Northeast, Russell Johnson decided to address them. He invited black leaders from Washington, Philadelphia, New Haven, and Boston to the summer institute at Geneva Point Camp on Lake Winnipesaukee in New Hampshire, a perfect conference center with cabins, a dining room, and a central meetinghouse.

Almost from the first evening, black leaders decided the conference offered a chance for them to get together. A waterfront house on the premises had often been allocated for people with special needs. The black leadership got together and decided that African Americans should use the waterfront house exclusively so they could talk about their own special needs instead of joining general meetings and following the planned agenda. At mealtimes, they took over a small dining room where they ate separately from those in the main dining area. They wanted their own agenda and to decide about their own issues rather than have the white community tell them what should be done.

Attendees at the AFSC institute tried hard to hear them. But Quakers in the Boston area, including Elizabeth Boardman, a volunteer in the Cambridge AFSC office, questioned whether to relinquish money or power. She had worked hard to raise money for an AFSC center in Roxbury, Boston's African-American community. She and other Quakers felt they should have control and that the black community should work with them on agreed-upon projects.

Many African Americans expressed their frustrations militantly in the mid sixties, and it was difficult to work together. At the AFSC institute, one delegate built a little stand and said, "I'm from the Berkshires raising money for the blacks here with no strings attached." He raised quite a bit of money in just a few days.

William Coperthwaite attended the institute. A native of Maine, he pioneered yurt building in the United States, lived in a Mongolian-style yurt, and wrote a book about living the simple life. During the institute, he drove off in his truck and returned with pieces of colorful suede. He provided scissors for cutting and needles for sewing the leather. He parked his truck right in the middle of the lawn and said to everyone, black and white, "In the afternoon, all of you come together. Help yourself to leather and make things." People showed up and made creative handbags and wallets. Blacks and whites passed scissors and needles back and forth.

Thanks to Bill Coperthwaite, we found a way to come together, cooperate, and slowly move to some mutual understanding.

Some participants, however, felt the black delegates and people with conventionally identified special needs should talk it through. To support the idea, we slept in sleeping bags on the lawn in front of cabins instead of inside. From his sleeping bag near me, Paul Goodman, the writer and social critic, announced at about one in the morning, "I can't sleep. This is not solvable. I'm leaving." He walked to his car dragging his sleeping bag behind him.

That was the last summer institute I attended.

In some ways, I had found limits on my ability to act, particularly in concert with the black community. On the other hand, AFSC offered me its great potential for working toward peace and justice. Tom supported my increasing commitment to antiwar work, and I found the cause that would define my life after the children grew up. Although AFSC's policies for multiculturalism and a community base did not precisely align with my concerns about ending war, I decided in the long run it was worth it to continue to work with AFSC.

*American Friends Service Committee sign that stood for more than
twenty-five years in Frances and Tom's front yard*

antiwar poster from 1968,
artist unknown

Very few—an almost imperceptible number—
qualified as COs in World War II. He felt the
same would be true for the Vietnam War. I
wanted to make everyone a CO. I wanted each
to develop his conscience and work against
war.

DRAFT COUNSELING

The Vietnam War escalated in the 1960s. This development wrenched society toward social change and propelled many of us to action. Not only did the tragic war exploit the people of Vietnam—a foreign and unfamiliar culture. The war also upended expectations of young Americans coming to maturity. The US draft interrupted and threatened to disrupt relationships, career plans, and families just as during World War II and the Korean conflict. This time, however, blatant lies and inequities outshone public relations spin, and people of all ages sought ways to resist.

Just before I counseled hundreds of young men to find their consciences and confront the draft in the 1960s and 1970s, I became active in the Women's Liberation Movement. Nineteen-sixties feminism, especially as advanced by Betty Friedan in her 1963 book *The Feminine Mystique,* affected women in Western Massachusetts as it did in the whole US. I was in my forties, and like many women then, I took part in women's groups and then consciousness-raising groups. The groups brought women together to talk about their lives and to examine their roles in the light of their personal choices while considering how societal forces influenced those roles.

My women's group meant a lot to me. We all were faced with examining our roles. I went to a therapist briefly to help sort out my life, and I found therapy helpful. I also took part in a group through the Friends Meeting that consisted of men and women trying to address issues raised by sixties and seventies "second-wave feminism." Tom took no interest in the Friends' or other consciousness-raising groups. He felt uneasy in such situations. Many in our group made major changes in their lives but I became affirmed in my role as a wife, mother, and woman.

Some women in the groups I took part in made decisions to go back to school or go to work. I decided, however, that I didn't want to go to graduate school, and I didn't want to get a job. In fact, I had already been to graduate school and, I thought, "I already have a job. And I'm going to stay with it." I kept busy with the outreach committee of AFSC and felt strongly that my work involved changing the culture of war, which I saw as the central issue.

Although we never sat down and made a conscious decision, Tom and I concurred when it came to feelings of social responsibility. He continued with Physicians for Social Responsibility and thrived in his work as a radiologist. All his life, he spoke against the dangers of cigarette smoking, and he always diligently wrote letters through Amnesty International in support of prisoners of conscience. He regularly wrote advocacy letters in response to action alerts put out by Physicians for Human Rights. He took satisfaction in my time spent on issues of peace and nonviolence.

In July 1968 we moved to our house on Langworthy Road. Caltha had graduated from Smith, Jarlath studied at National Technical Institute for the Deaf, and young Tom looked forward to beginning his days at East Hill. The summer before the beginning of school, I felt as if the children and their friends talked constantly about the draft when they sat around the kitchen table. The boys worried about what would happen to them if they were drafted, and Caltha and girl friends worried for them.

Patriotism and the lure of adventure pulled them in one direction while fear and concern about where war would take them pulled them in the other. The Vietnam War had been simmering since the fifties, and by 1964 with passage of the bogus Gulf of Tonkin Resolution, the US embarked on a full scale offensive with American troops on the ground. The Selective Service System operated at full swing as the means of supplying those troops.

I didn't know much about the draft nor what actually might face teenagers. I knew a Selective Service Act passed in 1917 required all men from ages twenty-one to thirty serve in the military. The practice stopped at the end of World War I but was reinstituted in 1940 by the Selective Training and Service Act and subsequent draft laws. I decided I needed to find out about the draft in general and the selective service law then in effect in particular. I wanted to focus on conscientious objector (CO) rights.

I heard that the Central Committee for Conscientious Objectors (CCCO), founded in 1948, planned a weekend draft counseling training in Philadelphia. That sounded like a perfect place for me to start. In the fall of 1967, I went to Philadelphia for the training. At the training, much discussion focused on specifics and interpretations of the draft law. Many in the group had served as draft counselors in World War II, and they felt that being a conscientious objector required a religious objection. I spoke with one of the instructors in the training course, and he said, "You have to come with religious training and a religious belief against war." Therefore, very few—an almost imperceptible number—qualified as COs in World War II. He felt the same would be true for the Vietnam War.

I wanted to make everyone a CO. I wanted each to develop his conscience and work against war.

When I came back to Northampton, I got a copy of the law. I read it very carefully and didn't interpret it the same way as they explained it in Philadelphia. The law says that conscientious objection comprises moral, ethical, philosophical, or religious grounds embraced by the individual opposed to war facing him in any form. When a young man holds moral and ethical objections with the same degree of intensity he would religious belief, he is entitled to the conscientious objector classification. During the Vietnam Era, conscientious objection meant that the individual would not be drafted.

You don't have to say what you would have done in the War of the Roses or hypothetical future wars. You don't have to say if you would have served in the First or Second World War. Those were not the wars facing the young men during the Vietnam War. The law applied to the war facing them. The way I read the law, a person qualifies as a conscientious objector and should not go into the military if that person holds a moral, ethical, or philosophical objection to the war facing him (or, now, her) with the same degree of intensity as he would if he held a religious belief against this war.

I wrote a letter. In 1968, the average person did not have access to photocopiers. I had to cut a stencil with my typewriter and then make copies on my clunky mimeograph machine. In my capacity as AFSC coordinator, I sent the letter to all ministers and lawyers in the area saying I planned a session on draft counseling the next Saturday morning and invited them to attend. I reserved a room in The First Churches in downtown Northampton. Nobody responded. Finally, on the Friday afternoon before the planned session, I got a call from Bill Norris, a new young lawyer in the area who wanted to come to the draft counseling session the next morning.

"I want you to read the packet of information I've put together," I told him. "I want you to look it over before you come. Why don't I bring it to you."

He lived in Cummington. It was winter and snowing. I drove the uphill twenty miles to Cummington. He and his wife invited me in. They had a cheery fire in the fireplace. They gave me a cup of tea, and we talked. That was the beginning of our enduring friendship.

I told him how I interpreted the draft law.

"You're absolutely right," he said. He explained that the ability to use moral and ethical grounds came about in 1958 when Dan Seeger, raised Roman Catholic but eventually becoming a Quaker, refused induction because he held his objection on moral, ethical grounds with the same degree of intensity he would if his objection were based on religious grounds. When the Supreme Court decided his case in 1965, he was released from prison. The Supreme Court ruled in United States v. Seeger that his conviction was mistaken because Congress in its statutory language "did not intend" using "the usual understanding" of "Supreme Being," but rather an interpretation that extended to Seeger's "compulsion" to "goodness." If you hold a moral, ethical, or philosophical objection to war, you are a CO.

"Great," I said. "That's the way I'm going to work."

I visited draft-counseling centers near Boston and New Haven. It seemed that angry, rebellious young men ran many of them. They talked about falsifying records, failing the physical exam by deceit, and getting a psychiatrist to write a letter affirming their mental deficiency. They recommended strategies such as adding protein to a urine sample, gaining weight or losing weight, or cutting off the right index finger—crazy demonizing things that disturbed me.

"No," I said. "That's not the approach I want to use. I want to help the men use the very best from within themselves." I knew their draft records would be available to anyone. If young men avoided the draft by illegal or marginal methods, they could jeopardize their ability to get health insurance or work they wanted later in life. I wanted to help them be conscientious objectors in moral and ethical ways. I decided to set up groups like the women's support groups I had been involved in so the men could support each other.

To run draft-counseling groups for potential COs, I needed training. I took a group-counseling course at the UMass School of Education. There I learned techniques for group counseling such as the importance of sitting in a circle, of responding not to the leader but to the group, of sharing stories and taking turns. Our house on Langworthy had a good place downstairs in its ample basement near my AFSC office to have such groups.

I decided to have the groups on Tuesday and Thursday afternoons and Friday nights. But the big challenge was how to publicize them. I tried to get an ad in the paper that said something like: "Young men, are you conscientiously opposed to participation in war in any form facing you? Come for draft counseling." At first, the advertising staff of The Daily Hampshire Gazette wouldn't publish the ad because they believed I planned to do something illegal.

"Talk to your lawyer," I said. "It is not illegal. I'm helping young men of draft age understand the law." Eventually, they changed their position, and I put in a small want ad: "Are you opposed to participation in war? Come to our group."

But nobody came.

The colleges did not provide bus service in those days, and not many students had cars. Like everybody else at the time, I picked up hitchhikers going back and forth among the colleges. One Monday morning, I set out in my station wagon. I had a stack of mimeographed sheets that talked about the draft and had directions to my house and the times of the sessions. I drove back and forth between Amherst, home of UMass and Amherst College, and Northampton, home of Smith College, and picked up hitchhikers all day. As soon as a young man got in the car, I asked him, "What are you going to do about the draft?"

They came up with various solutions, including lying, finding a psychiatrist, and going to Canada, where they would not be subject to the draft. I drove slowly and talked fast. When I dropped them off, I gave them materials and directions to my house.

The next day, I had a room full. The young men who arrived at my door all filled out a form when they came in, and I never had anyone who objected. They were very confident students. They gave their names, addresses, draft status, information about any of their possible physical exemptions, a little bit about other exemptions they might qualify for, and where they thought they wanted to go to do alternative service if it were assigned. I kept the forms so that if they were on vacation and the draft law suddenly changed, they could call me from Montana or wherever and I could look at their record and counsel them on the best course of action.

When they arrived, we sat in a circle. First, I asked each young man in turn to tell his story. Consciousness-raising groups and the course I had taken at UMass helped me feel comfortable about the approach. I asked the old John Woolman question: "Young man, what is it you are objecting to?"

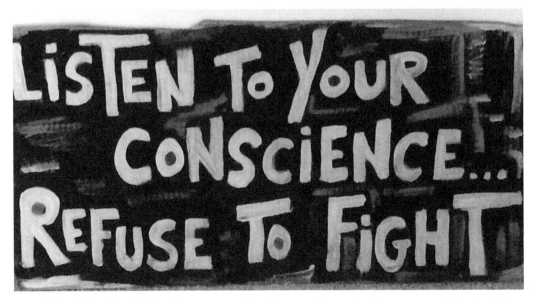

2000s Claudia Lefko banner reflecting sentiments Frances cultivated in Vietnam-era conscientious objectors (COs)

Some said they didn't want to be put in the position of killing someone or being killed. Others were more interested in their careers and not up-ending plans. As we went around the circle, each one said what he object-ed to. They began to gain confidence by hearing one another. Each could see he was not unique in his concerns.

"Yes," someone would say. "That's the way I feel."

"What's the basis of your belief, and where does it come from?" I asked. And "What do you think are seeds in your background for your ideas of conscience?"

One young man shared a story of accidentally killing a squirrel with a BB gun when he was young and how remorseful he felt. He said taking a squirrel's life impacted his conscience. Another told about reading *Johnny Got His Gun*, a popular antiwar novel, and how he then thought about war and killing. We talked about books, music, and films. We shared. Then those unfamiliar with particular resources found them and read, heard, or saw them to see if they were helpful in discerning their own beliefs.

I explained the law and supplied information about the draft and Se-lective Service regulations. Mostly the meetings proceeded as group dis-cussions. I asked questions, and we went around the circle to hear each person's response. Sharing stories helped the young men clarify their ideas of conscience. Even those young men who initially worried about interrupting their careers found that stories others told resonated. They began to find genuine ethical bases even if their original motive had to do with career. They took notes and, as new people came in, the experienc-es of those further along in the process helped newcomers clarify their responses to war.

We had coffee and tea, and sometimes people brought cookies, cheese, and crackers. I showed slide shows about Vietnam including Don Luce's "Remember Vietnam." It helped them get in touch with the current situ-ation in Vietnam and made them think about the reality of Vietnam as a place where people live and work. I bought a projector and showed films about the war, including John Pilger's *The Quiet Mutiny*.

After someone filed a CO claim, he had to fill out the 150 form re-quiring him to explain the nature of his beliefs in writing and where his beliefs originated. I helped young men see how they were brought up, influences on their lives, or their interest in nature and animals. Many things emerged to show their budding opposition to killing. Then they had to write about their beliefs and how they lived them. Eighteen-year-olds don't ordinarily express their feelings by standing in vigils. They didn't have guns, they didn't kill animals, and they tried to figure out the future. I helped them look into their own lives and list possibilities on paper. They drafted answers and came back later to read them to the group, which critiqued them.

They stayed late, and sometimes it was hard, on Friday night particularly, to get them to leave, because they had developed a group, a community. When they didn't start to leave by ten o'clock, Tom paced upstairs. He wanted me to wind things up and end the meetings. Nevertheless, Tom was very patient with the young men meeting in our home on Friday nights, and he truly supported my draft counseling activity.

The number in sessions ranged from a low number of eight to a high of seventy-nine. That first year from 1968 through 1969, I kept a tally each week of how many young men attended. There were 1,776 separate office visits with many young men coming back time after time. It's a grand number.

They helped one another. Articulate college students often were out of touch with their feelings while high school dropouts often were in touch with theirs. The group work provided a chance to help one another. One fellow was totally out of the system. He had never attended college and lived in a teepee in the woods. He had trouble expressing himself verbally, but he was a very good wood carver. The group encouraged him to express himself through his craft. He made a beautiful box, a cube. He carved Gandhi's face on one side, Martin Luther King on another, Cesar Chavez on another, and Dorothy Day on another, all heroes who espoused nonviolence. When it was time for him to make an appeal in person and state his beliefs before the draft board, he brought the box. At first, the draft board thought he had a bomb, but after they understood, he got his CO. He was very sincere and helped the college students enormously. In fact, I saw him a few years ago when he spent the summer in Granby. He's a well known artist now in Japan.

Eventually, some of those serving in the military showed up for the meetings as well as young men trying to decide whether they would go. A few girlfriends, mothers, and wives arrived, and even at one point a potential draftee's father who chaired a Holyoke Draft Board. He said he wanted to understand the law. He wanted to be sure to get correct information because his son had qualified for a CO in another district of Holyoke, and he wanted to be sure the draft boards' information corroborated.

I had all the legal books. I even subscribed to the *Law Reporter*. I realized that draft boards did not always follow the law to the letter. They sometimes drafted out of order or didn't follow the rules. Individual draft board members may have been appointed for political reasons and not because they had knowledge of, or even interest in, the draft law.

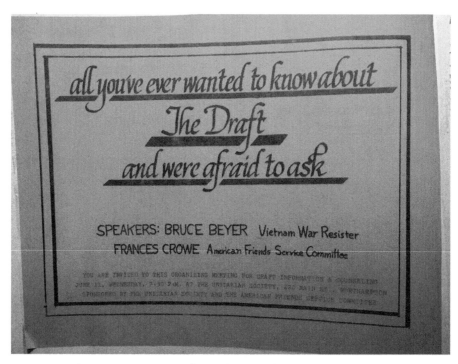

Vietnam War era flyer for a talk by Frances and Bruce Beyer about draft resistance

As part of my draft information work, I monitored the Northampton draft board. On their Monday meeting night, I parked in front of the draft board office on the second floor in a Main Street building. I sat outside in the car and watched to see who went in. On Tuesday morning, I went back to review the posted minutes to be sure they drafted individuals in the right order and didn't skip over people who had political connections.

The draft board had to follow certain guidelines. When I looked at the minutes of a meeting, I could see their actions and could challenge them if necessary. They knew about my monitoring. I never did challenge them, but I think it made them more careful. That vigilance made a difference, I think.

One of the most effective ways that people in the group helped each other was to role-play personal appearances in front of the draft board. After someone appeared before a draft board, he reported the questions the board members asked him. We kept lists of questions that some draft boards customarily asked. Draft boards traditionally asked four questions: What do you object to about war now, and what is the nature of your belief—moral, philosophical, ethical, or religious? Where did those beliefs come from, and what influenced you? How is that objection showing up in your life? And would you be willing to serve as a military medic? They sometimes asked stupid questions like, "Are you a vegetarian?"

94

as if that made a difference, and "What would you do if someone tried to attack your grandmother?"

The group coached them to respond, "That's not war, and my grandmother locks her doors. She doesn't have guns, and I don't have a gun." Young men figured out how to deal with draft board questions and, once they had dealt with them, returned to help others.

Often a young man who had been through a draft board interview came back and pretended he was the draft board chairman. He asked questions like those posed to him. We then helped others prepare for their personal appearances. It was lively stuff, and the young men loved it.

We kept data about many draft boards. I knew draft boards in New Jersey and on Long Island where quite a few Amherst College and UMass students originated. Because I knew those draft boards, I could say, "These are questions they are probably going to ask you." With such information, we were better able to be of service. After those who got their 1-0 classification as conscientious objectors came back and shared their experience, we celebrated. I ended up with many people who knew the law as well as I did and could use that knowledge to help others.

We discussed crystallization of conscience, that it is a slow evolution, that you take one step and decide how comfortable you feel and where you're moving, and that helps you take another step.

"What if the draft board says that you pay taxes so you obey the law?" some young men asked.

"It's illegal not to pay taxes just as it's illegal for me to go into the army if I object to the war facing me," I counseled them to say. I wanted to help them accurately use the law to support their moral and ethical objections to war.

One young man who came for draft counseling for himself told me about his older brother who had gone to Canada because he had resisted induction. He had applied for CO and didn't get it, and instead of reporting for induction, he fled to Canada where US law couldn't prosecute him. The younger brother came, and I worked with him to get his 1-0 classification. I told him that if his brother wanted to return to the US, I would be glad to help him. I thought perhaps he had been drafted out of order and, thus, would have a good reason to have fled.

He wrote to his brother and after his brother said he wanted to return, I looked through the draft board records and saw that, sure enough, the young man had been called out of order. That made his induction order illegal. I called him, and the next weekend, he came to my house. He got the illegal induction order vacated. He continued living in Canada but wanted to be able to see his family in the US. After the order was vacated, he could return without fear of arrest. He became a Quaker and came to the local Friends Meeting. He told me about his life.

I tried to help them all. I remember only one person who went to prison. He was eighteen and a Quaker from New Hampshire. He was determined to refuse induction even if it meant going to prison. He didn't register and said so publicly, and they came after him. There was a trial, and a number of us went. It was like Greek drama. He spoke eloquently, but the outcome was known. The judge simply said he was breaking the law and had to go to jail. I wept as I watched him taken away. I wrote him in prison. When he got out, I picked him up and drove him home, so I saw him through his choice. He ended up in New York State in the landscape business. But prison was hard for him. He thought he would eat only the very healthiest food and not do any work, but slowly they wore him down. If he did a little work, he could go running every morning. He found he couldn't change the system.

At least one person who came for counseling went into the army. He went in as a 1A0 and was assigned to Vietnam as a medic. His brother was already in Vietnam, and he felt that he wanted to be there too. But Tom always said medics in the service don't necessarily heal the most severely wounded first. Their orders tell them to get the least wounded back into battle. Tom said after he realized that, he would never want to take CO status as a medic. But this young man felt he wanted to be there.

We discovered that getting the draft board to award a 1-0 classification was like getting the first olive out of the jar. After a board gave out the first 1-0, the rest became easier. Each draft board had a quota of soldiers to provide. But I thought it was important to pass on to the young men that just the process of applying for 1-0 reduced the quota by one. You didn't go, but nobody went in your place. My reasoning was that, if everybody applied, nobody would go. I tried to get everybody to apply for CO status. "Look at the law," I kept saying. "Read the law. You are qualified. The government doesn't want anyone who is conscientiously opposed to the war. Under those circumstances, you actually violate the law if you go in."

The law stated that if a person qualified 1-0, he had to do two years of alternative service if called. If the draft board determined a CO had to do alternative service, we tried to find creative jobs for them if they were called. We got churches and nonprofit organizations to sponsor COs so that they worked for alternative schools, health care centers, food banks, and shelters, among other places. Many young men worked in hospitals. I tried to make sure they had useful work. The law says the work has to be something with national health or safety interests or for nonprofit organizations. The work also had to qualify as something that would at least slightly disrupt the CO's personal life, which usually meant moving out of his local community. I kept dozens of folders with job opportunities for COs all over the country. My background in personnel probably helped me to relate to potential draft resisters as clients looking for a way to do something important in their lives.

Many young men came and said they had flat feet or some other problem. But I always recommended they try for CO status first, because draft boards always sent them for a physical after they got a 1-0 classification in order to determine their fitness for alternative service. They would have an opportunity later to use physical reasons for disqualification from alternative service. If they didn't pass the physical, they did not have to serve. Eventually, I think many people classified 1-0 were disqualified for medical reasons. Then the draft board didn't have to provide alternative service, a cumbersome process for the draft board to carry out because it had to agree to alternative placements

Now when I run into COs, as I do after all these years, I ask, "What have you done with your life?" They have done interesting things. They are principals of high schools, and many are teachers, especially high school teachers, many in history, and some in college. Often they say they got turned on to social service or education when we got churches to sponsor them in daycare centers, soup kitchens, and shelters. One young man went to Haiti to work at the Albert Schweitzer hospital and came back and studied medicine.

Scarcely a week goes by that I don't run into somebody who was among the counselees. I went to an organic farm once, and the owner wanted to show me around. "You don't remember me," he said, "but I came. I was one of your people. And I've never really thanked you." He gave me carrots and potatoes.

In 1996, I received an honorary doctorate of humane letters from UMass. After the ceremony, someone from the crowd came up and said, "I can't believe you're still doing this stuff. I was one of your COs." His son was graduating, and he said, "I'm so happy you're here."

Some of the most difficult sessions involved those already serving in the military. They came, and we helped them. We encouraged them to think through their conscience. We gave them the GI Rights Hotline telephone number and gave them the names of lawyers who would help them discern their true moral, ethical, philosophical, and religious motivations about military involvement.

But some had to go back. One young man, who was AWOL, came, and we helped him talk through what he had to do. I didn't consider myself a military counselor, so I sent him to get military counseling to help sort through the issues. He decided to turn himself in and apply for a CO discharge. I helped him with letters of reference. I knew ministers in town who would talk to him, help him search his conscience, and then write a letter of support.

He went back into the military but refused to wear a uniform. He told us later that once he stood in his wooden barracks somewhere in the South wearing only his undershorts. The sergeant threw a gun at him and said, "You pick that up, or we're going to kill you." Picking up the gun would contradict his claim that he was a CO.

He didn't do it. He didn't pick up the gun. "I felt the group with me as I stood there," he told us. The military tested him, and he used his feeling of solidarity to withstand pressure tactics. I used his experience in later trainings to help people in our role-plays.

As for me, I didn't care if I took risks. I acted on my own conscience. I was pretty sure the government watched me. One evening, someone a bit suspicious came into a draft counseling session. He looked very uncomfortable and obviously had a tape recorder. I knew he wore a wig. "Look," I said, "take off your wig. It's too hot in here. Put your tape recorder away."

He mumbled something and fled.

Sometimes my neighbors objected to motorcycles and young men wearing torn jeans. Often there were lots of people. The Friday night we had seventy-nine, we had to break up into smaller groups all over the house and the yard. The neighbors couldn't miss that.

Sometimes mothers and fathers came, and many were skeptical. "What are you doing?" they asked. "Who are you? What's this all about?"

But I was just right out there. I was honest and trusting, and the young men trusted me. It was a good open process, and there was no media coverage of my activity. People had been socialized into an artificial patriotism filled with lies. Advertising, propaganda—it's unrelenting. People's minds were paralyzed and fearful.

I feel that parents have a responsibility to level with their children about their feelings and not just say, "It's your life. You have to decide." When their children are growing up, parents are responsible to promote their moral, ethical, and philosophical lives. During the Vietnam War, our son Tom was away at the East Hill School. He tried to be objective and, even with his mother deeply involved in draft counseling, he was skeptical. Eventually he said, "I think I'm going to go into the army and find out what it is really like."

His father and I did not want Tom to learn to kill or suffer the moral injury that would result from killing. I called him and said, "Tom, we want you to come home and spend a day with us. We'll talk this through

Vietnam-era antiwar demonstration on Amherst Common: demonstrators dressed as the Vietnamese to encourage empathy with them, Frances explained

Vietnam era flyer for a draft information session—a teach-in— sponsored by AFSC and Frances for high school students in the Amherst, Massachusetts, Bangs Community Center

because we feel this is not you. Come on a Wednesday when I don't have a group. We'll take the phone off the hook and won't answer the door. We'll be there totally for you."

He came, and he, his father, and I talked all day. We sat and talked it through. At the end of the day, he said, "I will apply for a CO on environmental grounds." For him it was to protect the earth. He felt that war damages the earth and animal life and endangers species and so he applied for his CO. He said, "I am not a Quaker," but it was his belief system that he tapped into. By then, the draft lottery was in place, and he got a number that did not put him at risk. I was very glad. Since then he has said, "That was really important what you did. If I had waited to go or volunteered, it would have been a big mistake." I think parents should get actively involved when their children are facing big decisions. It can make a difference.

Late in 1969 the government instituted a lottery to choose whom to draft. It changed things. Prior to the lottery, men were called from oldest to youngest. With the lottery, all men from nineteen to twenty-five could be selected. Days of the year were assigned a number. January first was number one and each subsequent day received the next number. The numbers went into a container, and then numbers were drawn one by one. If the first number drawn was the number ten, every man born on January 10 received a draft number of one and would be among the first called to be in the military.

With the lottery, the overall numbers of people seeking draft counseling declined. If someone had a high number, he was less likely to be concerned about being drafted. But we still had people. And more people already in the military contacted me. I didn't do a lot of military counseling, but I did help some get discharged or I referred them to someone who could help them. Bill Norris worked with them, or I sent them to Marj Swann in Voluntown, Connecticut with the Committee for Nonviolent Action (CNVA). Marj counseled men already in the military. They needed specialized information and counseling.

In the 1960s and 1970s, the draft applied only to young men. The last conscription occurred in 1972. Since 1972, the military has operated on an "all volunteer" basis. Required registration for the Selective Service System, familiarly called "the draft," resumed in 1980. The government requires all male US citizens between the ages of eighteen and twenty-five to register with the Selective Service System.

In the ensuing years, as young men had an obligation to register for the draft, I told them that, if they are opposed to war, they should register and say they are COs. If they don't register, they may not be eligible for federal loans for graduate or medical school.

I opposed war, and draft counseling gave me a way to work against the Vietnam War. My first arrest occurred at Westover Air Force Base in 1972 during an anti-Vietnam War demonstration. I was in a Women against the War group. We dressed as Vietnamese women and put white paint on our faces and red paint as if we were bleeding. We went to Westover on May 1 to read Vietnamese poetry. We didn't discuss risking arrest, but as we read the poems and cars kept entering the base, we decided just to move into the road and kneel down facing the base. Most of us were crying by that time. We were really into our role. We were arrested for blocking the road, arraigned, and released.

I managed to get home in time to fix supper, and I told Tom about the day when he came home. "You didn't tell me you were going to be arrested," he said with some surprise. Even though we had not discussed this new development, Tom understood what moved me to action, even when it led to arrest. As always, I knew I could count on his support.

About a week later, I heard on the morning WHMP radio news that Lieutenant Donald Dawson had become the first B-52 bomber pilot to refuse to fly in Vietnam. His mother came on the air from Danbury, Connecticut and said, "He's not a conscientious objector. His father fought in World War II, and Donald would have fought in World War II."

I went right to the phone. I got the numbers of all the Dawsons in Danbury and started dialing them. The first Dawson I got was Donald's mother. "I just heard you on the radio," I told her. "Your son will never know what he would have done in World War II. He wasn't even living then. The law says you have to be against the 'war facing you.' And he will never face World War II." I asked for his APO number so I could send him some literature. She gave it to me, and I immediately went downstairs and got a packet of stuff together and mailed it. He received it en route out of the battle zone as he was being court-martialed and returned to Westover.

Earlier, Donald had been at Westover during our demonstration for his month long Rest and Recreation leave. Even though he was on leave, his superiors called him to hold an assault weapon in case we came on the base. He said just holding the assault weapon aimed at us embodying Vietnamese women triggered his emotions.

That night he was watching *West Side Story* with his wife and just started crying. He couldn't figure out why. And the next day all the way back to the air base in Thailand, he was crying. Finally he realized it was because he had for the first time actually seen the Vietnamese people he bombed. From the plane, he bombed unseen targets that came up in the cross hairs. It so unnerved him that he went to see the chaplain and psychiatrist and said he could not participate in war any more.

The military court-martialed him but eventually gave him a CO discharge. I received a long letter from Donald in August of 1973 after he left the military. He told me the pamphlet I sent him convinced him to apply not for military status as a non-combatant but instead to apply for a conscientious objection discharge. The pamphlet explained the role of medics and their military obligation to treat the least wounded first in order to get them back into battle.

Donald's marriage did not last, and later, he remarried and had a family. He became a lawyer in Nashville, Tennessee where he worked against the death penalty by helping death row inmates prepare their appeals.

I think the counseling experience transformed the young men who participated. Humans are not made to kill each other, and once a person gets insight and support, it is easy to see how crazy it is for the government to train anyone to be a murderer. Now I frequently run into people in all walks of life who say, "I came to your draft counseling sessions and they were the turning point of my life."

Becoming conscientious objectors changed their lives forever. They faced the draft, took control of their lives, figured out who they were and what they wanted to do and why. They recognized that each of them had a conscience he could follow. I urged them to take responsibility, and I think it was a very positive experience for the young men. I know it was for me.

Over the years at AFSC, several college students worked with me in my Langworthy Road basement office. Those interns were invaluable assistants and brainstormers as we worked for peace and justice. They included Ruth Benn and Frida Berrigan who each went on to work with War Resisters League; Deirdre Cornell, author of *American Madonna* about Mexican veneration of the Virgin Mary and *Jesus Was a Migrant* about the value of migrants to the United States; Rachel King of the Sanctuary Movement; John Bonifaz who became a Boston lawyer specializing in constitutional law and voting rights; and Denise Mock who became the Development Database Manager at American Civil Liberties Union of Northern California.

Draft counseling and working with AFSC opened many doors for me to the peace and justice movements. In undertaking civil disobedience with others, I was finding my radical soul.

Frances in her Langworthy Road basement office for
American Friends Service Committee

In the China I saw in the 1970s, however, commerce involved only basic necessities, the things that people needed. People lived frugally and seemed to have what they needed. I felt inspired by the efforts the Chinese made to build a just society. I think the Chinese people felt they controlled their country. They worked at organizing their lives, which could be hard for them, but they persevered. During the trip, I saw happiness and optimism about the future.

CHINA AND VIETNAM

In a surprising turn of events in 1972, President Richard M. Nixon visited China. After twenty-five chilly years with no diplomatic relations between the United States and the People's Republic of China, Nixon's handshake in China with Chairman Mao Zedong marked a remarkable change. American foreign policy had for decades addressed China with suspicion and as an enemy, and likely only a Republican president could have pulled off the visit and warming of relations with China.

Soon after Nixon's visit, I got a letter from the US China Peoples Friendship Association (USCPFA) asking me to recommend someone from my area to go on USCPFA's first activist tour of China. Travel to China was nearly unheard of for any American.

It was one thing to work with young Americans who decided not to learn to kill in Vietnam. It would be another thing to meet Chinese people on their own soil, to experience their culture under the Maoist regime of the 1970s, and to see firsthand work people did to build a new society.

For an average American, even one devoted to peace and justice, to travel to China in 1973 was quite unusual. I tried five or six people, and no one was interested or could take advantage of the invitation to a fully funded trip.

When I got the letter from USCPFA about an activist tour, I asked Tom for ideas about who could go.

"Why don't you go?" Tom asked when it became apparent no one had shown interest.

"Me?" I asked. But the more I thought about it, the more I thought, "Yes, why not me?" I was still not deeply into organizing, but my children had grown and lived on their own. So I decided to go.

I've always felt that my work was right here at home. I've also always felt that we can learn from people all over the world and that piqued my interest in China and Chinese attempts there to establish self-governing communities.

As part of my work with WILPF, I got to know WILPFer Carmelita Hinton, who had a long history with revolutionary China. A progressive educator, Carmelita founded the Putney School in Putney, Vermont. Carmelita's son Bill Hinton was born in 1919, the same year that I was. An agronomist trained at Cornell, Bill worked in China as a staff member of the US Office of War Information during World War II. Intrigued by the great social experiment going on in China, Bill stayed in Shanxi Province and taught English. When the Communist Party took over the province,

Bill lived in the village of Long Bow where he learned to speak Chinese and worked side by side with people of the village. This experience became the basis for his generative book, *Fanshen*.

When Bill returned to the US from China in 1952 during the McCarthy Red Scare, US customs officials confiscated his notes and turned them over to the Senate Committee on Internal Security. After two years of legal battles, the US government returned his notes. Thus enabled to write *Fanshen*, Bill recounts how Long Bow adapted to Communism, including how the villagers pulled stools together in the winter to keep warm while they discussed ideas. *Fanshen* shares their stories of organizing and feeding the community.

Carmelita's daughter Joan Hinton, a physicist who worked on the atomic bomb as part of the Manhattan Project, joined Bill in China after she became disillusioned with devastation caused by the United States' use of nuclear weapons. There she met and married Bill's friend Sid Engst. For many years, Joan and Sid lived on the Red Star Commune south of Beijing, and our daughter Caltha visited Red Star when she traveled to China in 1975.

I was impressed by Bill's work and wanted to learn more about how the Chinese were building a new society with community input. That seemed to me an appropriate model for social change. Fascinated, I invited Carmelita to come to Northampton to share what she knew about the Chinese revolution. Carmelita spoke to a gathering of WILPFers about Bill's work, and then spoke at Smith College.

Everything I learned from Carmelita and from reading *Fanshen* gave me a foundation of knowledge about China, but I needed to learn much more in order to be ready for my trip and get the most out of what I could learn while actually in China.

Tom helped me get ready for the trip. We spent a weekend reading out loud to each other from books written by Americans who had traveled in China. Together, W. Allyn and Adele Rickett wrote *Prisoners of Liberation*. Allyn had studied Chinese language with the United States Agency for International Development (USAID) which then hired him to work in China. Adele accompanied him, and the Chinese arrested them for spying. They spent four or five years in Chinese jails before their release. They had no contact with one another during their imprisonment. In jail they went through the process described then as "thought reform." The Chinese released Allyn first. He went to Portland, Oregon, where sympathetic Quakers assisted him. "The Chinese were right," he said. "Without telling the Chinese, I sent material back to the state department about life in China and meetings in China, and I was wrong."

The Chinese arrested Adele because she typed Allyn's reports and distributed them. When she was released a few months later, even before knowing what her husband had said, she said, "The Chinese are right. The United States is empire-building at their expense, and it is wrong." It corroborated Allyn's account. He had refuge with Portland Quakers, and she joined him there. In *Prisoners of Liberation*, the Ricketts discuss China in transition from Mandarin to Communist society. They came to see that the US did not treat China fairly and openly. Eventually, Allyn served the Pennsylvania State University faculty as professor of East Asian languages.

Many felt that the Chinese brainwashed the Ricketts, but when I read their book I saw two thoughtful people attempting accurate descriptions of their experience.

When I traveled to China in 1973, most of the others in the group were missionaries who left during the Communist revolution. They wanted to go back to see how China had changed. One other traveler worked like me as a grassroots organizer.

China covers a vast area, of course. We toured a circumscribed region by bus. The group included twelve, and some spoke Chinese. To us, our guides spoke only English. They took their meals and slept separately from us. We questioned why we couldn't talk with them informally and were told it wasn't the custom.

We went to five cities, and I'm sure they showed us their best. Our trip was definitely controlled. Highlights of our tour included observing an operation conducted with acupuncture to serve an anesthetic purpose. The patient had part of his stomach removed. From the surgery theater above the operating room, we could see the patient on the table holding a copy of Mao's *Little Red Book* in his hand during the operation.

The Chinese government attempted to decentralize health care. Neighborhood committees organized health care committees. Government population control policies limited each family to one child. As under the Confucian system, local bureaucracies controlled local services. In order to implement population control policies, clinics kept a chart of each woman's menstrual cycle and, I imagine, monitored birth control measures.

Striving to build a new society, the Chinese we saw diligently studied music and valued education. Children seemed very happy. I took pictures of farm workers who appeared relaxed in conversation with one another. Grandmothers sat in a yard shelling beans or doing household chores. Old city housing revealed beautiful architecture. Society was highly structured and seemed to suit the people we saw. Breakfast was served where people worked and where the children went to school. Parents and workers could eat at either place. At the end of the day, people ate supper wherever they worked or in the schools. Communities sponsored plays and music in the evening. Families attended just as they had in Mandarin China when, not unlike in Italy and other European countries, nearly every town had an opera house. Early 1970s Chinese people lived very simply, I thought.

We traveled in China near the end of the Cultural Revolution, Mao's attempt to revive the values of the revolution. He required professionals to give up jobs in universities and colleges and live and work in the countryside as farmers and craftspeople. We were allowed to interview some who had been sent to the countryside. They told us theirs was a good experience and that they learned things they hadn't previously known. I'd love to see American politicians and Wall Street capitalists trade places with the poor. Maybe they would learn something.

The Chinese people we saw were by and large poor and had little to eat, but they appeared happy to work hard. They didn't have a lot to eat, but they took time to enjoy one another and impressively addressed concerns in their society.

By 1976 when Mao died, not long after my trip, the Chinese had discarded Mao's controversial re-education program and mechanisms for commune building unraveled. The China that evolved after Nixon's historic visit in 1972 reintroduced the profit motive and invited foreign investment. Under Communist Party control, the economy grew rapidly. Bill Hinton addressed the situation in a 1994 issue of *Monthly Review*. Chinese history became, Bill said, "the break-up of collective agriculture and the adoption of the family responsibility system . . . leading to the crucial choice now facing all peasants in China, the choice between rural stagnation rooted in hand-tilled, private noodle strips or growth based on scale production, a new form of organization that unifies land, machine tillage, crop and livestock technology, input supply, and output sales under community ownership and management."

When I made plans to go to China, I decided since I was in that part of the world, I would go to Vietnam. The US war in Vietnam had not officially ended, and travel to Vietnam would prove challenging, but in the end, I made the trip.

Russell Johnson had traveled in China earlier and then organized conferences in Asia for non-aligned nations, those who had allegiance neither to the United States and its allies nor, in those days, to China and the Soviet Union and their allies. Russell thought to show people from non-aligned nations the way people lived in China and other Asian countries.

Frances's collection of peace and justice buttons on a typical Asian robe with a Vietnamese farmer's hat

He had a slide show about Chinese agriculture that I liked, and at my request, he lent me his slides to take with me to Vietnam.

I wanted to go to the AFSC Quang Ngai Rehabilitation Center near the North Vietnamese border. There, AFSC operated a therapy center for civilians who lost arms and legs due to United States bombing and landmines. Specialists at the therapy center fitted them with artificial limbs. I wanted to see the facility and meet the people running it. I also wanted to show Russell's slide show about China, so I took the slides to Quang Ngai. I wanted to show them that peace held the promise of the kind of society the Chinese had.

I had to go through Hong Kong, still controlled by Great Britain. How shocked I was, after the simplicity I had found in China, to see the abundance of stuff in Hong Kong. Everything seemed to be about buying things. I felt that it was a terrible way to live and that China was on the right path, although by the time China began to finance US debt in the 1990s and 2000s, Chinese consumeristic commerce had largely replaced Maoist ideals.

In the China I saw in the 1970s, however, commerce involved only basic necessities, the things that people needed. People lived frugally and seemed to have what they needed. They seemed happier than folks in Hong Kong or China forty years later focusing on acquiring things. I felt inspired by the efforts the Chinese made to build a just society. I think the Chinese people felt they controlled their country. They worked at organizing their lives, which could be hard for them, but they persevered. During the trip, I saw happiness and optimism about the future.

In the early 2000s, I showed slides from my 1970s trip in Sigrid Schmalzer's History of Social Thought and Political Economy class at UMass. She teaches Chinese history, and the images gave the students a new perspective through a kind of seminar on the Cultural Revolution. Chinese students in the class said they knew almost nothing about the Cultural Revolution and President Nixon's visit to China in early 1972 to build rapport with the Chinese government.

When I arrived in Saigon, later renamed Ho Chi Minh City when the US lost the war in Vietnam, Paul Quinn-Judge and his wife Sophie met me. They represented AFSC in Vietnam. They found a place for me to stay, but first they gave me supper and then directions to my lodgings. The directions involved counting a number of streets and turns until I got to my destination. It was very dark, and with no streetlights. I walked down several streets and made what seemed like many turns all by myself and without knowing the language or being able to read a street sign. I had the key and knew the description of the building, but that was about all. Somehow I located the building, let myself in, and went to bed. The next morning I managed to get back to their apartment.

I told Paul and Sophie I wanted to meet Madame Ngo Ba Thanh, a Buddhist lawyer who fought for women's rights. Supported by the US, the Saigon police imprisoned her for several years. She had recently been released. Don Luce called my attention to her. On a fact-finding mission to Vietnam, he and Tom Harkin, then a Congressional aide and later a US senator from Iowa, investigated tiger-cage prisons where the Saigon police secretly held prisoners with US support. Harkin photographed the tiger cages and returned to the US where Don wrote about them for *Life* magazine. Outrage caused by the *Life* article forced the US to dismantle tiger cages and relocate prisoners once held there. Madame Ngo Ba Thanh brought tiger cages to the attention of the Vietnamese.

Paul and Sophie arranged for me to meet her. We had to take several trolleys in Saigon to get to the Buddhist pagoda where I was introduced to her and Buddhist nuns from her association. They had arranged a lunch. I knew they didn't have much food, but nevertheless they offered me extra food. It was uplifting. Although they were very poor, they had prepared tables full of food for my visit. They extended gracious hospitality, but our different languages caused a barrier preventing much conversation.

Then Paul and Sophie put me on a train from Saigon to the border between North Vietnam and South Vietnam. What a train ride! From the windows of the train, I followed the countryside moving before me. I saw firsthand the damages of bombing, defoliation, and burned simple housing. But always I saw the simple beauty of people humbly going about their daily routine. Bicycles provided transportation for everyone and everything. Many times I saw two or three smiling people riding the same bicycle and very much at ease with each other. I judged it a peaceful society disrupted by the violence of our war.

When I got to Quang Ngai, Julie Forsythe and her husband, Tom Hoskins, a young doctor from Putney, Vermont, and director of the hospital, met me. They had a group of local people come over in the evening to the medical center, where they also lived. I showed them Russell's slide show, and the Forsythes interpreted. I remember their gasps. They couldn't believe the prosperous rice fields in China and the extent of cooperation in society. When the program ended, I went to put my sleeping mat in the medical center living area, but I wondered why no one left. "Why aren't they going home?" I asked Julie in English.

"They can't travel safely at night because of possible ambushes connected with the war," she said. So they slept on the floor of the center.

113

When I came back from that incredible trip to China and Vietnam, I started a USCPFA in Northampton. For a while we were very active. We went to national conferences and endeavored to tell people about China. We also encouraged people to take advantage of tours organized by USCPFA.

That trip certainly sharpened my vision of the kind of society I wanted to work to develop—collective, open, and democratic. Mao's concept of a better society struck me as right on target. Unfortunately, humans being what we are, Mao and others in his era sponsored significant abuses. I don't condone them, and the supposed good end never justifies diabolical means. Power is the problem. But what I saw in China convinced me at the time that the way of life the people were cultivating had positive possibilities.

1970s poster showing Vietnamese people rebuilding their country after defeating the United States invasion and war

Western Massachusetts March against Apartheid, 1986

The film showed the South African black and white communities and damage apartheid did to both.

When the film finished, there was one question. "What will we do if we can't get good investments outside of South Africa?"

"We'll get another broker," Bromery said. Right then and there, the trustees voted to divest of their investments in South Africa.

NO APARTHEID

Because I have always believed that we must act to right our own government's wrongs, I found myself much engaged in international causes as the seventies evolved into the eighties and nineties. Our country traded with unjust foreign governments, covertly financed vicious and oppressive foreign regimes, and imposed sanctions on innocent civilians in other countries. Those of us interested in peace and justice had no choice but to expand our focus into foreign arenas. My involvement with AFSC gave me a perfect opportunity to advocate for peace and justice.

When the draft ended in the mid 1970s and I was trying to figure out what to do next, AFSC asked me if I would open a regional area office. Enthused, I said "Yes." By that time I saw myself as a Quaker and felt that AFSC, the social action committee of the Society of Friends, represented my deepest beliefs: action based on Quaker values of nonviolence and seeing what love can do. So this set my path clearly ahead to follow my personal philosophy:

• the means determines the ends
• the nonviolent struggle is ennobling for all who participate
• each individual is precious and worthy of concern

Once I said yes, I tried to figure out what having a regional office meant. It felt right to act on my personal beliefs through AFSC and my home office, but I had to decide where to place priorities and how to accomplish worthwhile goals.

I never actually changed the office downstairs in my home nor set it up any differently from when I counseled conscientious objectors. AFSC reimbursed me for postage and miscellaneous expenses, but I used our home phone extension, didn't charge rent, and didn't get paid.

Early on, I set up a committee that functioned as an unofficial board of directors. People came and went. David Kielson of Chesterfield volunteered early on. He and his wife, Gail, took interest in what I was doing. David served as treasurer/financial person. He went over the books. I had to document everything I was spending. He balanced the budget and applied for the reimbursement from AFSC.

Wendy Saviano from down the street volunteered to support the committee, which divided into subcommittees focusing on South Africa, Central America, and disarmament. Wendy made up agendas for committee meetings and sent out notices. Each subcommittee met every month or so. Wendy also helped with a little newsletter.

Like many socially conscious organizations, AFSC struggled with appropriate diversity. The committee wanted me to honor a wide variety of constituencies, and we eventually decided I needed a paid assistant. We tried hard to find someone with a culturally diverse background to work part time, and then AFSC decided not to hire someone else but instead to provide me with a stipend. By then, our son Tom attended medical school and my husband Tom wasn't well. I agreed to take a stipend. I had a real job! AFSC had a legitimate regional office. I received benefits, including health care. And it later meant I got retirement benefits.

From subcommittees, we organized ourselves into working groups. Michael Holroyde, who later directed outreach for the Traprock Peace Center, took a particular interest in southern Africa. Sarah Pirtle, who developed and taught peace education programs for Traprock, focused on disarmament. Lois Ahrens and Susan Triola coordinated the Central American group. One person from each subcommittee served on the board.

In the Southern Africa working group we tried to learn what we could about South Africa. Apartheid, a system of racial separation and segregation, had been a part of South Africa for much of the twentieth century. By the 1960s, entrenched apartheid manifested in an institutionalized system of laws that set up four racial categories: white, black, Asian, and colored, with schools and living areas determined accordingly. Black South Africans suffered the most under apartheid. Only blacks over the age of sixteen had be fingerprinted and carry passbooks as identification.

With others dedicated to working for peace and justice, we found the clear-cut apartheid issue appealing. We could foster opposition to apartheid. I think we found it easier to oppose racism in South Africa than racism in the US. Soweto riots appeared in the news, as we saw them frequently on television and in newspapers. Of course, we did not have computers and smart phones, so we relied on the prevalent media of the day. The issue of apartheid stirred memories of the American civil rights movement and encouraged many Americans to figure out ways to act. Some called for public institutions to take investment money out of South African companies. Eventually, widespread divestment had a significant effect on the South African scene.

In 1977, Reverend Leon Sullivan, a black minister in South Africa, drew up a list known as the Sullivan Principles that he felt that corporations should abide by. The principles endorsed separate but equal treatment for South African people of different races and required companies to pay people of different races equally and provide equal working conditions. Many of us felt that requiring a business to ascribe to the Sullivan Principles wasn't enough because the principles inherently supported apartheid. We wanted divestment so that American dollars would not support apartheid.

Arthur Serota, a Springfield lawyer, felt passionately opposed to apartheid. I met Arthur when I toured people around during my earlier days as outreach coordinator for AFSC. Arthur interviewed them for his daily radio program that aired from seven to eight in the morning and six to seven in the evening on WTTT at Springfield Technical Community College.

I worked with Arthur in efforts to organize the black community in Springfield against apartheid. Nazir Ahmed, an Amherst College student from Bangladesh, also volunteered. I got money for him to intern in the office for the summer. He lived with a college friend in town. We organized a film series because there were then quite a few good films on South Africa, six or seven, as I remember. We did the first showing at the Springfield library. Nobody came. We moved over to the office of the National Association of Colored People (NAACP). We thought maybe people would feel more comfortable there and come. I went around speaking in churches where I had a few contacts from my work during the Vietnam War. But we couldn't get people's attention.

Arthur hammered away at South African apartheid. We tried to break through what we identified as the helpless denial of many African Americans in Springfield. Since we couldn't get a film series going, Arthur said, "Let's have a clothing drive." We went into the black community and asked for clothing donations for South African blacks. We got some donations, but what a project it was to wash and sort and mend, and we could not use much of it. We worked hard to accomplish little.

Arthur kept at it every day, and when I walked up and down the street in the black community in the evening, I noticed that everyone listened to him on the radio as they sat on their steps in the evening. Arthur later continued the ideal of doing good work when he became executive director of the United Movement to End Child Soldiering (UMECS) in South Africa and Northern Uganda. UMECS endorses the end of child soldiering by supporting secondary and higher education.

We decided to celebrate South African Women's Day on August 9, which AFSC usually observed as Nagasaki Day, commemorating the United States bombing of that city. To advance the idea, I met Reverend Paul Fullilove, pastor at the Third Baptist Church, a predominantly black church on Walnut Street and Pendleton Avenue in Springfield. He said we could center observances of South African Women's Day in his church. We organized activities, games, and films cosponsored by many peace and justice groups.

1989 poster advertising a Jane Sapp concert at UMass to encourage opposition to apartheid in South Africa

On South African Women's Day, I had films showing inside the church when two Muslim women appeared with their heads covered. Reverend Fullilove was furious. We had also enlisted religious groups among co-sponsors, and we welcomed the Muslim women.

"Oh," he said, "I'm ending it. Absolutely I'm closing the church. I'm not having a Muslim here." We didn't know what to do. We slowly pulled ourselves together and tried to explain to him the need to be inclusive, but his strong feelings overruled our efforts. We didn't ask anyone to leave, but we slowed down activities and quietly began to pack up. Never again did we do anything with Reverend Fullilove. It dawned on me then that I had no business trying to organize in Springfield's black community. I didn't understand the dynamics and didn't know how to work there.

Many participated with the Southern Africa working group, Nancy Talanian among them. Founder of the Bill of Rights Defense Committee, she also gives endless time to the No More Guantanamos Committee. Michael Holroyde took a leading role in the group. He was very knowledgeable about the topic of South Africa and its system of apartheid for many years. He grew up in England and taught in South Africa the year after he graduated from college. He understood a lot about the situation in South Africa.

Michael told a story about his high school experiences in England. His school had scheduled a rugby match against white South Africans. Many opposed South African policies, and many felt it inappropriate to play a match with a South African team. Michael and some friends decided to stop the match. They sprinkled chalk all over the field at the beginning of the game. That act ended the game before it started. Michael and his friends took over with a perfect nonviolent act. The action stopped the match and got the attention of his whole school. I think Michael earned his reputation as an adherent of non-violence by that momentary act. Nonviolent actions have a way of helping us to climb Jacob's ladder, to bring problems to the top and to gain people's attention. I'm sure that there is a brief scene of this action in the PBS film *Last Stop at Johannesburg.*

The South African poet Dennis Brutus taught at Amherst College around the same time. He had been imprisoned at Robbins Island with Nelson Mandela. He was a living witness to what was going on in South Africa. Dennis organized a national effort to bar South African sports teams from playing in the US. We sent a couple of carloads of people to

South African poet Dennis Brutus and Frances during the AFSC 1980s anti-apartheid campaign in the Pioneer Valley

123

join a protest in Albany where a white South African team had a rugby match scheduled, and that match was stopped.

We had area meetings to discuss the situation. Most people at those meetings were less action-oriented than our group. They promoted the Sullivan Principles for corporate ethical practice and advocated working with the South African government to make moderate changes. I felt that it was up to the people of South Africa to decide what kind of government they needed. What we had to do was to end apartheid. Because US wealth helped fund South African businesses, divestment made sense as an important first step. Pressure needed to come from—and it eventually did—corporate America.

I approached Steiger's, a department store in downtown Springfield. They were selling blouses made in South Africa. I had an interview with Ralph Steiger, the merchandise manager, and after that, we set up a picket line on a Saturday two weeks before Christmas. He became very cooperative. He said that their company was against apartheid and that if selling blouses from South Africa disturbed people, Steiger's would stop. At first he felt that because the blouses had already been purchased, Steiger's had to sell them and then changed his mind. I decided the timing of our picket line was everything. We also picketed a coin shop in Springfield that sold South African Krugerrands. We were trying to carry the message to local businesses that the way to shut down apartheid was to refuse to do business with South African industries.

The Southern African working group also decided to encourage area colleges to divest of their investments in South Africa. The enterprise reflected a vibrant national movement. Our working group met weekly in my office. I sat in sometimes on their meetings, and they kept me informed. They all endorsed nonviolent discipline, and they left no stone unturned to get all the colleges to divest.

I had contacts with some students and faculty at UMass, including Bill Strickland, Ekwueme Thelwell (then known as Michael Thelwell) and John Bracey. We tried to reach the trustees. One day, Johnnetta Cole, a teacher at UMass who later moved to Hunter College, called me and said she had seen a fine film, *Last Grave at Dambaza,* that shows truths about South Africa.

I thought that a film would be a great way to educate people about apartheid in South Africa and wondered if maybe I could arrange to show it to the trustees at UMass. I learned that the trustees had scheduled a meeting for the coming weekend. Faculty and students had already planned a rally to coincide with the trustees meeting, and it looked like a promising scenario to pressure the trustees to divest of South African holdings. I suggested to Ekwueme Thelwell that I show *Last Grave*. He encouraged me.

I made an appointment with Randolph Bromery, the UMass chancellor, an African American, and asked if we could show the film at the trustees meeting. I didn't know Bromery, but he was open to my request. I trusted Johnnetta when she said it was a good documentary, although I had not been able to view it. In those days, you couldn't simply download a movie to see it. You had to get a physical reel of film from a place many mail days away and then set the film up on a projector.

Dr. Bromery wasn't sure the trustees had time to view the film. Their agenda was jam packed.

"What about when they're eating lunch?" I asked.

"If you have the film and are set to go, I'll ask them, and if they agree, you can show it during lunch," he answered.

Of course, I still didn't even have the film in my hands so I called Johnnetta. I think that was Wednesday. Johnnetta said she had scheduled the film in New York the next day and then could take it to the bus station for transport to Northampton in time for me to pick it up for the UMass trustees' lunch. That was the only way you could transfer something quickly in those days. She said there was a bus leaving Manhattan at seven in the morning to arrive in Northampton about ten. She agreed to put it on the bus.

I put my heavy, awkward thirty-five-millimeter projector and projection screen in my little yellow VW bug. Then I went to the bus station to wait to get the film and transport it the twenty minutes, barring unexpected traffic, to the university for noontime.

When I got to the bus station, no bus. I asked what happened, and the dispatcher told me that, since no one got on or off in Northampton, the bus had no reason to stop and went on to Greenfield.

I drove as fast as I could to the bus station in Greenfield. I got there in time to get the film off the bus—it came in heavy, large, round canisters—and then drove, I'm sure about eighty miles per hour, down Route 116 to get to the campus. Driving at eighty down today's Interstate Route 91 with a maximum speed limit of sixty-five would not be as dramatic, but Route 116 is a two-lane highway with a maximum speed limit of fifty-five. Luckily, I evaded any speed traps. The way was opening.

When I got to the driveway at UMass's Memorial Hall, the rally was in progress in front. Michael Holroyde and Ekwueme Thelwell directed me across the lawn and helped me set up the projector and the film as the trustees got ready to eat lunch. They agreed to watch the film during lunch, and I put it on.

anti-apartheid era poster declaring Mozambique the "apartheid second front"

I hadn't seen the film. Thankfully it is an excellent representation of South Africa. About ten minutes in, I realized that no one was eating the chicken salad. In 1977 when all this took place, that was the constant lunch menu: chicken salad and strawberry shortcake.

Their forks were on their plates.

As I watched, I knew that Johnnetta had called it right. The film showed the South African black and white communities and damage apartheid did to both.

When the film finished, there was one question. "What will we do if we can't get good investments outside of South Africa?"

"We'll get another broker," Bromery said.

Right then and there, they voted to divest of their investments in South Africa.

We re-showed the film in 2013 at the media series and it is still very convincing. This was one of many actions that persuaded me again and again that film is a great way to reach people.

The night of the UMass trustees vote, I went to a meeting of the Mount Toby Friends peace and social concerns committee. I told them the story. A staunch Quaker woman said, "Frances, we will buy you a copy of that film. We don't want you driving down the highway at eighty miles per hour."

When I got my own copy, I showed the film everywhere, and Michael Holroyde showed it even more widely.

We tried to get Amherst College to divest. Not directly related to any action of ours, students sat in at the admissions hall. Arrests ended the sit-in, but no divestment votes occurred.

At Smith, enthusiastic students took a stand. The Smith trustees felt Smith's South African investments rewarded the college. Students at Smith planned to sit in on behalf of divestment at the office of the president, Mary Maples Dunn.

The noon before the planned action, a Smith student came to my office and said, "Frances, we are going to occupy the hall of the president's office, and we want you to come over and do nonviolence training."

There wasn't time to do a training, as the action was planned for the next day, but I went over to Smith to talk to them about nonviolence.

During the action the following day, students filled up the stairs leading to the president's office. She was not there, but the students began their presence around four o'clock and stayed until they were removed several hours later. Meantime, President Dunn entertained the trustees at her on-campus home. She told the trustees a little white-haired woman had organized the demonstration.

Eventually, years later, Smith bought my AFSC archives, and over many years, I periodically went to campus for events and organized activities. In 2014, I secured an invitation for our Shut It Down Affinity Group to install an exhibition of our antinuclear memorabilia in the Smith Student Union gallery and participate in an intergenerational panel discussing activism and moderated by Smith faculty.

Encouraging colleges to divest took a lot of effort. The colleges wanted lucrative investment portfolios without much regard to social responsibility. Amherst, Mount Holyoke, and Smith refused to divest during our anti-apartheid campaign, but at least we planted the seed. By the mid eighties Mount Holyoke trustees voted to divest. Amherst and Smith followed suit in the later eighties.

In the Valley, Hampshire College led the way to divestment in 1977. The universities of Michigan and Wisconsin stood in the divestment vanguard nationwide but the University of Massachusetts was the first university to vote to divest. Unfortunately, in spite of the vote, the university dragged its feet for many years before it actually divested. It took more student demonstrations in the 1980s to get the university to actually do what it said it was going to do. A UMass student committee opposed government contracts with UMass for studying anthrax for use as a biological weapon. When the anti-anthrax committee explored the university's contracts and investments, it discovered that divestment from South Africa never occurred. Ten years after the trustees' vote, students took UMass to task for not honoring its vote, and the administration gave up investments in South Africa.

Tom and I had stock in the early Xerox, which appealed to us because Xerox emerged in Rochester during Tom's radiology residency. Tom's brother advised, "If you have any money, ten dollars, whatever you can, put it into Xerox. They are going to go some place." We bought a few Xerox shares, and they quickly appreciated. Unfortunately Xerox had considerable interest in South Africa. So we sold it.

Working for divestment underscored for me the reality that money is the root of evil. Of course, I had long realized that money finances wars and weapons. Apartheid and US investment in South Africa made it clear to me that money finances injustice of all kinds. Our work with apartheid may have been the beginning of my realization that eventually I would have to stop paying taxes to the US government in order unequivocally to walk my talk and find the heart of my radical soul.

Frances celebrates UMass divestment from South African holdings with Bill Strickland, UMass professor

Nancy Clover's photo captures Frances climbing a fence on August 1, 1983 at Seneca Army Depot, Romulus, New York, to stop deployment of Cruise and Pershing missiles

We shared experience in nonviolent action and carefully planned our moves. No signs on tent poles, for example. We acted deeply under weight of our concern for danger posed to the world by nuclear weapons. We planned carefully, and we had great faith in the potential efficacy of our action.

NO NUCLEAR WEAPONS

No weapon in the history of the world threatened humanity as vastly and profoundly as the nuclear bomb. As the earth warms, it may be that we prove ourselves capable of self-destruction with no weapons at all but our own arrogance, greed, and stupidity. In the meantime, the nuclear bomb never ceases to threaten annihilation of all life. When the US dropped the atom bomb on Hiroshima, I became convinced and still am that the use of such weapons could destroy life on this planet. Working against nuclear power and nuclear weapons has been at the core of my motivation and work.

Early in our marriage, our young family kept me very busy. We seemed to live in areas not particularly fertile for nonviolent opposition to nuclear weapons. When we moved to Northampton, however, we found and initiated opportunities for organized opposition. With the Committee for a SANE Nuclear Policy and Physicians for Social Responsibility, we found an active community of people working against nuclear weapons.

Dr. Ira Helfand chiefly orchestrates PSR activities in Northampton. As a young man in the seventies, Ira received his MD in general medicine from Albert Einstein College of Medicine of Yeshiva University in New York. During his residency at Mount Auburn Hospital in Cambridge, he met Dr. Helen Caldicott, then teaching at Harvard Medical School. Helen committed herself, with others, to revitalizing PSR. Later, Ira settled in Northampton where he dedicated himself to his medical practice and antinuclear work. He speaks widely, notably once in Oslo at a conference about what would happen in a nuclear winter. Ira serves as co-president of International Physicians for the Prevention of Nuclear War.

In the 1970s when the draft law changed and the draft was no longer compulsory, I stopped doing draft counseling. Nevertheless, I wanted to continue educating people to the dangers of violence, war, and nuclear weapons with slide shows and antiwar films. I had found a core of compatible people through AFSC. Traprock's Sarah Pirtle and Andrea Ayvazian, a nurse at Hampshire College student health services became allies.

Sarah and I founded the Northampton chapter of Mobilization for Survival (MFS), a national organization started in 1977 to abolish nuclear weapons. Mobilization had an office in a Cambridge church. We felt that we had to stop nuclear weapons or no one would survive.

Helen Caldicott, an Australian pediatrician opposed to nuclear power and nuclear weapons, joined the staff of Children's Hospital in Boston

Dr. Crowe Pens Articles On Fallout

An analysis of the result of radioactive fallout from nuclear bomb tests was given earlier this month in two articles published in Daily Hampshire Gazette, Northampton, Mass., by Dr. Thomas J. Crowe, a native of Waterbury and a son of Mr. and Mrs. Patrick Crowe, 481 Sylvan Ave.

A radiologist and staff member of a Northampton Hospital who has also conducted a private practice for 10 years in the Bay State city of about 30,-000 population, Dr. Crowe is also aligned with the Hampshire-Franklin Committee for a Sane Nuclear Policy, whose members have agreed to discuss publicly through the newspaper, problems regarding "Health Hazards From Bomb Fallout" and nuclear weapons, with which he is particularly familiar.

The 48-year-old radiologist received his elementary education in Mulcahy and St. Francis Xavier Schools, graduated with the Crosby High Class of 1930, and earned his college degree at Syracuse, N. Y., Medical College. His father, "Pat" Crowe, a retired Waterbury businessman, was at one time a driver of the locally famed gray horses and fire apparatus stationed in the Scovill St. firehouse.

After college, Dr. Crowe interned at St. Francis Hospital, Hartford, where he first became interested in radiology. He then studied and practiced it at Strong Memorial Hospital,

Tom Crowe offered analysis of nuclear-test radioactive fallout in a 1960s series published by The Daily Hampshire Gazette

around that time. Neville Shute's novel *On the Beach*, later made into a major movie, influenced Helen and other Australians with its Australian scenario about the end of life as we know it due to nuclear war. Australians and New Zealanders widely opposed nuclear testing, and Helen shared her profound concerns when she arrived in the US. As president of PSR, she led efforts to rejuvenate the organization. Her book *Nuclear Power Is Not the Answer* came out shortly after the Three Mile Island nuclear plant disaster in 1979 and ranks as a generative book on the subject. Her book and the subsequent film *If You Love This Planet* was reissued in 2009.

When Helen first came to Northampton to speak, our Mobilization group booked McConnell Hall at Smith College. Then the science building, McConnell has a capacity of maybe two hundred. We said we didn't think it was big enough, but the college administration and everybody working with us told us it would accommodate the program. On the afternoon of her talk, people streamed in, and the hall obviously would not accommodate everyone who wanted to hear Helen. I said to the other organizers, "We're going to go to Sage Hall." Sage is a much bigger auditorium across the street.

I don't know what moved me, but I jumped on the stage and said, "Follow me." Helen profoundly influenced me. We went to Sage, and the door was unlocked. We went in and took the stage. We finished the introductions, and Helen spoke. I think for me that experience of seizing the moment taught me that you have to be ready for any opportunity.

Helen speaks out against nuclear weapons and the whole nuclear industry. She draws crowds. She energizes us. In 2010, Helen spoke again at Sage Hall—this time the planned venue. I think the students invited her. I remember at one point when she started talking in her ironic, outrageous way, some students started to leave. Helen called out to the audience, "Lock the doors. You need to stay here and hear this. Don't let anybody out." Keeping students involved and interested poses a big challenge. So many issues face students today, and nuclear destruction may frighten them too much.

In 2013, Helen spoke in Northampton about the 2011 nuclear disaster at Fukushima Daiichi when an earthquake and subsequent tsunami caused three of six reactors to reach meltdown. Radioactive fallout from the Fukushima meltdowns harmed the Japanese people's health and food sources. Radioactive water seeps from the reactors into the Pacific Ocean and will contaminate the earth's land, sea, and air for centuries—even millennia—to come. Helen discussed the effect the Fukushima disaster should have on the US nuclear industry and observed that the federal Nuclear Regulatory Commission should implement additional safeguards at US reactors although it is very unlikely the NRC will do so.

Helen shared a potluck lunch with our Shut It Down Affinity Group dedicated to civil disobedience aimed at shutting down the Vermont Yankee nuclear reactor in Vernon, Vermont. Her advice to us was, "Take off your clothes if that's what it takes to get their attention." Entergy Corporation scheduled the shutdown of Vermont Yankee for the end of 2014, but it is unlikely that decommissioning and cleanup will proceed expediently. Shut It Down will continue to act for restoration of the reactor site to its state in the late 1960s before construction of the reactor.

I participated as early as 1962 in a demonstration against nuclear weapons. The New England Committee for Non Violent Action (NECNVA) in Voluntown, Connecticut told us about a scheduled christening at the General Dynamics Electric Boat Division in Groton, Connecticut, of a nuclear submarine designed to carry Polaris nuclear missiles. NECNVA waged an ongoing campaign to stop construction and deployment of these nuclear, missile-carrying submarines.

To facilitate the ongoing initiative, some from NECNVA acquired property in Voluntown near Electric Boat. They bought an old farm with a rundown house that they fixed up as their headquarters. Marj and Bob Swann lived there and directed the campaign. Marj and Bob also dedicated themselves to the "small is beautiful" movement as well as the peace movement and established an intentional community in the house. Because it is about twenty miles from Kingstown to Voluntown, it took considerable effort to maintain momentum. Fifty years after initial establishment of the community, the Voluntown Peace Trust wants to invigorate "the Farm" as a peace center.

The original group had a vision of a community dedicated to nonviolent principles, the eradication of nuclear weapons, and self-sufficiency. Many supported the endeavor, including Barbara Deming, a much revered peace worker and reporter for *The Nation*, and Brad Lytle and Erica Enzer, who committed their lives to working against the weapons system.

When I demonstrated, the launch ceremony at Electric Boat was centered on a submarine designed to carry Polaris missiles, two-stage solid fuel nuclear warheads. Launched simultaneously, the sub's total complement of sixteen nuclear weapons had a range of twelve hundred nautical miles. The system contributed vastly to the buildup of the US empire. US nuclear weapons proclaim to the world that splitting of the atom entitles the US to claim our planet as its empire.

First Lady Jackie Kennedy had agreed to christen the submarine USS *Lafayette* (SSBN-616) in Groton. A carload of us traveled to the ceremony. A row of women, we stood protesting as Mrs. Kennedy entered the christening area in an open car. She wore a Kelly green suit and pillbox hat. She stood regally waving this way and that to the crowd. I guess someone warned her about us on the right, because she turned to the left instead of waving to us. We had a sign that said something like "War is nothing to celebrate" or "Killing machines are not something to celebrate." We stood witness against missiles that targeted to annihilate millions, a US endeavor that still goes on and must stop.

Some twenty years later I participated in another action at General Dynamics Electric Boat shipyard in Groton, Connecticut. NECNVA mobilized people to risk arrest in protest of a Trident submarine launch at Electric Boat. Our action involved the disarmament subcommittee of Western Massachusetts AFSC. We got passes to attend the launch. Trident submarines carry Trident missiles, more powerful descendants of Polaris missiles. As is the usual complement for Trident submarines, the USS *Ohio* (SSGN-726) could carry twenty-four Trident missiles. Each of them provided as much nuclear destruction as six Hiroshima atomic bombs and had a range of four thousand miles. By the early 2000s, in spite of the nuclear

1980s anti-Trident submarine banner

freeze on building more nuclear weapons, the Navy and its contractors found a way to circumvent the Freeze by upgrading C-4 missiles to even more potent D-5s. As of mid 2014, eighteen US Tridents patrolled the world's oceans with a combined capacity to destroy the entire world many times over. The United Kingdom also has a fleet of four Tridents.

When we demonstrated in 1982, we mixed some of our blood with red paint in a little baby bottle. We planned to get up close, and it was my job to throw the bottle against the submarine. We planned to put up a sign with a message similar to our 1962 message, "Launching a killing machine is nothing to celebrate." We timed our action to coincide with our burgeoning campaign for a freeze on the manufacture of nuclear weapons.

Once we were at the General Dynamics launch site in Groton, we planned to hoist up the sign on aluminum tent poles so it would be easy to see. I carried the poles hidden in the hem of my skirt. I thought I was going to have time to put them together, but it took us longer than we anticipated to make our way to the submarine. Eventually I got close enough to the sub to throw the baby bottle. I was on the platform next to the path the sub would slide down. As it slowly glided into the water for launching, I threw the baby bottle of blood against the side of the sub—I had a pretty good arm. Then with some of the others in our group, I tried to get the sign up, but the tent poles kept falling.

People in the crowd were furious, and they came after us. They wanted to tear us apart, and others cheered them on. People pulled our hair and tried to rip our clothes off. That was one time I was glad to see the police and have them get us out of that melee. The police arrested, detained, and eventually released us after maybe four or five hours. We later went back to court, but the case never came to a trial.

Meantime, many of us got wrapped up in the nuclear freeze campaign to end United States manufacture of nuclear weapons with the United States and the Soviet Union agreeing to dispose of their existing inventories. Our strategy invoked time-honored, grassroots organizing methods to present voters with referendum questions so that once the public made its voice known on the ballot, legislators would honor their intentions and ban nuclear weapons.

Our regional effort focused on the nuclear freeze movement in the early 1980s around the time of the election of Ronald Reagan as president. The movement had its beginnings when Traprock Peace Center opened in the late seventies. Traprock developed on land in Deerfield bequeathed in 1953 by the Spruyt family to the New England Society of Friends. A building on the property housed Woolman Hill School, named for the austere and dedicated Quaker abolitionist, John Woolman.

My earlier contact with Woolman Hill occurred during inspiring weekend meetings sponsored by the Woolman Hill Friends committee. Among workshop leaders were pacifists Dave Dellinger and Staughton Lynd. I went to most of maybe fifteen stimulating workshops. Typically, a Friday night presentation opened a session with most of Saturday devoted to workshops and a Sunday morning session concluding with lunch. I experienced total immersion. We stayed in Woolman Hill's yellow house with bunk beds in the bedrooms. Unfortunately, diminishing finances ended the workshops.

I sat on a committee of Friends working to keep the workshops going. Others and I thought the place would make a fine international training center for nonviolence. People from all over the world could study nonviolence, be trained in nonviolent activism, and then put their activism into practice around the world.

When Randy Kehler finished his prison term for refusing to register for the draft, he came to the Valley to teach at Woolman Hill School, an alternative high school. Soon thereafter, although we didn't know each other personally, he telephoned me. We met in Amherst where I worked on building a cage to demonstrate how the US supported South Vietnamese underground tiger cages to torture prisoners of war. We talked about my experience with draft counseling and his experience as a draft resister.

When the Woolman Hill School closed after the barn burned in 1971, Randy joined the committee endeavoring to start a permanent peace and justice program at the site. Beverly Woodward, a war tax resister, teacher, and writer from Cambridge, and I really wanted to establish an international nonviolence center. We convinced the committee and hired Randy as first director of Traprock.

June 10, 1979 ad in The Daily Hampshire Gazette *during the United Nations International Year of the Child and three months after the Three-Mile Island nuclear power plant accident*

Frances, right, next to Andrea Ayvazian and unidentified others opposing United States cruise missiles during the Freeze campaign

The African-American tax resisters Wally and Juanita Nelson came to the Pioneer Valley while Randy and his wife Betsy Corner lived at Woolman Hill during the early days of Traprock. Juanita had been a news reporter during World War II in Cincinnati when she met Wally, imprisoned for refusing to serve in the army. Tax resisters who had lived in an integrated intentional community in Cincinnati after Wally's release from prison, the Nelsons were headed to Woolman Hill to consider living on the land. Somehow, the Nelsons had been detained by police on the New York Thruway and refused to cooperate. Randy went to Buffalo to rescue them and bring them back. They became fixtures of Valley resistance to war and taxes and influenced others to refuse to pay taxes, including Randy and Betsy, whose Colrain house was eventually seized by the IRS. In the award-winning 1997 film documentary *Act of Conscience,* videographer Robbie Leppzer of Turning Tide Productions in Wendell, Massachusetts shows war tax resistance actions and occupation of Randy and Betsy's house before the IRS seized it in 1989.

Juanita, Wally, and I often found ourselves together on Valley panels and at peace and justice events. Over the years, we became friends, and when I decided to become a tax resister, it was surely in part due to their influence.

When Randy returned in 1980 from a meeting of the Institute for Defense and Disarmament Studies in Brookline, he felt energized by the call to halt the nuclear arms race. He said that rather than work on the broad topic of training for nonviolence, the group should focus on abolishing nuclear weapons. He argued, "This is the focus right here. We've got to stop the arms race."

Randy Forsberg, a graduate student at MIT, created the nuclear freeze initiative and worked with Randy Kehler. She had been in Norway and Sweden with the International Institute on Peace when her husband was a graduate student there. After coming to the Boston area for her own graduate studies, she joined people interested in finding a way to reduce nuclear weapons. She had statistics and a plan for how we must freeze nuclear arms immediately in the United States and begin to reduce them slowly in cooperation with the Soviet Union. She provided data and summed up what was happening. Her group felt that it was time for a nuclear moratorium, to start reducing, to downsize slowly. They called it the Freeze.

Randy Kehler felt our group should join the nuclear freeze initiative. We all agreed. I wrote a grant proposal to AFSC for six thousand dollars that was earmarked for a local group who had a plan for nuclear disarmament. When we were awarded the grant, we began a search for someone to work at Traprock on the Freeze.

1980s Nuclear Freeze poster

Judy Scheckel, a nun, ran into the notice some place in Washington or Baltimore near her home. She called me and told me she had worked on the grape boycott. I said, "The job is open. Interviewing closes tomorrow night. If you can get here before tomorrow night, you can apply."

"I'll be there," she said. She got on a bus and called me when she got to Northampton. She stayed overnight with us and then in the morning I drove her up to Traprock in time for an interview.

Judy was hired—she had more than the necessary qualifications—and the Freeze took off like wildfire. So for a while everything centered on the Freeze.

We had one meeting in our living room of some thirty-five people representing groups organizing their communities. We didn't have any computers or fancy media because there weren't any widely available. So we wrote on flip charts listing why the world's nations should give up nuclear weapons. We calculated the number of nuclear weapons in the nuclear nations. After the meeting, under the auspices of AFSC and the Freeze initiative, I found people in many Western Massachusetts towns willing to work to put the Freeze referendum question on the ballot.

In 1980, the year Ronald Reagan won the presidential election, our group put requests for a nuclear moratorium on ballots in each of the state's congressional districts in Western Massachusetts. The referendum asked state senators to introduce a resolution in the state senate on Beacon Hill "requesting the President of the United States to propose to the Soviet Union a mutual nuclear weapons moratorium by which the United States and the Soviet Union agree to halt immediately the testing, production, and deployment of all nuclear warheads, missiles and delivery systems . . ." and "to transfer the funds saved to civilian use." It made clear sense to many others and me that we should not be spending all that money for weapons we cannot use when we need the money for human services—for day care and health care—right here in Northampton.

The referendum won in all state congressional districts except Springfield. In October before the election, I spoke at Amherst College at the International Living Center after showing two films: *Paul Jacobs and the Nuclear Gang* and *Hiroshima*. Judy Scheckel spoke in the Berkshires; Marta Daniels, a writer and peace worker, tackled "the myth of the Soviet threat"; and Daniel Ellsberg, author of the *Pentagon Papers* that exposed sordid details of US involvement in the Vietnam War, spoke in support of the Freeze at Springfield College. We placed ads in newspapers supporting the Freeze: one was signed by health care providers, including my husband, Tom; another was headlined "Say Yes to Survival" which was signed by John Olver, who was then state senator for Northampton, as well as a host of others.

TODAY, THE "TRIDENT MONSTER" IS MARCHING THROUGH AMHERST

. . . Creeping through UMASS, crawling down North Pleasant Street, comes the "Trident Monster." 560 feet long, it's as long as the Navy's latest nuclear baby — the Trident submarine program. The 408 black pennants represent the 408 nuclear bombs that the Trident is capable of launching in a nuclear war. Looks pretty scary, doesn't it? But don't worry, this monster is harmless, however . . .

ON SATURDAY, THE REAL "MONSTER" IS BEING LAUNCHED

Now, that is frightening! The first Trident sub is being built in Groton, Connecticut. On Saturday, the Navy, Rosalyn Carter, Senator John Glenn (D-Ohio) and the Electric Boat Company will celebrate the launch of the first Trident, the "U.S.S. Ohio." They'll be christening it with a champagne bottle. They are throwing a party.

But wait! *The launching of a Trident is nothing to celebrate,* instead, it is something to mourn. One Trident Sub can destroy 408 targets, with an explosion five times that which leveled Hiroshima. The Navy wants to build 30 of them!

On Saturday, people from all over New England will converge on Groton to protest.

STOP THE TRIDENT SUB! COME TO GROTON APRIL 7

ALTERNATIVE ENERGY COALITION
85 Main Street
Amherst, Mass. 01002
253-9998

1980s "Trident monster" poster encouraging demonstrators to stop Trident nuclear submarines

The night of the election, we were in our home keeping track of the vote on the radio and TV. On the back of a small calendar I was marking the towns and checking off each town as the vote came. Everybody was supporting the Freeze. We were devastated by Reagan's win but overwhelmed by the fact that town after town supported the Freeze. Before the election, I had talked with Senator Olver, whom we called John. He had been very noncommittal but one of the first calls I got on the day after the election was from John. "Where should I send a check?" he asked. He was right on top of it. He wanted to support us.

In the same election where Reagan prevailed even among Massachusetts voters (only Minnesota voted Democratic in 1984), fifty-nine percent of Massachusetts towns supported the Freeze. "I found a general profound concern about nuclear war," I wrote soon thereafter in a letter published in the *Amherst Bulletin*, "along with a sense of powerlessness to do anything about it, and also a lack of precise knowledge about the buildup of arms, the amount of money involved, the effect on the economy, and the outlook for national security. I think our little informal questionnaire 'Arms Race Survey' was a valuable tool to focus attention on these matters along with our thousands of leaflets. When people are informed, it seems they vote right."

State Senator Olver presented the resolution in the Massachusetts Senate, and it easily passed.

So although Ronald Reagan was elected, we saw a notable segment of the population advocating abolition of nuclear weapons. To follow up on success in Massachusetts, we went to national meetings in Washington, Saint Louis, and Chicago, where I spoke. Randy Kehler led the charge. He had left Traprock in 1981 to join the national Freeze campaign. He felt we had support in Washington and was very eager to take the Freeze referendum to a vote in the US Congress. I wondered if we had enough support. A Freeze resolution lost by two votes in the House in 1982, although a 204-202 vote seemed close enough to savor. When Reagan achieved reelection to the presidency in 1984, the Freeze was pretty well forgotten.

During our national campaigning in 1983, I got a call from Sister Jane Morrissey of the Order of Saint Joseph in Springfield. She wanted to organize an action by women of faith in Rhode Island, again to oppose Trident submarines and missiles. I thought, "Yes—keeping the pressure on." We remained in the thick in the nuclear freeze campaign, which would culminate with the 1984 elections when almost universally cities and towns all over America voted to stop production of nuclear weapons. But, of course, Sister Jane's call came before those votes.

Our women's group included Victoria Safford, Joan Ballas, and me from Northampton; Judith Scheckel of Greenfield; Jane Morrissey of the Sisters of Saint Joseph, Springfield; Judith Beaumont, Sisters of Benedict and Sue Ann Shea, Sisters of Notre Dame, both Hartford; and Ann Welsh, Sisters of Mercy, Pawtucket. The nuns wanted to focus on missile tubes designed to go around nuclear warheads before their positioning on a Trident submarine. The Navy and contractors stacked the tubes on a Quonset Point, Rhode Island dock for transport to Electric Boat and fitting to the submarine.

At meetings over some time, we planned our action. We agreed to go to Quonset Point for our presence designed to have all the elements of a Plowshares action: a ceremony, our blood splashed on missile tubes, and hammering on the tubes symbolically to convert "swords into plowshares."

We spent the night before our witness at a convent, beautiful beachfront property on the Rhode Island shore. We rose early to get to the installation before dawn. Two nuns from Providence served as our support and drove us. We used bolt cutters to get through the fence. Big signs warned of guard dogs and the intention of facility guards to shoot intruders on sight.

We cut through the fence, and the nuns led us fearlessly across a very dark area and out onto the docks to the missile tubes. We had a stencil that said, "Thou shalt not kill," and we used it to write on the tubes. We also had pictures of children in our families. Then, I had only one grandchild, Patrick. I taped his picture to the missile tube, and others taped their family members' photos. Then we formed a circle and prayed. We sang the Latin hymn, "Dona nobis pacem (Give us peace)." Guards discovered us as it got light. Accompanied by their guard dogs, they arrested us.

My grandson Sean once asked if we feared dangerous consequences from sneaking into a military base. We knew we placed ourselves in danger, but I don't remember being afraid. I worried that we wouldn't find the tubes or that I'd stumble and fall or do something foolish. We shared experience in nonviolent action and carefully planned our moves. No signs on tent poles, for example. We acted deeply under weight of our concern for danger posed to the world by nuclear weapons. We planned carefully, and we had great faith in the potential efficacy of our action.

After our arrest, the authorities took us to Cranston, Rhode Island for booking. Arraignment followed, and eventually, some weeks later, a trial. Mount Toby Friends Meeting members offered support. Becky Holmes of the Friends rented a bus, and they filled it with people to attend our trial. The Friends really rallied to our support.

*Connecticut police arrest Frances during a 1982
protest of a Trident submarine at General Dynamics Electric Boat
in Groton, Connecticut*

At trial, the judge enforced strict courtroom demeanor. I thought he was hostile to us. I was first up, but he wouldn't let me say anything or give my statement.

"I want to go into silence," I told him. "I'm a Quaker. Let's go into a silent meeting for worship. You won't allow me to say anything to defend myself. Since what we did was moral and ethical, I will use my time to pray."

He allowed me to pray. We wanted to say that our government waged an illegal war against other countries and what we had done was an act of civil resistance. We explained our action in terms of the US Constitution after exhausting legal means. We used an imminent danger defense, one occasionally but rarely viable for civil disobedients in an American court. The court found us guilty.

After the trial, the court set a sentencing date, and more Western Massachusetts people organized by the Mount Toby Meeting made the trip to Rhode Island for that. In the meantime the others and I went home for a few days and had a chance to get ready. At the sentencing hearing, the court sentenced us to six months, five of them suspended with thirty days to be served in the Adult Correctional Institution, Women's Division, then used for federal as well as state prisoners, in Cranston, Rhode Island.

After sentencing, the authorities took me off to jail. I was the first to go.

The first weekend, Ann Gere, a minister from Springfield, surprised me with a visit. She organized Springfield ministers for a justice and peace commission. With AFSC, we had organized events and activities involving churches. I was surprised to see her. Because she was a minister, the prison authorities admitted her even though visitors ordinarily do not have privileges for some weeks after an inmate begins serving a sentence.

Georgianna Foster of Mount Toby Friends Meeting told me that the Friends designated my husband Tom a minister so that he would be able to visit me in jail without the early rigmarole of being placed on a visiting list after filling out a questionnaire for approval by prison staff.

I did not find prison easy. It was noisy and smoky with an intercom constantly blaring instructions, like "Sentenced girls, line up for dinner." Dinner was at four in the afternoon. "Sentenced girls, line up outside your rooms. Sewing is starting." Most of the "girls" were in their twenties, about the age of my children. In my sixties, I was certainly the oldest person in prison.

Many of the women found themselves in prison because of prostitution or drugs or a domestic incident, often the result of their victimization by society and unscrupulous men. Many women spent their time smoking, watching TV, taking showers, and fixing their hair. The prison expected everyone to sew on machines, but most women resisted, so the guards gladly let me sew as much as I wanted. I liked it. I learned something I hadn't much known about before.

At night, the guards locked us in. Fortunately, Joan and I shared a room for a while. We wore prison clothes, and when we entered, they took all our belongings from the outside, including pre-addressed postcards and stamps I had brought with me to send to friends. A local priest helped us and brought us some books.

I liked to listen to other women talk about their lives, and they helped by telling me how to navigate prison life. They all called me Grandma. One young woman served a life sentence for killing her child. I found her intelligent and interesting. She had been drug-addicted and occupied by some strange religion when she killed her child six years earlier. She attended the prison's creative writing class and Alcoholics Anonymous meetings. She expected to earn her GED soon and to earn release on parole in fifteen years.

After a while I decided I wouldn't do any work for the prison, but I found out that I was required to work or be confined to solitary. My job was sewing overalls on their big sewing machine. I found it ironic that, after avoiding the overall factory in Carthage, I sewed overalls in jail. Eventually, I said, "You're making money from the overalls. I'll clean the toilets." I learned some things by cleaning the toilets. There was never enough warm water in the showers, so the showers were usually cold. I found out from other women that if the toilet flushed continuously as they were showering, cold water drained off, and then the water would be hot. It's funny how fast even a naive woman like me can become prison savvy.

Tom brought me some books to read: Martin Luther King, Jr. and Gandhi. I thought I would read them and pass them along to other inmates to read. When I was in a group cell, my cell mates weren't at all interested in that kind of literature. I guess I was naive again. Other inmates had some interest in Malcolm X, but generally, my fellow inmates did not seem to enjoy reading. In the common room, they always watched TV. Television news was so awful that I sat and read, holding the book on my lap and covering my ears. I tried to keep up with an exercise routine, a practice that seemed to rub off on other people, although mostly I did it to keep my body healthy.

The support I got in jail surprised me. Francis Holmes sent me an appropriate Biblical quote on a postcard every day. Bob Myers wrote a letter to the editor of *The Daily Hampshire Gazette*, and many letters and cards came from people I didn't even know. One day alone I received thirty-six letters.

Monday, Feb 9

Dear Tom,

It was was good to get your letter today. Joan & I are doing very well. It isn't exactly easy — everything is done to make one feel worthless & all the silly little rules the guards keep imposing on us) but the other inmates — the women are very friendly & helpful. They are young, mostly Black & with little going for them — & a very poor self image. We've sensed no anger towards us — they are curious about us & hopefully will be able to talk with them more & more about our work.

Re: the visiting — it takes about 10 days to clear the visiting permit — the birth date etc. — I guess they run each name thru the computer to see if you have a record etc. Clergy do not have to go thru that check — they can come in anytime — so it seems. Ann Gean from Cherapee came last nite — I was very surprised when she appeared — with her clerical collar on — she is a Methodist minister — a wonderful woman — she had her identification so they let her in. It was very good to see her. She told me she had called you.

Father Frederick is a Catholic priest

(left margin, written vertically) & but think could we can work here. Clergy can't come here. Clergy attn. even a little

one of Frances's 1984 letters to Tom during her incarceration at Cranston, Rhode Island for civil resistance at the Quonset Point Facility of Electric Boat in 1983

I think Tom found it hard that I was in jail. Mount Toby Friends Meeting wanted to bring him dinner every day, but he said no. Still, the Mount Toby Friends organized visits for me in jail and offered welcome emotional support to our family. Nevertheless, Tom took care of himself. None of the children lived at home then. He just had the dog. I have to admit it was such a luxury to have meals prepared for me.

Finally, after a month, they scheduled me for release. When I knew the time had come for my release, I said goodbye to the women who would remain. One, a jockey on the outside, served time in prison because she had fixed a race. She said, "I support what you're doing and will pray for you to be successful because you have made me aware of the danger of nuclear weapons. I have a daughter at home, and I want her to be able to grow up." I knew I had reached at least one person with the message.

While I was in jail, Smith College invited the presidential candidate Jesse Jackson to speak. Mary Wentworth and I worked on his campaign before my conviction, and I had helped with preliminary planning for the Smith rally. She and other organizers decided that when they put chairs on the stage for speakers they would keep one of the chairs empty, designated for me. They put a sign on the chair that said, "This space is reserved for a grandmother who is in jail."

Jackson asked about it, and when the event concluded, he called me in prison. Guards came to my cell and escorted me to the warden's office, where they allowed me to take the call. "What's a grandmother doing in prison?" he asked.

I tried to explain, but he wasn't very interested in hearing. "I'm going to offer a prayer for you because you're in jail to end war and these horrible weapons," he said. Then, on the phone, he prayed that they would release me soon and that I would be faithful.

Bill Strickland, chair of African American Studies at UMass and head of Jesse's campaign in New England, got the idea that, since Jesse planned a public appearance in Providence, he should get me released from prison. Then I would speak at a big rally in Providence. I learned later that Jesse didn't succeed in getting me released early, but his efforts had attracted sufficient attention that prison officials didn't want media around when I was released on the correct day.

I didn't know anything about any of it. But just after midnight on the day I was scheduled to be released, prison officials came, woke me up, and said that Jesse Jackson was there to take out me of prison. It seemed to me that Bill Strickland had arranged everything, although the prison officials had figured out how to maintain my release date. The Jackson campaign came to pick me up early that morning.

I got up, put all my stuff in the black plastic bag they gave me, and got dressed. When I left my jail cell, I looked to the end of the corridor, and there was Jesse Jackson. I had never seen him in person and remember thinking how tall he was.

"I'm here to take you home, but first we're going to stop in Providence for a rally," he said. The rally was scheduled for early in the morning, and the ride from prison to the rally took fifteen minutes.

So in the middle of the night, I rode in Jesse Jackson's limousine with a lot of media. I sat beside him talking about how unfair it was that prisoners could not vote. I told him it was wrong and he should work to change that law. But we passed large crowds, and he was busy waving to people. I don't think he heard me or paid much attention to what I saying. He had other things on his mind. I felt like a pawn in his chess game, a game I was willing to play for the exposure it gave to the dangers of nuclear weapons.

Jesse's campaign for president was building, and even though it was the middle of the night, people lined the road as we got nearer to the church hosting the rally. The church was filled, mostly with African Americans. I couldn't believe it. He spoke and asked me to speak. So I did, briefly. Then he reached down to kiss me, and a widely published photo resulted of Jesse Jackson and me in profile, kissing on the lips. *The New York Times* ran it the next day, and apparently it went on the AP wire, because it ended up on the front pages of the *Chicago Sun Times* and *New Haven Register* as well as in *Newsweek*. Who knows where else it showed up?

Betty Steinem from Deerfield wanted to write about my experience and arranged with the campaign to drive me home. First, we drove to Worcester where I spoke at a conference organized by Michael True, a professor of English at Assumption College. The next day, she drove me the hour and ten minutes home to Northampton. I was tired.

My driver dropped me off at home after the speaking engagement, and I walked in the back door as the phone rang. It was local media wanting to talk to me. I know Tom felt irritated with all the media attention. He had arranged a meal with a bottle of wine. He wanted to have a nice quiet dinner. Although he expressed little enthusiasm about the interruptions, I felt I had to take the calls to keep the story about nuclear weapons going and to get the message out.

Sometimes things get out of control. But when you put yourself in the grinder, you have to go with it. There's almost no option. You do the best you can to control it and not be used too much. But sometimes things don't work out quite the way you want them to. As always, Tom and I negotiated. I constantly walked a path between peace and justice work and my family. My family really counted as my first commitment. And Tom always understood. My concerns, after all, were his concerns.

During the Nuclear Freeze campaign, I went with Andrea Ayvazian and others from the Valley in 1983 to the Seneca Women's Encampment for a Future of Peace and Justice near Romulus, New York. Between July 4 and Labor Day that year, thousands of women participated and rallied against nuclear weapons and the patriarchal society that created and used those weapons. The purpose of the Encampment was to stop the scheduled deployment of Cruise and Pershing II missiles before their suspected shipment from the Seneca Army Depot to Europe that fall.

Andrea and I drove to the Encampment in her beige Toyota, later seized by the Internal Revenue Service because of Andrea's tax resistance. Andrea had a tent, and I slept in it with her during our stay at Seneca Falls, of course known as the birthplace of the women's rights movement since 1848. That's when local female Quakers organized the Seneca Falls Convention with Elizabeth Cady Stanton to assert women's rights.

At the Encampment, I showed films as often as I could, especially Robert Richter's 1982 short documentary, *Gods of Metal*. I also made arrangements to speak at the local Unitarian-Universalist Sunday service, where the congregation was very welcoming.

All of us at the Encampment decided to have a march and civil resistance action at the Seneca Falls Army Depot on Monday, August 1 to demonstrate the purpose of our presence in the town. Andrea and I had agreed in solidarity with about a hundred other women to walk onto the army base, thus risking arrest for trespass.

As we walked to the base, we realized that townspeople were not very happy about our presence in town. When we got to the base, the gate was shut. "Back away," announced the guard, "or you are under arrest."

Andrea decided to climb the chain-link fence with its barbed wire top. "Follow me," she called.

I hesitated.

"You can do it," she called.

Someone handed Andrea something to cover the barbed wire, and she went over.

"Frances, you can do it," she called to me. I was sixty-four, and Andrea was in her forties. Because I swam nearly every day and walked and hiked, I was in good physical condition, but the fence intimidated me.

"Frances, you can *do* it," Andrea persisted.

So I did it. I got to the top and someone handed me material to cover the barbed wire, and I went joyfully over. The guards helped me down as a young person said, "Even the old woman has come over."

Others came over. All were arrested, and they used plastic ties to lock our arms behind us. Then they took us to wooden barracks and put us into cubicles. Andrea and I were together and shocked at others doing the Can Can and flirting with the guards. I remembered there had been a global call for everyone to pause at six o'clock that evening for silence for peace. I announced it, and we all quieted down. Then Andrea gradually led us in peace songs and sharing of feelings. She took control and changed the atmosphere from trivial to contemplative. They booked us later that evening.

The Encampment brought so many of us together for peace and justice that summer, and then interest waned. Eventually the Encampment was sold.

Nancy Clover's photo captures the moment of Frances's arrest after climbing over the fence into the Seneca Army Depot to oppose nuclear weapons

But that climb over the wall moved my commitment to a more profound understanding of the depths of my radical soul.

I ran into Hattie Nestel at an Electric Boat/Trident demonstration, and she invited me to an Atlantic Life Community (ALC) retreat where east coast nuclear resisters gather twice a year. I went. Wife and husband Liz McAlister and Phil Berrigan, former nun and priest whose lives were dedicated to nonviolent civil resistance, organized the retreat with other members of the ALC. The Berrigans became nationally known both for leaving their previous religious communities to marry in the late 1960s and for pouring blood on selective service files in Catonsville, Maryland during the Vietnam war. The Berrigans and others founded the ALC and Jonah House, a Catholic intentional community in Baltimore, Maryland predicated on resistance. They tried to keep their consciences alive and do actions that were seriously nonviolent, turning swords into plowshares—to lift one another's spirit. The Atlantic Life Community believes a change of heart is possible and that faith-based resistance can result in profound change.

I particularly remember being arrested at the United Nations during an ALC retreat in the 1990s, probably protesting sanctions against Iraq. We were a large group arrested at the United States mission to the UN. The fingerprint machines were not working at the police station the authorities took us to for processing. So the police took a bunch of us women to a police precinct in the New York Transit Authority subway system itself. We were all handcuffed, and the process involved busing us, getting us off the bus, down at least one flight of stairs, and into the precinct situated on a lower floor as one would go down into the subway. There we were fingerprinted, and then the whole thing had to be reversed back to the original police station. We were quite the sight! Perhaps twenty of us were placed in a New York City holding cell when the jailers decided to move us. For years since, I've attended ALC retreats, often traveling with Daniel Sicken of Vermont, a former plowshares activist.

The ALC follows the Dorothy Day model of resisting the empire while feeding the hungry, clothing the naked, and housing the homeless—works of mercy and not just protesting. I found it very healing and strengthening to experience that balance. And I still do. The ALC, Catholic Worker movement, and their values abide as sustenance for my radical soul.

The Catholic Worker movement is growing with more than two hundred houses in this country. But the most wonderful thing is that many young people are running it now. They're children like my grandchildren who have finished college, who have a conscience, who are trying to figure out the next step in this society. My youngest grandson, Tomas, spent some

Frances converses with Philip Berrigan who, with his wife
Elizabeth McAlister and others, founded the Jonah House
faith and resistance community
in Baltimore in the 1960s

time at one of their houses. They live in the hospitality houses and they
work in the soup kitchens and they resist. They live on a stipend and do
that for a few years. They don't all stay but they are doing great work and
I'm sure that when they go on to a job and to raise their families, the experience in the Catholic Worker movement will stay with them.

As the 1980s progressed and encouraged by Western Massachusetts's
response to the nuclear freeze initiative, many of us wondered, "What
about Star Wars? The test ban agreement? Weapons in space?" And so we
had referenda on all of those every other year when there were Congressional elections: a referendum to abandon Star Wars, which was a plan
to set up an anti missile system in space; a referendum in support of the
test ban agreement to stop testing weapons in space; and a referendum
to develop a comprehensive test ban treaty. People went around getting
signatures on petitions, getting people to vote. It was a wonderful kind of
outreach, a way of organizing Western Massachusetts.

Towns throughout Western Massachusetts voted overwhelmingly to stop funding these programs. At one point I was working to get our US Congressman Silvio Conte to vote against Star Wars funding. On a map of Massachusetts, I put a gold star sticker on every town that had voted against Star Wars. When I took it to Congressman Conte and showed it to him, I said, "We've got to have your vote against funding for Star Wars. You have to take leadership in Congress."

He was surprised. "Even East Otis? Lee?" He had no idea that at the grassroots level people did not want Star Wars funding. He looked at my map and said, "I can't believe it," and from then on he opposed all the votes for Star Wars even though he was a Republican.

The last time I went to see him was in 1987—he died in 1991. He said, "I want you to know that last vote on Star Wars cost me something." Nineteen-eighty-six was the centennial of the dedication of the Statue of Liberty. Renovations had been done, and there was a big celebration on the Fourth of July to announce the reopening. Conte said that he was given an invitation to go out on a battleship. He said that he had taken his mother who was in her eighties, his children, and grandchildren.

They headed out to the battleship in Manhattan with their invitations and were told their invitations had been rescinded. Someone in the Reagan administration had pulled them. "I was so embarrassed in front of my grandchildren and my mother," he said. So he took his family up to the World Trade Center instead.

"You probably had a better view of things," I said.

He didn't seem to regret his decision, however, and said that what he did affected many things including the Reagan proposal for the Strategic Arms Reduction Treaty (START), part of a two-phase treaty between the US and the USSR that would reduce overall warhead counts of any missile type and was eventually signed by George H. W. Bush and Mikhail Gorbachev in 1991.

After the fall of the Soviet empire, with no Cold War, some of us believed we could encourage the US government to disarm the Trident submarines. I went to a workshop in Connecticut attended by many in the anti-Trident movement. We thought submarines could explore the oceans and be underwater conference centers. We believed we could hope for transition from a war economy to a peace economy.

Over the span of the Trident campaign, I spent days and weeks in jail and found solace, calm, and understanding I hadn't previously experienced. I felt I was accomplishing something, and I knew there was much, much more to do.

more than a decade after the end of
the Nuclear Freeze campaign,
Frances and others obstructed a
Trident submarine launch in 1998, and
Frances received this citation for trespass

Peace activist found guilty

By JUDY KELLIHER

A longtime peace activist was found guilty Thursday of a trespassing charge after 15 of her supporters were removed from the courtroom when they caused a disturbance.

"I said, 'It's like Nazi Germany in these courts, nothing is permitted,' and that's when they (the supporters) clapped and the judge made everyone leave," said 66-year-old Frances L. Crowe, who was tried before a six-member jury in Springfield District Court.

Crowe, of 3 Langsworthy Road, Northampton, added that the judge was "clearly nervous and overreacting," and it was an "attempt by him to isolate the defense."

Judge Robert J. Moran had court officers clear the courtroom of all persons, except one witness, when a number of Crowe's supporters clapped in response to her statement.

Crowe was accused of trespassing in the Springfield Federal Building while taking part in a May "sitdown" to protest a U.S. embargo of Nicaragua.

"I felt powerless," said Crowe, after the courtroom was cleared. "It was very unfair because there was no warning of any type."

Crowe was sentenced to 10 days in the House of Correction in Framingham. Her sentence was suspended for one year under unsupervised probation on the condition that she is not arrested within that year. If Crowe is arrested, she will have to serve the 10-day sentence.

Crowe's husband, Dr. Thomas Crowe, a retired physician, said of the order to clear the courtroom, "I felt very indignant. It was very arbitrary and there was no warning of any kind."

He said that not all of the supporters in the courtroom clapped, and he did not applaud.

Frances Crowe was one of 135 persons who staged a protest May 7, 1985 at the Federal Building on Main Street in protest of President Reagan's decision to impose a trade embargo against Nicaragua, which went into effect May 1.

Of the more than 100 persons arrested for trespassing, Crowe was the only one who refused to pay the $50 fine and appealed her case to a six-member jury trial.

Crowe said that she considered herself not guilty and that in good conscience, could not pay a fine for her actions on May 7.

Union photo by Don Traeger

Peace activist Francis Crowe, right, greets her husband, Dr. Thomas Crowe, and friend Isabella Halsted outside the courtroom where she was found guilty Thursday of trespassing.

Frances greets Tom after her conviction for trespassing at the Springfield Federal Building on May 7, 1985 during a "sitdown" to oppose the US embargo of Nicaragua—Don Traeger of the Springfield Union *newspaper caught the moment*

Villagers had undertaken twenty-four-hour vigils. Eight of us joined them setting our alarms and taking two-hour stints through the night. People practiced impressive solidarity. We experienced the magic of being Americans vigiling under the Southern Cross in solidarity with campesinos who lived under a constant threat of American bombs and military maneuvering.

Tom wrote me a poem about the San Juan del Sur.

CENTRAL AMERICA

During the 1980s, I continued to learn about United States actions on the international stage. I didn't much like what I discovered, and our machinations in Central America revealed the worst. The more I learned, the more I became convinced that not only would I have to act in opposition but I would also have to withhold my tax dollars. But I wasn't ready yet.

Tom and I went to Nicaragua with the newly-founded Witness for Peace in 1984. As I prepared this memoir in 2014, Witness for Peace continued its nonviolent mission to "support peace, justice, and sustainable economies in the Americas by changing US policies and corporate practices that contribute to poverty and oppression in Latin America and the Caribbean."

Central America was everywhere in the news in the early 1980s because the US government under Ronald Reagan actively supported governments or insurgents fighting any group that had ties to or supported Communism. In El Salvador the US supported the government in the civil war that pit left-leaning insurgents against a conservative incumbency. In Nicaragua the US looked upon the Sandinistas, the revolutionary government following the tenure of the repressive Somoza family, as a Communist threat. The US supported the Contras, a group of rebels trying to take down the government.

When an opportunity arose to join Witness for Peace as a volunteer to stand in solidarity with the people of Nicaragua and their elected government, we took it. It fit perfectly with the Central American working group of Western Mass AFSC. Witness for Peace had offices in Durham, North Carolina, Washington, DC, and Santa Cruz, California. A large group from North Carolina had previously stood witness in Nicaragua—maybe thirty people who stayed a weekend. Witness for Peace planned to send a smaller group from New England to stay longer. Ours was one of the first small delegations to go and we stayed for two weeks.

Most participants had affiliations with religious groups, and many of the young women studied at Harvard Divinity School. Frank Dorman, Massachusetts coordinator for Witness for Peace until 1990, invited Tom and me to join the delegation. Frank and I had worked together in his previous capacity as an organizer for Western Massachusetts Clergy and Laity Concerned. When he ended his tenure with Witness for Peace, he went to work for Harvard Divinity School.

Tom and I really wanted to go to Nicaragua and stand in resistance to US policy. It was the first time Tom and I joined in an action. He took par-

1980s poster supporting Nicaragua in the face of
United States bombing and interference

ticular interest in the medical situation in Nicaragua. He heard that hospitals were well-run and that the Sandinistas, the group in power opposed by the United States, worked diligently to upgrade facilities. Although Tom wanted to tour hospitals and medical facilities, in the end he didn't visit many large hospitals. Mostly he visited village medical clinics run by the government and open to everybody. Tom gave a positive evaluation to the Sandinista health care system. He brought his Nicaraguan colleagues copies of the manual *Where There Is No Doctor*. Originally written in Spanish but now updated and translated into many languages, it provides simple-to-use methods for health care providers at all levels.

Before our group went to Nicaragua, we notified the American Embassy. When we arrived, we went to the embassy in the capital, Managua. We advised the ambassador of our plans to witness for peace. We vigiled at the embassy. The ambassador welcomed us and said our witness wasn't really necessary. "There are no problems," he said.

We were surprised to find that even though news media experienced censorship, people willingly spoke with us and gave opinions about the government. We felt those we spoke with generally supported the Sandinista government while also offering criticism of governmental shortcomings in meeting the needs of all the people.

We planned to go to the border of Honduras and Nicaragua at Jalapa to stand where the Contras bombed and attacked Nicaraguans. We lived and ate meals with residents of Jalapa. One woman often cooked rice and beans for us in her yard. We slept in other homes around the town in basic accommodations. One night I tried to sleep in the shed where several of us, including Tom and me, stayed. Outdoors, rain poured down, and inside, rain dripped down on the bed. To take a shower, we poured buckets of cold water over our heads. I tried it once only.

The goal of our group was to explore the society built by the Sandinistas in Nicaragua and also the role of the Catholic Church, an institution at the time complicit with US imperialism. We met priests not-so-institutionally inclined who practiced liberation theology and interpreted scripture in the light of social injustices. They used the pulpit to support the revolution and Sandinista government.

We demonstrated in serious marches through villages. People supported us. Many of us did not speak Spanish, however, and could not speak with our supporters. Our delegation included ministers and nuns. We went to churches, had a foot-washing, and practiced religious disciplines to help us center. Eventually, we heard the Contras might attack at the border, so we went there.

When we heard that the US had started bombing at San Juan del Sur on the Pacific coast, we got on a bus and moved our vigil there. San Juan del Sur is a beautiful town in southern Nicaragua. When we arrived, we saw evidence of attacks along the beach—bits of shrapnel, bullet holes in trees, and remnants of rockets. Villagers had undertaken twenty-four-hour vigils. Eight of us joined them setting our alarms and taking two-hour stints through the night. People practiced impressive solidarity. We experienced the magic of being Americans vigiling under the Southern Cross in solidarity with campesinos who lived under a constant threat of American bombs and military maneuvering.

Tom wrote me a poem about San Juan del Sur:

Change of the Watch at San Juan del Sur

When I left you sitting silently on the sand
Close to the almost inaudible sea,
While a few small fishing boats bobbed in the little harbor
Their bare masts swaying slowly,
And as I turned to walk back the cobblestone street
Of the silent dimly moonlit town
I saw the Southern Cross had tilted slightly from its zenith
Continuing its fixed-focus journey around the southern sky:
A sign of suffering and of hope to oppressed people.

Tom Crowe's handwritten poem,
Change of the Watch at San Juan del Sur

After three or four days, we went back to the American embassy to tell the ambassador that, despite what he had told us, there were problems.

"We know what we're doing and what we're doing is the right thing," he told us. "You are very conscientious, I'm sure, and I respect what you're doing, but the US is doing what it needs to do." What the US did involved spreading the empire by force without permitting Nicaraguans to take control of their government, which was moving toward a society for the people.

In Managua, we met Daniel Ortega, ruling leader of the revolution and government. He told us that times were hard for Nicaraguan people. Nicaraguan voters did not re-elect Ortega in 1990 but returned him to office in 2007.

When we returned home, we made public appearances to update audiences about conditions in Nicaragua where the US backed Contra insurgents and the Sandinistas continued to hold their power. We staged a demonstration at the Federal Building in Springfield when the US decided to place an embargo on Nicaragua. Tom and I went with perhaps seventy other people. We wanted to convince our federal representatives, then Congressman Conte and Senators Edward M. Kennedy and Paul Tsongas, to lift the embargo against Nicaragua and stop supporting the Contras.

The demonstration resulted in many arrests, including of Tom and me, for disturbing the peace. Tom paid bail. He was released and never tried. Because my civil resistance means that I am acting to demonstrate the greater wrong of the government, I never pay bails or fines. I won't cooperate with the government. Eventually, I went to trial where the court found me guilty. I served a week's sentence at the Massachusetts Correctional Institution—Framingham (at the time it was called Framingham State Prison), the only all female prison in the Commonwealth.

Again, I found prison difficult. Because my sentence required me to stay only a week, the prison assigned me to the intake section, usually preliminary to longer stays. Seven of us shared a cell crowded with double decker beds. A woman in the adjacent bunk seemed catatonic. She spent all her time on her back repetitively moving her arms and legs. When the social worker came around to see how we were doing, I said, "This woman should not be confined here in this way. I feel she has serious problems." They moved her out, and I was grateful they paid attention. I hope they treated her appropriately.

As before, I was old enough to be grandmother to the other women. Once more, many had been convicted of drug offenses and some of prostitution. Although I had a few conversations with some of them about the Contra War and Nicaragua, I had an easier time conversing in Rhode Island about nuclear war and nuclear weapons.

Later, AFSC's Central America working group and others occupied US Representative Conte's office in Holyoke to encourage him to vote against federal subsidies for the government of El Salvador. The Salvadorian and US governments terrorized dissenters, and we felt it wrong that the US government funded the terror. Judy Scheckel of Traprock helped to organize the sit in. All twenty of us from the working group took part.

We crowded into Representative Conte's office to discuss our concern with him, but he was in Washington. An independently minded Republican Congressman, Conte often voted with the Democrats. He responded conscientiously to his constituents. When we asked to speak to him on the phone, his office staff said we could not and that he had made up his mind and planned to vote for the funding. Finally they threatened us with arrest if we didn't leave. Some did, but Judy and I said, "We're going to stay." We sat prayerfully all day. They locked the bathroom and wouldn't let us use the toilet. I don't think we had any drinking water with us, but nevertheless we stayed.

The others vigiled and rallied outside after they left the office. Reverend Donna Schaper, a minister and one of those outside, called the press. Finally at about five in the afternoon the secretary told us, "Congressman Conte is on the phone." He knew the building would close soon and, if we didn't leave, his staff would have to ask police to arrest us.

Conte knew me from previous AFSC work and interactions. Once, during the Vietnam War, I organized a group of clergy to meet with public officials. Father John Roach of Shelburne and Father Leo Hoare of Springfield College with several others participated in the delegation. We took a bus to a demonstration in Washington where Conte, a Catholic, said he would meet with the priests. When I introduced Father Roach to Conte, he said, "When I was a priest in Pittsfield, I used to go jogging in the morning around the lake in front of your house. It's such a beautiful place, and I always prayed for you as I jogged by."

Conte eventually voted the way we urged him to.

When we talked to Conte on the phone during the sit-in about funding for El Salvador, we told him to pay attention to the legitimate concerns of the people of Central America. We said the US should not impose its military on El Salvador and support a repressive regime out of fear that the people would take a path similar to the one of the Sandinistas in Nicaragua. Many El Salvadorians lived in poverty and fought for peace and freedom.

Notice:

All packages, briefcases, handbags and similar objects are subject to examination upon request when you enter this building.

Frances, standing, and others, including, from left,
Lois Ahrens, George Markham, and Arky Markham,
all of Northampton, sitting in at the
Springfield Federal Building to stop the US embargo of Nicaragua

1980s poster outs the hidden war in El Salvador and decries US bombing of the country

Frances, front left, and her grandson Patrick, walk in a 1980s Springfield march to oppose funding of US war on El Salvador

working with AFSC and Mount Toby Friends Meeting, Frances and others brought several Guatemalan refugees to the Valley in 1985

We talked with him for some time, and eventually he said, "Yes, I will refuse to send any more aid to El Salvador." He kept his word and voted against funding for military support of El Salvador. When we left the building, we told the vigilers what had happened. We felt we had accomplished something.

Sitting in a Congressman's office doesn't always work. I tried the same thing many years later with my then-Congressman Richard Neal. But when the staff left and I was the only one there sitting on a chair, the police came, slid me to the door in the chair, and dumped me out on the hall floor. Next time I'll sit on a couch and not in a chair so they can't slide me out.

When the US funded wars in Central America, students mobilized on campuses in opposition. Elliot Abrams, Reagan's Assistant Secretary of State for Human Rights and Humanitarian Affairs, was scheduled to speak at Wright Hall at Smith College. We at AFSC had a good slide show depicting US bombing of people in Central America. Some students suggested we present the slide show before Abrams spoke. I had the projector and the slides and agreed to preempt the program by showing the slides once Abrams appeared.

Of course, I couldn't use the Smith projection room because we didn't have the key. So I went in to the hall before the audience arrived for Abrams's speech. I brought in a little table and put my slide projector on it. After the Smith president welcomed everyone and Abrams was introduced, one of the students in our group turned out the lights. I got the slide show going and tape recorder on before he could start to speak. The action worked. He never spoke. He fled instead in his limousine. His appearance was a total washout.

Affirmed by the action, students felt empowered. They spoke up, and they got him off campus. Unfortunately, he never stopped working with the dictators in Central America.

As I planned the trip to Nicaragua, I was still on probation for the Electric Boat action that got me a month in Cranston, Rhode Island federal lockup. I had to get permission from the judge to break probation in order to take the trip. He gave it and said, "I want you to know that you gave me a hard time the Christmas after I sent you to jail. My daughter in college came home, and she was very supportive of what you did."

"You must be very proud of her," I said.

Also during the 1980s, Western Mass AFSC and others supported the Sanctuary Movement, begun when people died during our covert war in Guatemala. Nuns and volunteers from Protestant churches harbored fugitives from Guatemala who escaped our war by traveling through

171

Central America and Mexico and into Arizona. We at AFSC got involved through an intern in the AFSC office. Rachel King, a student at Smith, worked in the office as an undergraduate, and when she graduated, I asked, "So, Rachel, what are you going to do next?"

"I think I'm going to Tucson to see what's going on with the Sanctuary movement," she answered.

About two weeks after she left, Rachel called from Tucson. "Frances," she said, "I'm heading a caravan to bring Guatemalan refugees across the US. We are going to seek sanctuary for them in American communities. We're going to deliver them to supporters in Kansas, Chicago, and Michigan. I want you to get Mount Toby Friends Meeting to host them and give them sanctuary. After Western Massachusetts, I'm going up to Weston, Vermont. It's up to you to get permission from Mount Toby to offer two young men sanctuary."

"Rachel," I said, "I'll do what I can, but you'll have to call me in a few days." Cell phones, email, and other methods of instant communication didn't exist then.

I belonged to the Mount Toby peace and justice committee. At a special meeting, I proposed offering sanctuary to the two young Guatemalan men. After a good discussion, the committee agreed to bring it to Monthly Meeting. They had previously sponsored Cambodian refugees and were again open to the concept. When the two Guatemalans arrived at Mount Toby, they agreed to welcome them and offer support.

We had a potluck supper and an ecumenical welcoming. Brothers, the men assumed the names of Pedro and Joaquin. One, a poet, was thirty-four and the other, a radio announcer, was twenty-three. They wore kerchiefs to disguise their identity because of uncertainty about their welcome or status in the US. We told the US immigration service we had offered them sanctuary. "We are offering sanctuary to people who had to escape from Guatemala," we said. "They were politically active in trying to stop the violence and risk reprisals if they return." We had no repercussions from the immigration authorities, so after that Pedro and Joaquin felt no need to wear masks in public.

They stayed at the meetinghouse, and Mount Toby Friends took turns staying with them at night. Friends brought meals to share, and a sense of community developed.

Providing sanctuary created an occasion for community building at Mount Toby Meeting. It pulled us together because we shared a common concern. Newspapers ran articles and pictures of the young men. We had potluck meals and after about two weeks in the meetinghouse, we set up a committee to find housing and work for them. Ruth and Bruce

Hawkins coordinated help for Pedro, Joachin, and their families. Tom organized medical care among sympathetic physicians and dentists. Eventually, Aiden Thayer in Northampton offered them an apartment in her home on Henshaw Avenue. Julie Rapaport, who had traveled in El Salvador and spoke Spanish, acted as interpreter. Paul Sustick of Paul and Elizabeth's, a natural foods restaurant in downtown Northampton, offered them work in the kitchen, and Collective Copies, a printing and copying business in Amherst, hired them. They learned English and made friends.

As years went by, the two Guatemalans who settled here got their relatives to come—parents, cousins, nieces, and nephews, so there is quite a Guatemalan community in the Valley. Ruth Hawkins helped them get green cards so they could work here legally. One of them married Julie Rapaport, and both settled into long-term jobs in the Valley. One made a career at Whole Foods and brought his wife from Guatemala. Joaquin and Julie's daughter Victoria Elena Oliva Rapaport was valedictorian of her 2011 Amherst High School class and matriculated at Tufts University.

In the 2000s, when we showed a film about Guatemala, Pedro introduced the film and spoke about his arrival in Western Massachusetts, his welcome, and his subsequent good life here. He remembered mistreatment and torture in Guatemala. How wonderful that Mount Toby Meeting came through for them.

Not all Guatemalans who arrived with the sanctuary movement stayed in the US. I know that those who went to the Weston Priory returned to Guatemala. Traditionally Mayan, they felt more comfortable in familiar territory.

In 2013, issues of sanctuary returned to the news with the trial of Efraín Ríos Montt, military dictator in Guatemala in the 1980s. A progressive woman judge convicted him, but the conviction was overturned through a complicated set of legal maneuvers. Ríos Montt consistently acknowledged US financing for his repressive regime and political support from Elliott Abrams and Ronald Reagan.

United States activities in Central and South America have been complicated almost since the beginning of our country. In the 1980s, those of us interested in resisting our government's covert activities there found a thicket of intrigue. We learned, as one always learns, that people are people everywhere—the good and the bad—and that it always rewards the soul to tend toward the good, as Tolstoy said. Witness for Peace, the Sanctuary Movement, and other endeavors sometimes brought goodness to bad times in Central and South America.

Frances works the phone in the AFSC office

We didn't solve the problems of biological weapons, homelessness, or conflicts around the world, but with our actions we started the process. We laid down a challenge, and others followed through. It was good work, and it furthered my conviction that I must continue to explore the roots of injustice in the process of finding my radical soul.

RADICAL COMMUNITY ACTION

We were busy in the AFSC office in the late eighties and the nineties. We focused considerable energy for some time in the eighties on US biological weapons, specifically anthrax research at UMass. Some students from the Committee to End Militarism on the UMass Amherst campus came to us. When they investigated university ties to the US Department of Defense, they discovered that UMass contracted with Fort Detrick, Maryland, and the Pentagon for research about biological weapons. The students came to AFSC for help.

John Bonifaz of Amherst graduated in 1987 from Brown University in Providence, Rhode Island. He participated actively in Brown's South Africa divestment campaign. Back home in Amherst, he tried to figure out what to do next: whether to go immediately to law school or take a year off.

"John," I said, "if I get some money for you, maybe you could spend this year working on the anthrax issue." John agreed, and I talked to Ira Helfand at PSR, which agreed to fund an initiative for John to coordinate resistance to research in the Valley about biological weaponry. The campaign turned out very effective. Victoria Dickson, a Quaker, whose husband taught at the University in the engineering department, agreed to help out. She kept records and managed correspondence. She put together careful, detailed files.

Through the Freedom of Information Act we got a copy of the contract UMass had with the Department of Defense. That took a while. When we received it, we took it to Boston to Jonathan King, a microbiologist at MIT. He edited a newsletter called *Science for the People* dedicated to humanizing science. After reading the contract, he offered his opinion: "This is not research to prevent anthrax. This research is for weaponizing anthrax."

We engaged a microbiologist from New York University School of Medicine to come to Northampton and examine the contract. He verified Jonathan King's opinion. "UMass is developing anthrax as a biological weapon and not working on a vaccine or some other prevention," he said.

The Amherst Board of Health conducted a hearing that didn't go the way we wanted it to go. Although we wanted them to address the ethical issues of experimenting with anthrax for its use as a biological weapon, their authority extended only to whether the experiments posed danger to the community. Most who spoke at the hearing opposed anthrax research on grounds of safety, not morality. They objected because anthrax spores could escape and result in an anthrax epidemic beginning in Amherst. The board of health concluded that UMass did not endanger the town because it handled anthrax with sufficient care.

However, we did not want to make the point that anthrax could be dangerous to a community. We objected on ethical grounds to using anthrax (or any biological contaminant) as a weapon. Basing our case on a 1970 World Health Organization report, we argued that developing biological/chemical weapons is against international law. But the board of health believed its jurisdiction had to do only with safety, not law or ethics.

UMass contracted with the Biological Defense Research Project at Fort Detrick, Maryland. Because of previous United States treaties—not to mention sound ethical practice, including medical ethics and the Hippocratic Oath—biological weapons research at Fort Detrick did not constitute moral or ethical activity. Curtis Thorne, a UMass professor in the microbial genetics department, previously worked as branch chief at the Fort Detrick biological labs in Fort Detrick. As an expert on anthrax with connections to Fort Detrick, he naturally understood the projects advanced there and had the ability to secure funding to do related research at UMass.

Students staged several large demonstrations protesting Ames Strain anthrax research at UMass. They filled Memorial Hall for a couple of days and fasted to oppose anthrax research. Ira Helfand, then practicing medicine in Northampton and continuing his avid involvement with PSR, worried about the students' health because of the fast. I went over to the nearby campus with him one night. He climbed in a front floor window. He examined the fasting students and told them how important it was to drink plenty of water. The fast ended the following day when police arrested the students.

At first, campus police and town police collaborated in arrests during the anti-anthrax campaign, and often they treated people roughly. In some arrest situations, people who were not students participated in demonstrations. Once, after a sit-in at the chancellor's office, police carried eighty-eight-year-old Margaret Holt of Amherst out in a chair. She posted bail because of her advanced age, but others didn't. At a later trial, the court convicted them and sentenced them to time in the Hampshire County House of Correction.

Students continued to demonstrate publicly against anthrax research in the days ahead. John Bonifaz worked with them through several arrests. At Herter and Goodell halls, where anthrax research was underway, they staged sit-ins in hallways. Police pulled them out. Claiming that research focused on developing a vaccine against anthrax for American troops in the event of an anthrax of attack, trustees would never talk to students. From our Freedom of Information Act research and the MIT and NYU microbiologists, we knew UMass researchers intended to develop weapons, but the trustees would never admit it.

Meryl Nass, a PSR physician from Amherst, dedicated considerable time to our campaign to end anthrax research at UMass. Meryl informed herself about anthrax. She traveled to Africa for interviews when she became convinced the US government had used anthrax as a weapon there. Meryl emerged as an authority on anthrax and eventually established her medical practice in Bar Harbor, Maine.

The press took note of the campaign. I recorded the Amherst Board of Health hearing on audiotape and videotape. We gave copies to the board of health and Amherst's public library, Jones Library.

Finally, quietly, the university dropped the contract. In 1990, the researcher Curtis Thorne decided not to reapply for the defense department's biological defense research program. In 1994, *The Daily Hampshire Gazette* reported in a little news item on the back page that on the retirement of Curtis Thorne, the university would no longer accept biological defensive contracts.

After working with us for a year, John Bonifaz went on to law school. He passed the bar to practice law and founded the National Voting Rights Institute. He advocates diligently for a Constitutional amendment to negate the 2012 Citizens United Supreme Court decision that gives corporations the same rights as people. In 1999, he received a MacArthur Fellowship, a so-called genius grant, for work with National Voting Rights Institute.

In 2013, Dusty Miller, an old friend from Northampton, wrote a mystery novel, *Danger in the Air,* about the anti-anthrax campaign. A retired psychotherapist, Dusty professionally wrote books on health. In retirement, she writes mystery novels to bring important issues and nonviolent direct action to a wide audience. She bases her central character, Alice Ott, on me and uses my photo on her book covers. In 2014, Dusty released a second Alice Ott mystery, *Danger at the Gates,* about the campaign to shut down Entergy's Vermont Yankee nuclear power reactor.

When mysterious anthrax mailings went to US elected officials in Washington not long after 9/11, a reporter from the *Springfield Republican* interviewed me about the anti-anthrax campaign and wrote a story for the newspaper. The Smith College archives now house our anthrax campaign files.

AFSC and I participated in many initiatives in the 1980s. "Take off the boards" advocated nationally for housing for the homeless. We realized that empty, boarded-up buildings could be used for homeless shelters and low-income housing. Mike Kirby, a writer from Northampton, noticed

advocacy for the homeless and people of low-income extended from the "Take Off the Boards" campaign of the late 1980s to an initiative at Northampton State Hospital where Frances, right, holds a sign in 2005 with Lee Hawkins of Northampton

the area had no homeless shelters. All buildings associated with the former Northampton State Hospital on Grove Street on the outskirts of Northampton stood empty. A boarded-up former superintendent's house remained in good condition. Mike wanted to "take off the boards" and occupy the building as a possible eventual shelter or dwelling. He invited me to participate in the initiative. Although I had not previously advocated for the homeless or for low-income housing, I agreed to participate.

Mike carefully selected his action group. Teresa Rodriguez, a local housing advocate; Margaret MacDonald, among other things a Sunday school teacher from the Florence-Northampton Unitarian Universalist Society; Mike, and I comprised the group. We went to the former state hospital before dawn on Saturday morning of July Fourth weekend in 1988. I went to the back door of the former superintendent's house, broke the glass, reached in, and turned the knob. When we walked in, we saw that although the house was basically sound, it hadn't been occupied for maybe twenty years. Plenty of dirt and dust had accumulated. We brought rags, pails, and bleach as well as our own food and air mattresses and prepared to stay.

Mike brought others for support. Don Ogden of Wendell began planting a backyard garden. Although no one else came in to the house, others occupied the yard. Teresa, Margaret, Mike, and I occupied the house and began cleaning.

After we had worked for three hours, state troopers arrived. I have no idea who called them. We were, after all, working in a state-owned building, so our occupation would seem to have been the jurisdiction of state troopers and not local police. We told them we were participating in a national effort to recognize housing needs of homeless and low-income people. We said the building should be used as a homeless shelter. The troopers eventually said we could stay as long as only four of us stayed in the building. They provided a note that said we could stay for the weekend and no one else from outside should come into the house. They attached the note to the front door.

The four of us busied ourselves with cleaning. Mike was so energetic that he cut a vein in his arm on a piece of glass and had to be rushed to the hospital to have it sewn up. He was lucky that it wasn't more serious. He managed to go to the hospital and return without the police knowing. And they didn't know at the hospital that he was a part of this effort.

Someone brought a television for us. We had a VCR, and I had a film that I wanted to show about Steve Biko from South Africa who had been brutally killed by police during apartheid. His death mobilized many in opposition to South Africa's racist policies. Then Sunday night as we watched the video, state police arrived to arrest us despite the note on the door. I don't know what changed their minds.

They took us to jail in Northampton's state police barracks on King Street, and we stayed over the weekend until arraignment. The troopers seemed very angry with us, maybe because it was the weekend of the Fourth when they would be extremely busy addressing many local matters including drunken driving and domestic violence. The policewoman in charge of me allowed no privacy in the bathroom. She went in with me as if I were going to be using drugs or hiding something in my underwear. I have since realized no one gave me any special treatment and that her behavior was standard protocol.

Luckily when we left the house and they arrested us, I impulsively grabbed the note the state police had tacked to the door and took it with me. Perhaps the shift had changed and the information about the note had somehow not transferred from one group of troopers to the next, resulting in a weekend arrest. Although the law provides generally for arraignment within twenty-four hours, if there's an intervening holiday and court is not in session, short of a special court session, arrestees like us routinely sit in jail over the holiday.

When we finally stood for arraignment on Tuesday, Tom Lesser, the lawyer who represented us pro bono, produced the sign. It said that because it was a holiday weekend we could stay through to Monday. When the judge read the sign, he dismissed our charges of trespassing.

Victoria Safford, Margaret MacDonald, and others of the Unitarian Society of Northampton and Florence supported us, and Unitarians took leadership to obtain housing for the homeless. They permitted a group of homeless people to put up tents on the church lawn. Consciousness grew, and the group acquired the state hospital superintendent's house we originally took over on behalf of the homeless.

Now called Grove Street Inn, the building serves as a homeless shelter, the first in Northampton. Financed largely through donations, it houses some twenty people.

AFSC, Valley Quakers, and others concerned about peace and justice, participated in a number of demonstrations, actions, and initiatives during the 1970s, 1980s, and 1990s. We stood with signs to support the American hostages taken by Iranians in 1979. We endorsed the freeing of Mumia Abu-Jamal, first sentenced to death in 1981 after what I believe was an unfair trial with the sentence commuted to life imprisonment in 2011. We marched against the death penalty. In 1996, we confronted Massachusetts Governor William Weld about casinos.

Brattleboro Reformer
12-21-79

END
U.S.
INTERVENTION
IN
OTHER
NATIONS'
AFFAIRS

UPI

UNITY DAY — Residents of Greenfield, Mass., turned out for a vigil on the town Common Tuesday to show their support for American hostages in Iran.

Frances carries a sign proclaiming "End US Intervention in Other Nations' Affairs" during a 1979 Greenfield, Massachusetts vigil intended to show support for American hostages in Iran, as reported in the Brattleboro Reformer

Frances, left, and Margaret Holt support Mumia Abu-Jamal in the early 1980s after Abu-Jamal's conviction of murdering a Philidelphia police officer during a trial widely considered unfair

1980s flyer invites gathering at the Unitarian Church on Main Street, Northampton, Massachusetts, for a March Against the Death Penalty organized by Frances and others

MPSHIRE GAZETTE

Established 1786

TON, MASS., FRIDAY, JULY 12, 1996   28 PAGES — PLUS HAMPSHIRE LIFE — 50 CENTS

JERREY ROBERTS

Gov. William F. Weld listens to local activist Frances Crowe on the subject of possible casino gambling in Holyoke during his visit yesterday at Elwell State Park in Northampton.

Arky Markham, Frances, and others, from left, confront Massachusetts Governor William Weld in 1996 to demonstrate their disapproval of casinos and encourage the governor to stand firm against them. as reported in The Daily Hampshire Gazette

1990s poster announces a Five-College Conference on the Conflict in the Former Yugoslavia and its World Wide Implications, sponsored by the Friends of Bosnia

During the Bosnian War from 1992-1995, Paula Greene, a practicing Buddhist and psychotherapist from the little town of Leverett north of Amherst, felt called to bring techniques of conflict resolution to international adversaries. The Harvard University Negotiation Project and its program, Getting to Yes, served as models. Paula invited me to be on the board of her nonprofit organization, Karuna Center for Peacebuilding established in 1994. Of course, I accepted her invitation.

Karuna means compassion, active sympathy, gentle affection, and a willingness to bear the pain of others.

I attended several early programs, including one organized by the Harvard team in New York requiring negotiation between native Bosnians and native Serbians. Early in the session, hostility was very evident, but by the end through mediating and people's conscientious desire for resolution, everyone wanted to avoid violence and war. We didn't discuss political solutions because Karuna's approach involves recognizing each other's humanity.

I also took Paula's first-week long course in conflict resolution during January term at Hampshire College. Groups in conflict contacted Karuna Center for assistance, and Paula started a summer course at the School for International Training in Brattleboro, Vermont.

Even after she retired as Karuna's director, Paula traveled to Sudan in 2014 to assist with conflict resolution and many times traveled to work with Palestinian and Israeli women to find common ground.

We didn't solve the problems of biological weapons, homelessness, or conflicts around the world, but with our actions we started the process. We laid down a challenge, and others followed through. It was good work, and it furthered my conviction that I must continue to explore the roots of injustice in the process of finding my radical soul.

Frances whips up a banner in her AFSC office, about 1996

*banner by Claudia Lefko for the
Northampton Committee to Lift the Sanctions (later the
Northampton Committee to Stop the Wars)*

Our government lied to the world about Saddam Hussein's weapons of mass destruction and, in the wake of 9/11, too many people were anxious for war. As a Quaker, I am compelled by my faith in the Peace Testimony to try to live my life "in the light" that takes away the occasion of war. My action of trying to leaflet the workers at Lockheed-Sanders on December 10 was an act of conscience.

NO SANCTIONS, NO WAR

Sanctions and war comprised the focus of my resistance work in the 1990s and early 2000s. In community and civil disobedience, I worked with others to block sanctions and then war in Iraq, war in Afghanistan, drones, and US support for repressive regimes everywhere. More and more, I acted with others in nonviolent direct action that could result in arrest. Eventually, I stopped paying federal taxes and truly identified my radical soul.

In the early nineties during the presidency of George H. W. Bush, we at AFSC became involved in actions against the First Gulf War, which lasted four months from August 1990 to January 1991. Our Northampton coalitions opposed the war.

Although the war ended quickly, the United Nations imposed brutally oppressive economic sanctions on Iraq that persisted from August 1990, when the war began, until March 2003 when the US again invaded Iraq, this time during the presidency of George W. Bush. The UN officially sponsored sanctions. However, the US chiefly enforced sanctions, and without the US, sanctions wouldn't have devastated Iraq's infrastructures and undermined Iraqis' health and security. At least five hundred thousand children died because of sanctions, according to the most conservative estimates.

President Bill Clinton's secretary of state Madeleine Albright famously told *60 Minutes* interviewer Leslie Stahl in 1996 that "The price was worth it" when asked about the deaths of so many Iraqi children. We abhorred sanctions and the deceit and duplicity associated with them and acted to stop them. We also protested against the use of depleted uranium in US weapons, supported campaigns against land mines, and waged civil resistance initiatives against defense contractors.

During sanctions, delegations from Western Massachusetts brought nonviolent direct action to Electric Boat in Connecticut; Westover Air Force Base and the defense contractor Raytheon Corporation in Massachusetts; British Aerospace, for some time affiliated with defense contractor Lockheed-Martin, in New Hampshire; the defense contractor Bath Iron Works in Maine; the Pentagon and White House in Washington, DC; and the School of the Americas in Fort Benning, Georgia.

I have long since lost count of how many times police arrested others and me with charges like trespassing or disturbing the peace during those years. Sometimes, the court convicted us and we served time in jails, although never very long—perhaps five days at the most. I remember Cumberland County Jail in Portland, Maine and Goffstown State

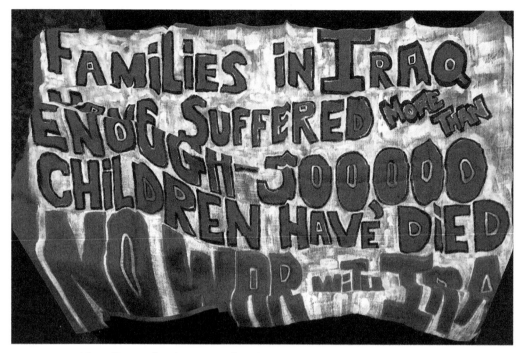

*Claudia Lefko banner decries the devastating effects of
US sanctions on the children of Iraq*

Penitentiary in New Hampshire. Through prior agreement with others
in my affinity groups and in solidarity with the poor, I never paid bail or
fines and, thus, sometimes served jail time instead. Sometimes judges
assigned community service, which some of us refused. Sometimes, some
resisters paid bail while others, including me, refused. I remember once
acting with Hattie Nestel and a large group of others at Westover during
sanctions when only Hattie and I stayed behind.

In early 1997, Hattie, Marcia Gagliardi, Jessica and Audrey Stewart,
Pat Garrity, Mary and Mike Donnelly, Lisa Guido, Ardeth Platte, Carol
Gilbert, and I trespassed at the Portland, Maine Bath Iron Works facility.
We acted soon after the federal court convicted the Prince of Peace Plowshares group led by Philip Berrigan. Susan Crane participated in that
plowshares action and expected to serve eighteen months in the Cumberland County Jail as a result.

Susan lived with Ardeth, Carol, and Phil at Jonah House, the Berrigan
community in Baltimore. After our arrest, we ended up in the same jail
as Susan during a judge's convention. Mike Donnelly went to the men's
pod (as it was called), and the rest of us went to the women's. Although
states generally arraign prisoners within twenty-four hours because of
US Constitution habeas corpus provisions, arraignment was delayed several days because of the convention. Ardeth and Carol, both Dominican

nuns, orchestrated a wonderful retreat for us during our stay. Also every day, some of us played volleyball with longer-term inmates during the recreation period.

When we finally appeared for arraignment in the Cumberland County Courthouse in Portland, Maine, it turned out that the prosecutor had been a childhood playmate of the Donnelly children. He refused to prosecute us. We pointed out that it might be wrong for him not to prosecute us. "No," he said. "I can make this decision." We went back to the pod to get our few prison belongings before reclaiming our outside gear at intake. It was nearly time for volleyball, and the other inmates asked us to stay. The guards asked if we wanted to stay, and when we said "yes," they allowed it. We played for a while, and when the guards told us our rides had arrived, the inmates hugged us and asked us to return. Of course, there would be only one way to accomplish that (and we did, at least once, although not all of the same inmates remained).

I phased out my career with AFSC during the mid 1990s and retired on October 1, 1995. The work of AFSC continued with full-time executive directors, who were, in succession, Anna Megyesi, Jo Comerford, Doug Renick, and Jeff Napolitano. Jo went on to be Director of Programs at the Western Massachusetts Food Bank and then executive director at the National Priorities Project, before becoming campaign director at MoveOn. In the middle 2000s, on her own time, Jo acted with our Shut It Down Affinity Group at Vermont Yankee.

During US sanctions against Iraq, I often passed out leaflets at the Northampton Recycling Center, and Claudia Lefko, whom I had not previously known personally, came by one day with her household recyclables. From the newspaper, I knew Claudia was a prominent member of the Northampton School Committee. We got to talking about sanctions. As we conversed, I suggested that Claudia take an interest in anti-sanction activities.

I found a new volunteer commitment with the Northampton Committee to Lift the Sanctions Against Iraq, later Northampton Committee to Stop the Wars. Claudia became instrumental in that work even as she established her Iraqi Children's Art Exchange and made periodic trips to Baghdad to foster the exchange and bring aid to the Iraqi people. The Northampton Committee was a natural transition for AFSC supporters and me, and the committee often collaborated with AFSC. Northampton and the Valley have a substantial core of dedicated workers for peace and justice, and together they pitch in to support endeavors aimed at righting wrongs perpetuated by government and corporate policies.

AFSC sometimes organized vigils in Northampton over the years. The first vigils opposed the Vietnam War or brought attention to situations in South Africa and Central America. When Anna Megyesi was the AFSC staff person working closely with my friend Ruth Hawkins, they organized vigils to oppose the Persian Gulf War from August 1990 to February 1991 More often, however, we supported the vigil from noon to one Sundays on the Amherst Common, which began during the Vietnam War and is ongoing as I write this.

Many people have vigiled with the Northampton Committee, which also continues as I write this. I came across a Northampton Committee email list from the middle 2000s, and the people on the list include Al Belkin, Nick Camerota, Jo Comerford, Joel Dansky, Bill Diamond, Harriet Diamond, Nancy Felton, Ed Ferguson, Susan Garrett, and Ruth Hawkins.

Others on the list are Peter Kakos, Claudia Lefko, Rose "Arky" Markham, George Markham, Rick McDowell, Harold Rouse, Marguerite McMillan, Dusty Miller, George Munger, and Mike Nagy.

Also on the list are Dimitri Oram, Richard Sanders, Daniel Sheehan, Mary Siano, Irvine Sobelman, Mary Trotochaud, Kathleen Winkworth, Paki Wieland, and Jack Wright.

Of course, the list constitutes only a snapshot of one era of the vigil, but I think it gives a sense of who was involved. Many, many others vigiled over the many years of the vigil. We developed a caring community that has existed for years.

The justice and peace community I have seen emerge in the Valley in the past fifty years embraces the Northampton Committee and many initiatives. Our community grew out of AFSC, Social Workers for Peace and Justice, Physicians for Social Responsibility, and the Mount Toby Friends Meeting.

George Markham was a newspaperman and union organizer who with his wife Arky provided the social glue for our community with their New Year's Eve parties and then their dinners at The Great Wall Restaurant that included so many of us. Arky was a good fund raiser and organized events for AFSC around the January birthday of Martin Luther King, Jr.

Carl Saviano organized the Crescent Street Irregulars, a group meeting occasionally for brunch in our homes on Sunday mornings. The Crescent Street Irregulars included Leonard and Lisa Baskin, the Markhams, the Crowes, Emma and Sidney Kaplan, Henry Rosenberg and Katie Hicks, and others. We wanted to change the priorities of war and build a democratic community here.

poster acknowledging the source of war:
US defense contractors and the lure of profit,
agreed-upon cause of war for Stop-the-Wars vigilers

poster featuring the American tradition of dissent
honored by Stop-the-Wars vigilers

As the Northampton Committee developed, many of us also involved ourselves with the Women's Congress for Peace, which was created in response to the events of September 11, 2001 and our country's subsequent actions. The first congress gathered more than 250 women from all over New England on November 10, 2001, an all-day event at First Churches. The congress later observed Mother's Day in the spirit of Julia Ward Howe's 1870s proclamation "Appeal to Womenhood throughout the World," a call for women to unite for peace, written in reaction to the carnage of the American Civil War and the Franco-Prussian War. For many years, the Women's Congress for Peace staged a Mother's Day march through Northampton to encourage women to unite for peace.

The Women's Congress remained active for many years and helped spawn many activities that continue to this day, like the politically satirical singing group, Raging Grannies, fostered particularly by Ruth Hooke. The Women's Congress brought attention and support to the Bill of Rights Defense Committee, Iraqi Children's Art Exchange and the Women's Congress for Peace Proclamation.

during the period of US sanctions against Iraq in the 1990s when planes taking off from Westover played a role in enforcing the sanctions, Claudia Lefko of Northampton presents a box of vitamins to a Westover Air Base, Chicopee, Massachusetts police officer with the intention that the officer pass the box on for delivery to Iraq

In 1998, Claudia threw herself into organizing and documenting the Northampton Committee to Lift the Sanctions, separate from the Amherst vigil. We were from Amherst, Hadley, Northampton, Springfield, and more. Our avowed work was "to educate and inform our fellow citizens so that we can bring effective pressure on our government to lift the sanctions on Iraq." We chose to stand in front of the courthouse downtown with signs and banners, many on burlap hand-painted by Claudia, an artist and educator. With other materials from the vigil, they may be found in the archives at UMass.

I had been arrested at Raytheon, manufacturer of the Patriot missiles that we had used in Iraq. I had heard Claudia was interested in writing, so I said, "Maybe you would like to come to the trial and write about it for the papers."

In March 1998 during our years-long campaign against the Raytheon Corporation, police arrested eleven of us for trespass at the Raytheon

Raytheon Peacemakers, from left, front, Tom Feagley,
Jane Bernhardt, and Scott Schaeffer-Duffy; back, Marcia Gagliardi,
Frances, Hattie Nestel, Susin King, Michael True, Suzanne Carlson,
Chris Allen-Doucot, and Ken Hannaford-Riccardi outside the Law-
rence, Massachusetts, District Courthouse after their 1998 convic-
tion for blocking the Raytheon Corporation gate

facility in Andover, Massachusetts. I remember the arrest very well: there were twenty-seven police vehicles from New Hampshire and Massachusetts, and a SWAT team arrested Hattie, Marcia, and me. We had vigiled weekly at Andover's Raytheon plant for months before this arrest and, as with most civil resistance initiatives, had spent months planning the action that might lead to our arrest. Scott Schaeffer-Duffy of the Francis and Thèrese Catholic Worker in Worcester and Chris Allen-Doucot of the Hartford, Connecticut, Catholic Worker coordinated our planning. Other Raytheon Peacemakers were Jane Bernhardt, Suzanne Carlson, Tom Feagley, Ken Hannaford-Riccardi, Susin King, and Michael True.

Scott orchestrated our defense at our three-day trial in Lawrence District Court in October 1998. Ramsey Clark, former US Attorney General, advised us in employing the necessity defense. In keeping with the necessity defense, we asserted we had to trespass in order to thwart Raytheon in the same way we would trespass at a burning house in order to save an endangered child. Ramsey Clark's presence attracted daily media attention. We lined up expert witnesses including Thomas Gumbleton, Bishop of Detroit; Kathy Kelly of the Chicago antiwar organization Voices in the Wilderness; and Allen Pogue, a photographer who documented the effects of US Patriot missile attacks on Iraqi civilians.

Supporters in Andover sponsored a potluck the night before the trial. I thought perhaps Claudia would like to come with us and report for *The Daily Hampshire Gazette*. She rode with Hattie, Marcia, and me to the potluck and trial. About seventy-five people attended the potluck chaired by Jane Cadarette of North Andover in the Franciscan Center. As always before a significant trial, we were quite excited. Kathy Kelly described conditions she had observed firsthand in many visits to Iraq during sanctions: crowded hospitals, children dying for lack of clean water and food, and to add to it all, the danger of missiles falling on civilians.

When the jury trial opened the next day, we all admitted we had trespassed because it was necessary to save people dying in Iraq from Raytheon's Patriot missiles. If we could stop manufacture of the missiles, we argued, we could save the people of Iraq. In an unusual but not unique development (although I have experienced perhaps twenty percent of all my courtroom trials under similar circumstances), Judge Ellen Flatley allowed our testimony.

Murat Erkan, the prosecutor in his mid twenties, held Islamic prayer beads throughout the trial. He argued there was no proof that weapons were deployed at the moment we trespassed and so "no imminent danger" existed. He also argued there was not even a glimmer of possibility that Raytheon would stop producing weapons as a result of the trespass.

Claudia Lefko photographed Frances witnessing against
US sanctions during the 1990s in Greenfield with
Sunny Miller, left, then director of the
Traprock Center for Peace and Justice, and others

He said we had other means at our disposal, like publishing a book or forming a grassroots organization. That suggestion brought a laugh from our supporters in the courtroom and from us when we thought about all the books written and grassroots organizations set up to stop the manufacture of military weapons. Erkan said that Raytheon manufactured defensive weapons, not offensive.

Finally Scott laid out the defense. Advised by Ramsay Clark, who attended the trial for the first two days, Scott pointed out that Raytheon and the US violated Nuremberg principles and committed war crimes against peace and humanity. Scott said Raytheon indeed manufactured offensive weapons and that their use in Iraq required the eleven of us to intervene to put an end to the killing they caused. Despite Scott's argument, Judge Flatley decided without comment that we could not use the necessity defense.

We took the stand one by one, some of us enumerating instances of Raytheon weapons causing death and destruction. Eventually, nevertheless, a twelve-member jury convicted us all. Judge Flatley sentenced us to a year's probation and a thirty-five-dollar witness fee or seven hours of community service. Hattie refused both the fee and service, but the rest of us worked for seven hours in an Andover homeless shelter.

Claudia wrote an extensive article, and *The Daily Hampshire Gazette* gave it prominent coverage. Massachusetts newspapers widely covered the trial, which also went national on the Associated Press wire.

With some of the same people, I also participated in a long-running campaign during the late 1990s at the Sanders facility of Lockheed-Martin, later a British Aerospace factory, in Nashua, New Hampshire. Among the resisters was Ruth MacKay of Concord, New Hampshire, who had vigiled every week at Sanders since 1983 to oppose the manufacture of weapons there. The US depended on Lockheed-Martin and British Aerospace for weapons to enforce the sanctions no-fly zone.

Judge Martha A. Crocker allowed us to make statements at our sentencing. My son Jarlath, who attended, kept my statement:

> I am here to plea for a revolution in moral consciousness. I plea that the citizens of this state will reclaim their democracy from the military-industrial global corporate media empire of Lockheed-Martin.
>
> Is it right that the workers at Lockheed-Sanders are held hostage to making electronic parts of weapons delivery systems sold to Turkey and used to bomb the Kurds or sold to Indonesia to be used to bomb the people of East Timor?

I plea for the democratically elected leaders of this community and state to take leadership in securing Federal funds for serious conversion work.

For instance, Lockheed-Sanders could make windmills to be placed five miles off the New Hampshire coast to generate energy for New England. There are many other sustainable energy technologies in need of development.

Our military stood by during the pillaging of Baghdad's historical treasures in favor of securing oil fields and soon deposed the dictator Saddam Hussein.

Our government lied to the world about Saddam Hussein's weapons of mass destruction and, in the wake of 9/11, too many people were anxious for war.

As a Quaker, I am compelled by my faith in the Peace Testimony to try to live my life "in the light" that takes away the occasion of war. My action of trying to leaflet the workers at Lockheed-Sanders on December 10 was an act of conscience—and a last resource for me. I have worked full time since 1968 to try to abolish war and the instruments of war. The basement of our home was made into a peace center where I worked with many volunteers.

I have petitioned, vigiled, organized meetings, organized referendums, spoken publicly, written letters to the editor, traveled to Washington to see my Congressional representative and yes, gone to jail.

I know of no other way to raise the issues of my tax dollars being spent to subsidize Lockheed-Martin's weapons development instead of sustained economic development and meeting human needs.

I plea for a revolution in our thinking from corporate profits to societal needs.

Only responsible action based on conscience can begin to create a future for all of us.

In the first of three similar outcomes, the judge sentenced us each to a one-hundred-dollar fine that we refused to pay. Therefore, we each served five days in the Goffstown state prison for women. Usually when prisoners first arrive at a prison, they spend a number of days in quarantine, and that was the case at Goffstown. Because we were an uneven number of women and sentenced for a very short time in an area with double bunks, I volunteered for solitary confinement.

After writing the article about the Raytheon trial, Claudia became more caught up with the unfairness and brutality of sanctions. With the Northampton Committee to Lift the Sanctions, we brought people to Northampton to speak, including Denis Halliday, formerly an assistant UN secretary-general, and Scott Ritter, a UN weapons inspector assigned to divest Iraq of any weapons of mass destruction. In New York on his way to work at the UN, Denis sometimes encountered Kathy Kelly and an anti-sanctions demonstration. After conversations with them, he had compunctions about his work and realized that people suffered brutally and needlessly because of sanctions.

In conscience, Denis resigned his position, and told me he felt his resignation was a direct result of conversations with Kathy and others as

Frances advises resisting another US invasion of Iraq

a poster by Tom Lewis asserts No US War in Iraq

he experienced the strength of their commitment and fasting. Even the person who followed him in the job, Hans von Sponeck, later resigned for the same reasons. Scott Ritter made it clear that there were no weapons of mass destruction in Iraq even as Bush's Secretary of State Colin Powell insisted at the UN that Iraq had great stockpiles of nuclear weapons.

Attacks on New York's World Trade Center and the Pentagon on September 11, 2001 invigorated the work of the Northampton committee. We continued our vigil to end the war and intensified our education programs. We opposed the pending United States-led NATO invasion of Afghanistan. It began with the US Operation Enduring Freedom military onslaught into Afghanistan on October 7, 2001, the start of a thirteen-year war, the longest in US history and an exercise in US terrorism of innocent civilians not unlike the horrors of the Persian Gulf War. In the lead-up, the George W. Bush presidential administration propagandized Operation Enduring Freedom as a very quick clean-out of Taliban and Al-Quaeda, which had claimed responsibility for the September 11 attacks.

Northampton Mayor Mary Clare Higgins issued a proclamation in 2005 to honor the dead, the wounded, and the suffering on all sides of the war against Iraq. Claudia led the Northampton committee initiative adopted by Mayor Higgins in keeping with a February 2003 resolution adopted by the Northampton City Council to oppose the pending US invasion of Iraq.

Nine of us dressed as Iraqis on Martin Luther King Day, January 15, 2003, to block the gate at Westover Air Reserve Base in Chicopee, where planes departed daily with personnel and supplies for the invasion. When the action came to trial in May, Judge Mary Hurley Marks would not allow the necessity defense. Five of us pleaded out and paid fines while four of us proceeded with the bench trial, including Carl Doerner of Conway, Kathleen Winkworth of Leverett, Claudia, and me. The judge found us guilty and fined us.

After the war began in Iraq, the committee's name changed to Northampton Committee to Stop the Wars, and the committee's agenda expanded. We maintained the weekly vigil, participated in fasts, brought speakers to the area, sponsored films, and participated in regional, state, and national demonstrations and marches to encourage an end to the war. Some committee members posted tally signs showing the number of Iraqis, Afghanis, and Americans killed in the wars. Some of us supported Hattie when she disrupted the speech of US Secretary of State Madeline Albright when she spoke at the Smith commencement in May, 2003.

Denis Halliday, Kathy Kelly, and the Northampton committee's resistance to the wars moved Claudia profoundly. She joined Ramsey Clark's

Frances dresses in prison orange in downtown Northampton to invoke empathy for prisoners held without reason and tortured by the United States at Guantanamo, Cuba and Abu Ghraib, a suburb of Baghdad

Frances confers about Northampton committees matters with Lois Ahrens of Northampton, top, and vigils against the 2003 US invasion of Iraq with Sally Zorn of Northampton and Diedrlck Snoek of Easthampton, bottom

missions to Iraq to bring material aid to people suffering under US sanctions. Because she was an educator, she carried art supplies, crayons, and paper for Iraqi children. The reality of poverty, illness, and damage done to children through US bombings, sanctions, and war swept Claudia off her feet when she saw them. She developed a working relationship with the director of a Baghdad children's hospital. When she returned, she encouraged partnerships among US hospitals and medical schools with the Iraqi hospital.

The concept of peak oil became clear to me in part because US greed for oil motivated the two wars in Iraq and the war in Afghanistan. Karl Davies, a forester and Mount Toby Friend, introduced me to the idea that humans had consumed more than half of the world's oil, which eventually would run out. Unless humans found a replacement for oil, inevitably our way of life would change drastically because of heavy reliance on oil for energy. Karl and I carpooled to meetings at Mount Toby.

When we drove together, Karl explained the concept of peak oil. Oil is not a renewable resource. Karl communicated online with people all over the world about peak oil, and he often shared his conversations with me. I thought about lifestyle changes and began to consider giving up my car, using less energy, eating only local food, and otherwise supporting renewable and sustainable concepts.

Karl unfortunately developed colon cancer. I drove him to the doctor when he got the diagnosis. I realized how much the issue and finding a solution to the peak oil dilemma mattered to Karl. "Let's start a group that can work on this topic," I suggested. Karl liked the idea, and I found people willing to pursue the subject and help educate others. Sometimes when he was sick, we met at his bedside. He planned to marry, but the day of the wedding, he died. We were all there with him.

It was really, really sad. He was only forty years old. He had spent his inheritance buying land, which he left to his fiancée with the request that she obtain a conservation restriction for it so that it would remain open and undeveloped. Karl's own family did not approve of his position on fossil fuel. His grandfather had been an executive with Standard Oil of New Jersey, and the family mind set was corporate. Karl had just cut himself off from his family. However, his fiancé invited them to Karl's memorial service. The family attended, and Karl's fiancée became a powerful bridge to heal the rift.

Karl organized our group, modeled on the West Coast Gosalo program. We called ours CommuniGo, based on a ride-share opportunity developed in the San Geronimo Valley of California. Richard Heinberg, author of *The Party's Over*, spoke to us about peak oil. With the goal of conserving petroleum products, our group developed ideas for a hitchhiking system modeled on a California project. The system would work this way: If you were willing to pick up hitchhikers, you would be vetted and then get a sign on your car door announcing your qualifications to pick up hitchhikers. Likewise, approved hitchhikers would have a little sign. We established stops throughout the Five College area so that approved hitchhikers and drivers could travel among the campuses of UMass and Amherst, Smith, Mount Holyoke, and Hampshire colleges or among the college towns.

We got good publicity for Gosalo, but we couldn't find enough drivers. We found plenty of potential hitchhikers, however, so we asked some of them to congregate at a convenient parking turn-off on Route 9 between Amherst and Northampton. We hoped to flag down drivers to break the ice on the hitchhiking project, but alas, no one stopped. We had coffee, muffins, and students, but no one to drive the students. Perhaps we were ahead of our time. Perhaps the Valley will one day accept the hitchhiking project.

We recognized the realities of peak oil, our society's penchant for excess, and our country's addiction to war and its weapons as I moved into my nineties. I wanted to stay involved and active, and my conscience compels that I be involved. Because I believe that exercising the body helps keep the mind fit and keeps me useful, I maintained activities like walking and swimming even when it felt physically challenging. I also recognized a need to resist the excessive consumption of society. I looked toward the goal of giving up my car and eating only locally-produced food. While I have not yet entirely achieved these goals, I find that they certainly are in keeping with my understanding of my radical soul.

*Frances blocking the Entergy Vermont Yankee gate with
the Shut It Down Affinity Group in April, 2007, including to right, from
Frances, Dorthee (her full name), Ellen Graves, Hattie Nestel, Paki
Wieland, and Julia Bonafine*

The Clamshell Alliance occupation of Seabrook with its previous and subsequent demonstrations remains a high point of community nonviolent action. Many Clamshellers attend reunions and reminisce about their days trying to shut down Seabrook. Humans need one another. It's not enough to protest and write your letters alone. You have to come together in groups and act, which provides an unequaled sense of friendship and community.

NO NUCLEAR ENERGY

The United States government perpetuates lies concerning the safety and "greenness" of nuclear power. For me, those lies stand in the long line of official misrepresentation and obfuscation about nuclear power and nuclear weapons. How I wish we would see the light and invest our talent and treasure in safe, renewable power. How I wish we would invest in truth. But wishes don't make things happen, and so I have spent my eighth and ninth decades acting to bring an end to nuclear power.

Although dropping the atom bomb on Hiroshima and Nagasaki catalyzed my activism, I soon realized that the whole nuclear energy industry was closely related and equally dangerous. In 1974 five years before the Three-Mile Island disaster in Pennsylvania, the issue of nuclear energy exploded on the scene in Western Massachusetts when Sam Lovejoy toppled a tower that was the precursor of a proposed nuclear reactor in Montague, Massachusetts.

Through AFSC and draft counseling, I learned about the plans when I spoke about the draft and conscientious objection at Chestnut Hill Farm in Montague one evening in the early seventies. The farm, a commune founded in 1968 by Marshall Bloom and others from a breakaway faction of Liberation News Service, was part of the back-to-the-land movement of the seventies. Among those living there were Harvey Wasserman and Anna Gyorgy. Young people there dedicated themselves to growing organic food and living cooperatively. We met in a barn, and I sat on a bail of straw and talked to them about the draft. They told me about the proposed reactor. They knew far more about the nuclear power industry than I did.

One morning in 1974 I got a telephone call. I learned that the test tower for the eventual nuclear reactor had been toppled. It was the Paul Revere moment that really alerted people to the dangers of nuclear power.

The power company Northeast Utilities had put up a tall weather-testing tower with blinking lights on the Montague Plains outside of Turners Falls in the town of Montague to test whether weather at the site would be suitable for a nuclear power station. You could see the blinking light from Woolman Hill. To build a nuclear reactor on Montague Plains would disrupt a magnificent agricultural flood plain and its aquifer. It made opponents sick and sad to think of degrading the landscape by building a nuclear reactor there.

Sam Lovejoy, an Amherst College graduate turned organic farmer at Chestnut Hill Farm, went to the tower on Washington's Birthday, February 22 and cut the guy wires holding it up. Sam did an extraordinarily courageous and dangerous thing because, aside from potential legal ramifications, when he cut the first guy wire, it whipped around uncontrollably. The wire could have decapitated him—never mind the possibility of the tower falling on him. Luckily, he eluded the wire, cut a second wire, and ran down and out of the way as the tower crashed down. Then alone in the February cold, he picked up his tools and walked down the road that he had come on.

He walked alone in the dark on that icy, clear night. A police car drove by and offered Sam a ride. He accepted the ride to the police station, where he told them he had toppled the tower. At first they didn't believe him, but when he pointed out to them that the strobe light on the top of the tower no longer flashed, they did.

Lovejoy's arrest mobilized people. Obviously guilty, he went to trial. Howard Zinn, well known historian and Boston University professor, spoke at the trial about the necessity of standing up to evil. John Gofman, a University of California, Berkeley professor and an authority on nuclear power, spoke of its danger.

Because of a technicality, the court acquitted Sam. The state had accused him of destroying personal property, but the tower was real property. The judge threw out the case. Sam didn't serve any time and became a national folk hero. He organized many concerts and events to raise money for the Clamshell Alliance that worked against nuclear energy. Dan Keller of Green Mountain Post Films documented the tower toppling in his film, *Lovejoy's Nuclear War*. Sam woke up people not only in Massachusetts but around the country by empowering them to believe they could act to stop nuclear reactors. Northeast Utilities never built the planned Montague twin reactor.

Also in the 1970s, I acted with the Clamshell Alliance to oppose constructing New Hampshire's Seabrook nuclear reactor just across the strait from Hampton Beach State Park. At their request, I provided nonviolence training for a planned action at Seabrook Station, the reactor construction site. My only prior experience involved offering training for nonviolent civil resistance to the young people working at Chestnut Hill Farm in Montague. Richard Greg's book, *The Power of Nonviolence*, provided just what I needed to know. It serves as the bible on nonviolence. Of course we didn't have the Internet, and I couldn't Google for techniques of training in nonviolence. I concluded we should role-play direct action scenarios.

From my own involvement in actions, I knew how important it is that everybody be focused and clear. Each person in the group must support each of the others and not divert attention from the main point of the action. For example, if you're going into an action, you don't permit a media person to come and stick a microphone in your face and ask, "Why are you doing this? Do you think it will be effective?" You instead refer to the group's spokesperson.

Each person in the civil resistance scenario must understand the discipline of the action so that people won't overreact no matter what they're faced with. Together, resisters should experience the same spirit and share common mind. Solidarity defines the character of action. Small groups enhance the possibility of solidarity, and small affinity groups within a large group assist people in recognizing their common purpose. Role-plays vitally assist action planning. Resisters put themselves in imagined situations or watch others confront imagined situations in order to clarify how people should stick together.

Once during a pre-surgical interview, the woman interviewer asked, "Have you been in stressful situations? Are you likely to get anxious?"

"Well," I replied, "not medically stressful, but I've been in stressful situations where I've done acts of civil resistance and been confronted by police dogs and horses, so I think I'll be okay."

She seemed uncomfortable with my answer. Maybe she wondered, "What is this old lady talking about? Does she have all her marbles?" Perhaps she had never encountered a civil resister before, or maybe it had never before occurred to her that civil resistance provides a mechanism for calming oneself and centering.

Just before a 1977 action at Seabrook, with others, I provided a day of nonviolence training in the UMass student center. We trained several groups. It took about two hours to do one group well. We decided to form into affinity groups, a concept made popular in Germany during antinuclear demonstrations there. Before the training session, I hadn't much thought about my own role in the pending actions, but by the end of the day, I joined an affinity group of students. I was the old lady of fifty-eight, but we had gotten to know each other during the trainings and felt comfortable.

The Clamshell Alliance attracted resisters from all over the United States, even, and thus several affinity groups trained at UMass became part of a much larger demonstration. Clamshell occupied the Seabrook site in imitation of a resistance demonstration involving more than twenty thousand people at a German nuclear power plant site.

Several earlier demonstrations at Seabrook had resulted in a few hundred arrests each. We felt tremendous energy on Saturday, April 30 as we occupied the site of the prospective Seabrook nuclear reactor. We went

an Associated Press photographer captured the scope of the
1977 Seabrook Clamshell Alliance demonstration
where Frances spent weeks in community in a
New Hampshire armory with others

prepared to stay with our backpacks, sleeping bags, tents, veggies, and trail mix. We felt very sure we could stop construction of that plant, that with our bodies and solidarity, we would say no to nuclear power.

Once on site, we became a community. We varied in age and demographics and embodied in microcosm the larger community of people not present that day. After meals and music, we slept overnight in our tents. Sunday morning featured a big, satisfying outdoors Friends meeting. We gathered in a circle with several rows of us sitting on the ground. People spoke from their hearts about the day when we would live without nuclear power.

Helicopters began circling by early afternoon. The police arrived and told us to leave or expect to be arrested. More than fourteen hundred people refused to leave, and slowly police arrested us for trespass. In the end, the authorities booked 1,414 people. They held us mostly without food or water in school buses from three in the afternoon to three in the morning. The police processed our affinity group together, and together we experienced the long wait. We overwhelmed the New Hampshire State Police, the New Hampshire National Guard, and the Public Service Company of New Hampshire, owner of the proposed plant, with our numbers.

The police held us because, in pre-planned solidarity, no one accepted bail. New Hampshire did not have enough jails to house us, so the authorities converted armories to jails. School buses took some groups to Portsmouth Armory where they separated men from women; others went to Dover and still others to Somersworth. My group ended up all together in Manchester Armory. By the time we arrived, we were so tired we spread our sleeping bags on the floor and slept with our knapsacks as pillows. The next day, the police brought folding cots, and our group put our cots in a circle.

Long tables had been set up in the big room, and Claire Bateman, one of the women from Western Massachusetts, suggested we put all our food out to share. That was great. It enhanced the building of community spirit that would grow during our time in the armory. Those two weeks qualify as two of the best weeks I've ever experienced for learning something about building community.

They stuffed perhaps four hundred of us into the armory with only about two toilets. The government brought in food, and we ate cafeteria style.

In the armory, our affinity groups organized us. Each group and each individual decided what its gifts were. We had massage groups, theater groups, media groups, tai chi groups, yoga groups, storytelling groups, and more. We set up morning and afternoon schedules, and people signed up for workshops. We got political education and learned about one another. At night we returned to sleep with our affinity group. Throughout, many of us refused to post bail, and so the officials could not clear out the armories.

Every day, each affinity group elected a spokesperson to attend the daily assembly called a "spokesmeeting." Most of us took a turn doing it. When I represented our affinity group at spokesmeetings, I felt conflicted about the constant talking and discussing. Because our views about how to end nuclear power at Seabrook ranged from anarchist to conciliatory, spokesmeetings posed a challenge. Governor Meldrim Thomson tried to persuade us to post bail, and while many continued to refuse, some had obligations that would not permit their staying. Sometimes, consensus eluded us. Eventually, we came to agreement with government officials who had not understood how to deal with our non-hierarchical structure.

Frustration ran high sometimes. One night we had a rumble—a big march around the armory. I don't know quite how that started, but people took garbage can lids and sticks. They pounded, sang, and shouted for an hour or more. People seemed to feel better after releasing energy, and we finally fell into our own cots and slept.

I particularly enjoyed getting to know people from the Movement for a New Society in Philadelphia, a group of seasoned organizers. Bill Moyer (not the reporter Bill Moyers) of that group presented workshops about how change occurs in society. He helped us learn to understand and gauge public opinion and how to present information in appealing ways. My insights and capabilities grew as a result of the two weeks in the armory and the workshops and other activities there.

My being in the armory for two weeks did not make life easy for my family, however. All those years before email and smart phones, my husband Tom wrote me a few letters, one around our wedding anniversary. He told me he didn't know much when we got married—young as we were, but he at least knew enough to choose the right woman. What a very loving thing to say as he spent two lonely weeks in Northampton while I refused to bail out of the armory. It especially concerned him that we couldn't predict the length of our stay. My daughter, Caltha, wrote to tell me she was proud of my activity.

Eventually, Governor Thompson and the spokespeople negotiated an agreement. Authorities released us without bail and gave us trial dates. At our affinity group's trial, we duct-taped our mouths to show that by not putting an end to construction of the nuclear reactor, the corporation and authorities robbed us of our voices.

The Clamshell Alliance occupation of Seabrook with its previous and subsequent demonstrations remains a high point of community nonviolent action. Many Clamshellers attend reunions and reminisce about their days trying to shut down Seabrook. Humans need one another. It's not enough to protest and write your letters alone. You have to come together in groups and act, which provides an unequaled sense of friendship and community.

Public Service Company of New Hampshire eventually built one nuclear reactor at Seabrook. They scrapped plans for a second because of cost overruns and delays in the first unit. Seabrook continued to produce nuclear power as I prepared this memoir. Nevertheless, the Clamshell Alliance energized the national movement to oppose nuclear power. Demonstrators forced some fully licensed, operating, and expensive reactors to close well ahead of their proposed lifetime, including Trojan in Oregon in 1998, Fort Saint Vrain in Colorado in 1989, and Yankee Rowe in Massachusetts in 1991. Rancho Seco in California closed by referendum in 1989 and now has solar panels and half a million shade trees.

It makes sense to close dangerous nuclear reactors, dirty coal plants, and natural gas plants fueled through fracking activities. Sustainable methods of generating electricity make more sense, and I favor solar and wind. President Nixon said that he wanted a thousand nuclear reactors built by the year 2000, and the George W. Bush/Dick Cheney secret energy committee of the middle 2000s fostered plans for building almost four hundred new plants worldwide. Industrious mathematicians calculated in 2007 that, if all proposed Bush/Cheney plants opened and operated, the world's uranium would be depleted by 2040.

United States policy advocates building nuclear reactors in India and China, among other developing countries, and the government touts the activity as good for the economy. Nothing, however, can justify construction of such dangerous facilities. Several first-generation American nuclear power plants closed between 2012 and 2014 in the wake of the Fukushima, Japan nuclear meltdowns. We can only hope that more will close. Still, a hundred American nuclear power plants operate as I write.

From the 1960s to the 1990s, I protested the Rowe Nuclear Power Plant in northwest Massachusetts, the first reactor in New England. Under the auspices of AFSC, we demonstrated to oppose Yankee Rowe

Yankee Rowe closed for good in 1992 because of an embrittled reactor; the federal Nuclear Regulatory Commission declared the reactor fully decommissioned in 2007; Frances participates in effigy in this 1980s protest at Yankee Rowe

when management offered school tours of the reactor. We didn't let our children attend because of the danger of exposure to nuclear emissions.

In the 1970s, Al Giordano, a radical young man who moved to the Valley from New York City, asked me to be part of a group planning nonviolent civil resistance at the Rowe reactor. He had experience with Clamshell. I did not want to go to Yankee Rowe because of low level radiation emissions there, so I sent an effigy of myself with a sign attached that said "I'm with you in spirit but not in body. I don't want any more radiation."

I also attended meetings in Charlemont of Citizens Awareness Network (CAN), organized by Fred and Deb Katz. With others, the Katzes orchestrated the demise of Yankee Rowe. The reactor closed prematurely in 1991 ostensibly because of a crack in the containment tank and largely from the work of CAN and the Union of Concerned Scientists. Rowe shut down in the thirtieth year of a proposed forty-year existence.

As of 2014, I had worked with others for nearly a decade to close Vermont Yankee, a nuclear reactor operated by the Entergy Corporation in Vernon in southern Vermont. The government commissioned Vermont

a Brattleboro police officer asks Shut-It-Downers to move away from the Entergy Headquarters gate they block in Brattleboro in April, 2006; the actors are, from left, Hattie Nestel, Paki Wieland, Claire Chang, Marcia Gagliardi, Dorthee (her full name), and Frances; Jo Comerford also acted that day and is not visible in the photo by Harvey Shaktman of Citizens Awareness Network, which supported the demonstration

Yankee in 1972, and in 2012 the reactor got a twenty-year extension on top of its forty-year license from the Nuclear Regulatory Commission against the wishes of the Vermont legislature.

New England Coalition on Nuclear Pollution introduced Tom and me to Vermont Yankee. NEC's annual dinner meeting features knowledgeable, antinuclear speakers like Helen Caldicott and John Gofman. Led by President Diana Sidebotham, NEC represented many antinuclear organizations, some of them associated with Clamshell experience. A number of demonstrations including civil resistance attempted to prevent construction of Vermont Yankee, but they didn't succeed. So the reactor stood and operated in Vernon, Vermont. I did not think much about it for many years.

Then in 2005 Hattie Nestel, Raytheon Peacemaker and longtime friend, encouraged me to demonstrate again against Vermont Yankee.

"We have to put our bodies out there," Hattie said. And Hattie is right. When you have exhausted your administrative remedies, when you've petitioned, gone to Washington, been on the radio, written letters to the editors and op-ed articles in the paper, showed films about the dangers of nuclear power and still the nuclear reactor operates, all you can do is put your body on the line—put your whole self in as the song goes.

The prospect of shutting down Vermont Yankee occupied much of my energy. I care about the people of Afghanistan, Iraq, Pakistan, and every place where US bombs fall and drones kill, but Vermont Yankee poses an immediate threat to the region where I live. A dangerous old nuclear reactor threatens an accident that would make this area of New England uninhabitable for generations. As the crow flies, Vermont Yankee operates only thirty-five miles from Northampton. Clever planners of nuclear power knew that Vermonters in the state capital of Montpelier have little concern about a nuclear reactor 124 miles away. Planners also knew that opponents would have difficulty finding effective ways to encourage Massachusetts and New Hampshire legislators and executives to oppose a Vermont reactor.

Builders situated Vermont Yankee in a beautiful rural area on the Connecticut River, compromised by millions of gallons of overheated water dumped in it daily from the reactor's functioning. As a consequence, the river's high temperature adversely affects spawning habits of fish. Measurements detect Strontium 90 in the fish themselves. It reminds me of those years when I unsuccessfully encouraged my children to drink powdered milk because of our concern with Strontium 90.

Aside from specifics about Vermont Yankee, the federal government has not solved the problem of nuclear waste. We have no safe way

Shut-It-Downers Ellen Graves, Paki, Frances, and Hattie got through the security gate at Vernon's Vermont Yankee Nuclear Power Plant on Yom Kippur, 2009, thus demonstrating inadequate security

to dispose of highly radioactive nuclear residues, but we continue to generate nuclear power and create radioactive waste. We have figured out how to reprocess some of it into plutonium for nuclear weapons, depleted uranium to enhance the killing capabilities of conventional weapons, and even so-called durable construction materials (that emit radioactivity). Options for re-using radioactive waste result in weapons or contamination, and none makes an acceptable alternative to waste storage that we can not seem to provide. We accumulate nuclear waste that will emit killer radioactivity for generations, a huge unacceptable burden for the future.

Citizen's Awareness Network (CAN), the organization instrumental in shutting down Yankee Rowe, Millstone Unit 1, and Connecticut Yankee, staged a large legal demonstration at headquarters of Vermont Yankee's owner, Entergy Corporation in Brattleboro, in December 2005. CAN made room for civil resistance, although not many wanted to take part. A few of us crossed the line in an arrest scenario choreographed by CAN in collaboration with the Brattleboro police. In a harbinger of things to come, police arrested us, but the state's attorney dismissed the charges. Only once has a group of us gone to trial.

Again a few months later, CAN staged a demonstration. Our women-only group—the Shut It Down Affinity Group—is the only affinity group to demonstrate continuously against Vermont Yankee. Our women range in age from thirty-seven to ninety-five. By the middle of 2014, we had acted there more than forty times.

Our affinity group has grown from seven women to about thirty Vermont, New Hampshire, and Massachusetts women. We have acted in groups as large as fifteen and as small as two. We encouraged friends to join us. Deb Reger of Corinth, Vermont designed our hand-painted, individualized tee shirts. Once a month, we meet at my house for a delicious potluck meal and decide through consensus on our plans. We have an agreed-upon mission statement outlining our solidarity. The character of our demonstrations evolves. In an early action at Entergy headquarters in Brattleboro, we wanted to shut it down, lock the doors, and put it out of business. For a while, we used paper chains to shut it symbolically and avoid obstructing the office building's fire exits. Because many of us wanted to use real chains, we agreed to block the gate at the nuclear reactor itself where we could chain ourselves to trees, posts, or fences without causing a fire hazard. When we chain ourselves, Entergy's guards and Vernon or state police have to cut us free with bolt cutters.

Hattie often feels moved to spray paint danger warnings in the driveway to the reactor. Some of us could not picture themselves spray-painting, and we gained strength from discussion. In consensus, we decided that those willing to paint would paint and those not willing would, in solidarity, accept the same charges. We practiced in my garage to be efficient at what we would paint and tested a number of different messages. I knew I didn't have the strength to push the spray-paint button, so I used a brush. Hattie sprayed paint in an outline, and I filled in with a brush.

Police arrested all of us who participated in that action, but only I was arraigned because the police identified me as a painter. However, the judge dropped the charges at the discovery phase, and I never went to trial. I was let off on a technicality. The court arraigned me for "unlawful mischief." I said I had not acted mischievously; I said I was dead serious, and the judge was very happy to let me off. Citing the expense of prose-cution and trial, the Vermont state's attorney rarely presses charges for our actions. Entergy itself rarely presses charges, so police often arrest us on site and release us rather than face the expense of trial.

Frances was arraigned in October, 2010 for unlawful mischief in connection with spray-painting a warning on the Vernon reactor driveway, an unusual prosecution because the state's attorney consistently dropped charges for action after Shut-It-Down action. Hattie and others supported Frances on her court day, when the judge dismissed the charges. Frances explained that she was not "mischievous," she was "dead serious."

Only one action ended up going to trial. We blocked the gate at the reactor in August 2011 after the flooding following Hurricane Irene. Some of our group questioned the wisdom of acting then and wondered if police would be too busy with the aftermath of the storm. I remembered Martin Luther King, Jr. and his letter from Birmingham Jail. He writes that sometimes it is not convenient to do an action, but it is never convenient to condone wrongdoing. I agree with him. We acted and went to trial in November 2012 when the court convicted us. Some months later, the judge, John Wesley, ran in to Hattie in downtown Brattleboro and congratulated her on our having done a good job in court. On conviction, he had fined each of us $350, which each of us refused to pay.

Unlike New Hampshire when we acted at Sanders/British Aerospace, Vermont did not provide for jail in lieu of fines. Judge Wesley told us he would not send us to jail even if we preferred it to a fine. Without being asked, a business competitor of one of our affinity group offered fifty dollars to the fine fund. From there, a subcommittee of our group composed of women not convicted in the action accepted donations for the fine. Eventually, they collected more than five thousand dollars and paid our fine during a public rally in January of 2013.

Our affinity group refined our approach to our work. We plan actions carefully after considerable discussion. Following each action, we submit press releases to regional media and often receive press coverage. Reporters from Vermont newspapers, radio, and television sometimes cover our actions. Hattie invites the press, which sometimes shows up to film us or write about us. Smith College invited us to display our banners, photos, and slide show at an exhibition in the student center in 2014.

the state of Vermont successfully prosecuted Shut-It-Downers for unlawful trespass after they acted on August 30, 2011 by blocking the Vermont Yankee gate in Vernon; from left, after arrest at the Vernon police station are Frances, Nancy First, Hattie, Paki, supporters Mary-Ann Palmieri and Sandra Boston, Ellen, and Betsy Corner

227

VALLEY PEOPLE

NO STOPPING HER: Thirteen. That's how many times longtime Northampton activist Frances Crowe, 92, has been arrested for her involvement in protesting the Vermont Yankee nuclear power plant.

Her most recent arrest took place Monday, when Crowe and 10 other women who are members of the Shut It Down Affinity Group, occupied the offices of Entergy Corporation and attempted to make a citizens' arrest of the board and officers of Entergy, operator of the Vernon, Vt., plant.

All were arrested on charges of unlawful trespass and directed to appear for arraignment in January in Superior Court in Brattleboro, Vt. Along with Crowe, other Valley women arrested in the incident included Paki Wieland and Susan B. Lantz, both of Northampton, Annele Corbett of Florence and Jean Grossholtz of South Hadley.

Crowe's arrest this week comes on the heels of the dismissal of charges of unlawful mischief stemming from an incident this summer at the Vermont Yankee.

According to an email from fellow protester Marcia Gagliardi of Athol, Crowe and other protesters were arrested June 30 after they brush- and spray-painted a message on the power plant's driveway. The message said "Solar under the grid." This was the first time charges against group members were not dropped by the state's attorney.

Speaking of her actions, Crowe said, "I want the power plant to convert from nuclear to solar energy. It will be safe instead of dangerous, and it will preserve jobs."

Representing herself in proceedings that began with a Sept. 6 arraignment, Crowe submitted a motion for dismissal of the unlawful mischief charge, arguing that she did not intend to damage property at Vermont Yankee, Gagliardi's email states. While she admitted that she brush-painted the word "Solar" on the driveway as part of the longer message, she said she used water soluble paint.

When informed on Sept. 6 that she had been charged with unlawful mischief for the June 30 action, Crowe answered, "I was very serious. I want to warn people about the danger at Vermont Yankee, and I want to shut it down for good."

At the arraignment, Deputy State Attorney Steven M. Brown requested that Crowe's release from court custody include her signing a pledge not to return to the Vermont Yankee nuclear plant, which is owned by Entergy Corp. Crowe refused to sign. "If Entergy will close Vermont Yankee for good, then I will not return," Crowe said. "It is up to Entergy now."

Before pleading not guilty, Crowe said, "I have been working against nuclear weapons and nuclear power since 1945, as they are both extremely dangerous. I am not guilty of mischief behavior. I am deeply serious about nonviolently shutting down Vermont Yankee."

— PHOEBE MITCHELL

Frances Crowe of Northampton, left, and Julia Bonafine of Shrewsbury, Vt., paint part of a message on the driveway of the Vermont Yankee nuclear plant in Vernon, Vt., on June 30. The message stated "Solar under the grid."

Frances Crowe speaks at a 2010 public forum on the resolution to "Bring Our War Dollars Home" at JFK Middle School in Northampton.

The Daily Hampshire Gazette *focused on Frances's activism in 2011 and featured a photo of her painting on the Vernon Vermont Yankee driveway with Julia Bonafine*

Sometimes an action will work out better than our plans. We visited at Vermont Yankee headquarters in Brattleboro in 2007 with an affinity group including Jo Comerford, one of my successors at AFSC. We entered the Entergy headquarters vestibule and blocked the door. A walkie-talkie hung on the wall for communication with Entergy's main office, and spontaneously, Jo called and asked for Larry Smith, Director of Communications for Vermont Yankee, to come down and meet us. Of course, no one came except, eventually, Brattleboro police who arrested us. And then, as usually happened, the state's attorney dismissed charges of trespass.

Then on December 12, 2011 during the Occupy Wall Street movement, we discussed our unlikely hope that we might walk in to Entergy's

Brattleboro headquarters from the lobby. Our support people dropped us off, and we tried the door thinking it would be locked as usual. To our surprise, it opened. We went through a second door and then upstairs. All our decisions occurred spontaneously in the building, and it was a dream come true. We were inside Entergy headquarters where we could confront executives with the heinous facts about how they earned their money while purveying nuclear power.

Nobody seemed to be in the headquarters building. We went into what looked like a conference room with a long table surrounded by chairs. We "occupied" Entergy headquarters. We had brought crime scene tape that we were going to use at the entrance that said, "Caution, do not enter . . . ," and we taped up the conference area. Paki Wieland, my longtime friend, read our statement and did an occupy-style antiphonal mic check.

Finally, accompanied by Windham County Sheriff Keith Clark, Larry Smith, Entergy's vice president for public relations who has since resigned, came to speak to us. He expressed his anger at our trespassing presence. The sheriff arrested us and charged us with trespass, but the state's attorney dropped the charges. That exciting action evolved from our good luck in seizing the moment to occupy the Entergy conference room, and I loved it!

Brattleboro Reformer *featured the Shut-It-Down occupation of Entergy Headquarters above the fold the next day*

Mary Beth Hebert, then chief of Vernon police, recognized my advanced age whenever she arrested us at the reactor and helped me up the driveway and into the front seat of the cruiser. "You do your part," I once told her. "We do our part."

During one action planned with what I call a walk of the dead with black robes and white masks, we had incorrect information about the Governor Hunt House on Entergy's property near the entrance to the Vermont Yankee reactor. We planned a walk of the dead through the Hunt House because we believed it housed some of Entergy's offices. However, as we walked through, we realized it was more of a conference center. With a bit of spontaneous conference, we changed direction and brought our action outdoors where Vernon police soon arrested us.

On March 22, 2012, the expiration day of Entergy's original license to operate the nuclear reactor, our affinity group joined hundreds of individuals organized into affinity groups in a vast action at Vermont Yankee headquarters. Cort Dorsey served as emcee that day. Acting on behalf of Safe and Green in coalition with other antinuclear nonprofits, Randy Kehler, Leslie Sullivan-Sachs, and spokespersons from affinity groups ironed out choreography with Entergy officials and Brattleboro police for the arrest of more than three hundred people. Brattleboro police recognized each of us in our affinity group and booked and released us on site. Vermont state troopers transported other demonstrators that day to their barracks in Rockingham for booking and release, so for many it was a long day.

Supported by the antinuclear Buddhist order Nipponzan Myohoji, we chained ourselves to the reactor gate the day before the mass action at Entergy headquarters. Neither our action at the reactor nor the massed action the next day at headquarters resulted in prosecution, because the state's attorney dropped all charges.

In March 2013, we appeared at a federal Nuclear Regulatory Commission (NRC) annual assessment meeting in Brattleboro High School. In a habitual maneuver, NRC trotted out a panel of experts to tell us how well Vermont Yankee was doing. NRC works in the back pocket of the nuclear industry and never refuses to extend a nuclear reactor license regardless of a reactor's age or how many unsafe incidents it experiences.

We dressed in black with white masks and performed a walk of the dead during the meet-and-greet before the March 2013 meeting. We snaked silently through the room single file with our signs. We positioned ourselves with our white masks near the presenters' table. The NRC moderator said the hearing would not proceed unless we sat down, but

in January, 2012, some months after the Fukushima reactor meltdowns in Japan, Shut-It-Downers staged a death walk in driveway of the Vernon reactor before police arrested them; a month later, on Valentine's day, they distributed valentines in Brattleboro to urge love for the earth— from left, front, Robin Lloyd, Martha Hennessey, Frances, Ruth Hooke, Hattie, Connie Harvard; back, Anneke Corbett, Susan Lantz, Mary-Ann, Nina Swaim, and Deb Reger we refused for a while. We offered a mic check opportunity for Occupy-Wall-Street-style call and response, and the audience began to join us. Cate Woolner came forward. More and more people came to the front until almost three quarters of the audience stood to oppose nuclear power.

The NRC panel left the room. With others, we read statements expressing opposition to nuclear power. It became a kind of hearing. Then the NRC panel returned but stood just inside the door. NRC panelists made no move to regain control of the meeting they had called.

The next year we planned to repeat the experience at the annual NRC hearing in Brattleboro. We enacted a walk of the dead and then occupied the floor in front of the NRC panelists. They refused to continue the meeting unless we moved. Instead of white masks, we wore the image of Gregory Jazcko, former chair of the NRC who resigned because of disagreements with the rest of the NRC about relicensing. We read a list of problems Jazcko had enumerated at Vermont Yankee and other US plants in the wake of the Fukushima nuclear meltdowns in Japan.

Still the NRC refused to start the meeting while we stood in front of them. People in the audience seemed to wait politely to address the NRC. So, although it broke our solidarity and confused some of our affinity group members, some of us chose to sit down without processing through the group in order to give attendees a chance to speak. Two young women were among informed speakers challenging the NRC. Neither was with an activist group. They were local people concerned for themselves and their families who shared their concerns

In the spring of 2013 when then-Nuclear Free Future Coalition of Western Massachusetts (NFF) invited Helen Caldicott to speak about the Fukushima disaster, Helen came to my house before the program for our Shut It Down potluck. Helen arrived early at my house. When I greeted her at the door, she said in her direct way, "I'm Helen Caldicott." She still has special sharpness and passion in communicating with people. We worried that no one would come to her talk, but more than two hundred people showed up.

Entergy Corporation, which bought Vermont Yankee in 2002, announced in the fall of 2013 it would close the reactor at the end of 2014 in spite of its 2012 twenty-year license extension. The corporation said it was closing because the reactor did not make a profit. When the reactor is shut down, that event will not mitigate the danger of thousands of spent nuclear fuel rods stored seven stories up in a spent-fuel pool on the banks of the Connecticut River. Because radioactive fuel rods in the pool flaunt the possibility of attack or natural disaster, Entergy should move spent fuel rods to on-site dry-cask storage as soon as possible. Only complete decommissioning and cleanup of the radioactive Vermont Yankee site will suffice. Entergy must not equivocate about its obligation to make sure safe, thorough decommissioning occurs. Although Entergy says it plans to move fuel rods to dry cask, on-site storage by 2020, there are no guarantees. The New England anti-nuclear community must be vigilant to ensure that the fuel rods are moved. Entergy is a corporation that has not always been forthcoming with the facts about radioactive leaks, contamination, and other dangers. We must hold Entergy accountable.

Even after the reactor closes, the women of the Shut It Down Affinity Group plan to keep our eye on Entergy's actions and the progress decommissioning. If we are called to act, we will until the site is restored to green field status. My vision is a field full of solar panels on the cleaned up site of Vermont Yankee. What a beautiful sight that would be.

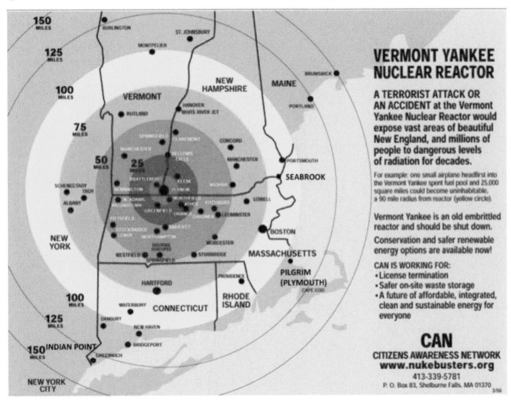

Citizens Awareness Network map shows the areas that would be devastated by a Vermont Yankee reactor accident even after plant closure; the Nuclear Regulatory Commission estimates that the reactor will not be decommissioned and safe until at least 2040

Democracy Now! *host Amy Goodman converses with Frances at
a WMUA-sponsored celebration for Frances's ninety-fifth birthday*

Democracy Now! broadcasts the truth every day. Amy Goodman gives real news without the glamor of mainstream media. She broadcasts the truth about global problems and interviews people immediately involved. She finds interview subjects who stand up for progressive change, peace, and justice all over the world. If we do not get accurate news, we are slaves to corporate conspiracy. I say, listen to Amy and resist, resist in every way that you can.

MEDIA AND DEMOCRACY NOW!

In every aspect of my peace and justice work—I want to call it my vocation, I have relied on media of all kinds. From early days when I lugged Russell Johnson's slide show to Vietnam or sped down the highway with bulky canisters of film to show the UMass trustees, I have used media to make a case. We supplemented draft counseling information with films and slide shows and showed John Pilger's early film on Vietnam, *The Quiet Mutiny*. I have always found films, slides, tapes, and later DVDs and CDs more convincing than my voice alone.

And in 2001 I discovered Amy Goodman's TV/radio program, *Democracy Now!*

When the September 11, 2001 attacks on the World Trade Center and Pentagon occurred, I was in Maine visiting my son Tom and his wife. They had planned to fly to Italy on September 11 for a two-week walking tour. I went to their house to take care of my grandchildren while Tom and Nancy traveled. At about 9:20 in the morning, we had just about everything organized after the children went to school. Tom made final rounds at the hospital.

Nancy waited with me for Tom to pick her up to go to the airport. The phone rang. A friend called and said, "Turn on the television." We did and, thanks to the miracle of media, witnessed the shocking situation. Not certain if they would be able to travel, Tom and Nancy went to the airport where the Federal Aviation Administration had grounded all flights. Instead, Tom and Nancy took their vacation in Toronto.

Each day after I got the grandchildren off to school, I listened to a Maine radio station, WERU as I walked along the shore. I found Amy Goodman and *Democracy Now!* on WERU. I had never before heard the one-hour program, which began airing in 1996. The reporting of Amy and her colleagues blew me away. Right away after 9/11, she interviewed Pakistanis and provided broad context for circumstances surrounding the attacks and aftermath. After listening to *Democracy Now!* for two weeks, I decided Amy Goodman offered the most balanced daily news account on the airwaves.

The weekend after I returned home, I attended a program in New York City at the progressive United Church of Christ Judson Memorial Church near Greenwich Village's Washington Square. Still in shock after the attacks, the resilient city went about its business. New Yorkers all, Judson congregants had become accustomed to the looming World Trade towers and, of course, missed them on the skyline. Amy introduced one of the panels.

When I met Amy, I explained that no Western Massachusetts outlet provided *Democracy Now!* in our area. She suggested that I ask my local National Public Radio (NPR) station, WFCR, then Five-College Radio located on the UMass campus, to broadcast *Democracy Now!*

On my return, I approached WFCR. Martin Miller, general manager, said *Democracy Now!* was not WFCR's kind of program. I felt then (and have never changed my mind) that Miller equivocated because of the nature of the content of *Democracy Now!* Refused at WFCR, I approached college radio stations about airing *Democracy Now!* They all said no, although in the North Quabbin in 2005, Hattie Nestel easily arranged to show *Democracy Now!* on Athol-Orange Community Television (AOTV). Friends contributed money for the required satellite dish and other equipment to broadcast the program, which has aired continuously in prime time on AOTV ever since.

I couldn't understand why Valley stations would not air the show, because I feel *Democracy Now!* offers important, responsible research that no other broadcast program carries. I thought it would be easy to find a way to broadcast *Democracy Now!* in the Valley. But no one would touch it.

Hoping to persuade someone in the Valley to broadcast *Democracy Now!*, I circulated a petition advocating its broadcast and collected hundreds of signatures. Still the stations ignored me. Because Valley residents hear the strong frequencies of the Albany, New York, NPR station WAMC in Albany, I went there to request that they air *Democracy Now!* I felt frustrated and defeated when they, too, refused. I thought maybe only a sit-in at the WFCR or WAMC office or other drastic approach would produce results.

One day, a young area man stopped by the weekly vigil in Northampton. "Frances," he told me, "I heard you were interested in getting *Democracy Now!* on a local station, and I just wanted to let you know that I'm broadcasting it from the top of Mount Holyoke."

"How do you do that?" I asked.

"In the morning," he said, "I download the program from my computer to a CD. Then I drive up to the parking lot at the top of Mount Holyoke, park the car, load my backpack with a battery and my laptop, and walk up to the mountain's high point. Then I throw the antenna in a tree and put the disc into my laptop running from the battery and attached to the antenna. I send the program out every weekday from 4:30 to 5:30 in the afternoon. So tune in." He chose the frequency 92.3 because it wouldn't interfere with other local frequencies. Of course, both he and I knew he

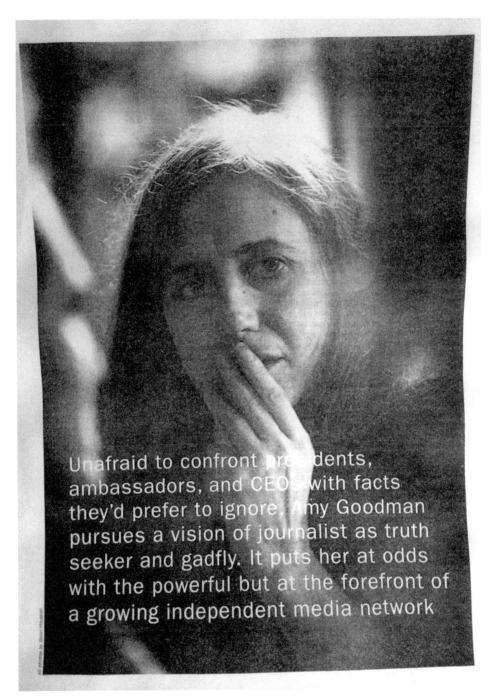

Unafraid to confront presidents, ambassadors, and CEOs with facts they'd prefer to ignore, Amy Goodman pursues a vision of journalist as truth seeker and gadfly. It puts her at odds with the powerful but at the forefront of a growing independent media network

promotional poster for Amy Goodman describes the journalist's unfailing pursuit of truth, the quality that appealed to Frances and encouraged her devotion to Democracy Now!, Amy Goodman's daily media broadcast

pirate radio tower in Frances's back yard

violated Federal Communications Commission rules in a delightful act of civil resistance, which is why I am not revealing his name here.

When Monday came, I turned my radio dial to 92.3 FM at four-thirty in the afternoon, and there was *Democracy Now!* as clear as crystal.

I knew the road to the top of Mount Holyoke would soon close for the winter. I went to the Fitzwilly building in downtown Northampton and asked Solidago Foundation, with offices on top floors, if I might put the broadcast antenna in their building. They didn't want to deal with it. I also talked with Jim Levey, a friend knowledgeable about computers and broadcast requirements. He provided a list of tall buildings in town, and I approached many people, but nobody was interested except for Peter Ives, minister of The First Churches of Northampton. He said the steeple would be a good place for the antenna, but the young man who set up the frequency would have to climb up into the steeple. Unfortunately, because he has a disability, he could not do that.

"Frances, let's try your yard," the young man suggested. "You're higher than downtown." He came into my yard and threw the antenna into my walnut tree. "Let's see what it will do," he said. Then he drove around Northampton with his car radio tuned to 92.3. When he returned, he said he could hear it all over town almost to Amherst.

"All right," I said. "You choose an appropriate antenna and transmitter. I'll buy them and figure out how to put up a pole in my back yard." I think the transmitter was eight hundred dollars or so. I would soon become a broadcaster.

I got a carpenter to put up the pole and place the antenna on top. Then I had little cards printed up with the call numbers 92.3 and the times I would broadcast *Democracy Now!* with the young man's assistance. I gave the cards to everybody I could think of. I went around to restaurants and stores and stuck them under the glass top of the tables. Every day, I picked up the CD from the young man, and at 4:30, I put it into the player connected to the antenna in the tree. We were on the air every afternoon from 4:30 to 5:30. People began listening and getting addicted. If for any reason they couldn't tune in to Amy's program, people called to ask, "Where is *Democracy Now!*?" I knew the show had caught on.

My children worried about my piratical broadcasts. We knew the penalty for illegal broadcast was a fourteen-thousand-dollar fine for each offense. My children worried, "You'll lose your house and your savings."

"All right," I said. "I will set up a family trust. I'll put the house, the investments, everything in a trust." All well into their fifties with their own careers, my children cooperated fully with our lawyer and me.

Everybody I knew advised me against signing my assets over to my children.

"One can never trust one's children," said my tax person. "They will do you in."

"We'll see," I said. I told them what he said and, of course, as I knew, they never have nor will they ever do me in.

The FCC never bothered me, although around that time, the agency closed down an illegal Brattleboro station. Some people warned me that I would be shut down, but it never happened. Evidently no one complained to the FCC about my one-hour/one-program station, and (if the agency knew about it), the FCC let it operate.

I appealed to WFCR's board of directors. They listened to me and then said, "Oh, there are so many requests. We can't honor them all." WFCR's lack of interest disappointed me. I have supported WFCR since the beginning of the station in the 1960s. When I did outreach for AFSC, I often took visitors to WFCR for interviews. The late Bob Paquette, longtime WFCR news director, interviewed AFSC's Russell Johnson whenever Russell visited. Once, WFCR stopped airing the Spanish language program *Tertulia*, and our petitions persuaded the management to restore the programming. My history with WFCR goes back a long way.

When Roger Conant of Amherst heard about WFCR's unwillingness to broadcast *Democracy Now!*, he said, "Frances, I think you should do an alternative pledge campaign." He emailed everybody he could think of to urge them to let WFCR know they would withhold their financial pledges to WFCR until the station agreed to broadcast *Democracy Now!* In one week, the station heard that Roger's contacts would withhold forty thousand dollars in pledges.

Martin Miller called me. "Frances, come over," he said. "We need to talk." He told me that WFCR would download *Democracy Now!* and stream it to WMUA, the UMass station if WMUA were willing.

I didn't want to accept that deal. We hadn't exhausted our possibilities. I wanted to have a rally and a sit-in at WFCR. I wanted to chain myself to the door to shut the station down if they wouldn't air *Democracy Now!* I felt that we ought to go further.

Others voted me down. "No, Frances," said Lisa Baskin. "This is enough. This is a good solution." I reluctantly agreed.

I became a member of WMUA's community committee. It was uncomfortable for a while, but several of my friends joined the WMUA committee, and eventually we encouraged a student to download parts of *Democracy Now!* to broadcast during his regularly scheduled program.

Kate Harris, WMUA community representative, worked at promoting airing of the entire broadcast of *Democracy Now!* on WMUA. A young woman, she worked better with students than I could. Eventually, the student board conducted a poll about whether to broadcast *Democracy Now!* as a regular program. Kate worked with campus organizations who endorsed airing the program. Finally, daily at eight o'clock every morning, fresh and live on 91.1 on the FM dial, anyone in the listening area of WMUA can hear the program. Donations pour in to WMUA because of *Democracy Now!* and they have more listeners.

"Having *Democracy Now!* on WMUA has been a godsend for us," Glenn Siegel, WMUA's administrative adviser, told me. "Their honest, uncompromised program has greatly expanded our listening audience and is a model for our students for what ethical journalism sounds like in the twenty-first century." WFCR still streams it to WMUA, which routinely announces its appreciation to WFCR for this service.

In the early two thousands, Prometheus Radio, a nonprofit developer of local radio stations, conducted its annual meeting in Northampton at our invitation. My guests were people I met in 2001 from the Maine radio station WERU, where I had originally heard *Democracy Now!* Tom and Nancy introduced me to them. Prometheus Radio worked with students so they could obtain a low-power license. Under the auspices of Sut Jhally's Media Education Foundation (MEF), they established WXOJ as Valley Free Radio in 2005 using 103.3 as its bandwidth.

WXOJ broadcasts twenty-four hours a day. It airs *Democracy Now!* daily at five in the afternoon and much other good programming all day long. They air Free Speech programming from Pacifica. They air programs on Native Americans and on Valley history. One of my favorite programs, *Farm to Fork*, provides information about farming, the environment, and sustainability. It dovetails nicely with my commitment to the local food movement.

Amy Goodman came to UMass in March 2014 to interview me publicly when I turned ninety-five. She brought UMass graduate Mike Burke with her. As a student, he had a late night music program on WMUA and now serves as a senior producer on *Democracy Now!* UMass was the first college in Massachusetts and one of the first in the country to carry *Democracy Now!*

Democracy Now! broadcasts the truth every day. Amy Goodman gives real news without the glamor of mainstream media. She broadcasts the truth about global problems and interviews people immediately involved. She finds interview subjects who stand up for progressive change, peace, and justice all over the world. If we do not get accurate news, we are slaves to corporate conspiracy. I say, listen to Amy and resist, resist in every way that you can.

Not long ago I was talking with Mary Clare Higgins, former mayor of Northampton. I said, "When you were mayor, one of the best things you ever did was to bring the local community television station into the twentieth century. We owe you." We had a community television station that no one ever watched. There was a community board, and it was very cautious. I had heard that the license was up for renewal. I went to the mayor and said, "If you renew their license and they don't broadcast *Democracy Now!* I'm going to organize a sit in at your office." She knew I was serious. I had been calling Comcast in Springfield at least twice a week and they kept saying it wasn't their kind of programming. Then Mayor Higgins gave them an ultimatum. They capitulated and now they broadcast *Democracy Now!* at eight in the morning, at noon, at seven in the evening, and at midnight.

During the Vietnam War I noticed that people often wouldn't make eye contact with me if I was walking downtown. Sometimes they would cross the street if they saw me coming. Who knows why. Maybe they thought I was going to offer a pamphlet. But now they say, "We really are grateful for *Democracy Now!* Thank you for your work on it." People really listen. And if they do, they get addicted to it and begin to think differently.

I think people really need to talk, that it isn't enough to listen and get the truth. I wanted to go out every morning and instead of saying, "How are you today?" say, "What did you think of *Democracy Now!* today?" and to talk about the issues.

When I read in the paper that the Media Education Foundation had bought the old fire house on Masonic Street in Northampton and were going to set aside a community room where non profits could meet and organize, I got in touch with Sut Jhally, the director of the foundation. I knew he was very sophisticated and interested in politics and opposed to the war in Iraq and Afghanistan.

Sut Jhally is a professor of media at UMass. He started his own company, the Media Education Foundation upstairs on Center Street in Northampton. MEF produces and distributes documentary films and other educational resources to inspire critical thinking about the social, political, and cultural impact of American mass media.

Then he bought the building that housed the old firehouse on Masonic Street in Northampton and remodeled it so they could make and show films. On the first floor he set up the community room. The Woodstar Café occupied the front.

I talked to Sut Jhally about the role of media in the panels we had and the effectiveness of the visual and dramatic arts. DVDs were just coming out to make all kinds of films accessible. So I asked him if the Northampton Committee to Stop the Wars could have the community room for Friday nights. This committee had come out of the vigil that Claudia Lefko, Ruth Hawkins, and I started in 1999 to stop the sanctions against Iraq.

Bush's Brain was the first film we showed. It is about Karl Rove and his role in the Bush presidency. I said, "No refreshments, just the film and then discussion." And people came.

We advertised the films on northamptoncommittee.org, our website managed by Winston Close, an independent computer programmer and website designer. We kept to the rule of no refreshments. We simply showed films and then we put the chairs in a circle and talked about the films. At one point we decided that so many of the films were depressing that we should show films about what people were doing to change things in a positive way. So we started to include films about people using nonviolent activism to make a difference: *A Force More Powerful, Gandhi in India, The Democratic Front of South Africa* and films about what was going on in Poland during World War II, what the Danes had done to say no during World War II, civil rights in the US, and what the people of Chile had done to overthrow Pinochet. There are lots of good stories out there, stories about people being faithful and making a change.

We found films about what's going on in Bolivia and Argentina. There's a lot of successful organizing in South America, but we don't hear that much about it, like the women of Cochabamba in Bolivia who protested the privatization of their water and were successful in stopping a corporate takeover of their water supply. There's another film, *The Take,* about how people in Argentina organized themselves when their economy collapsed and they took over the factories and built a new society. We showed a new film about Monsanto and the genetic engineering of seeds and also one on the history of US relationships with Iran. We often had speakers too, experts who came and filled in with background information about the film. We co-sponsored them with the Northampton Committee to Stop the Wars, Valley Committee Against Secrecy and Torture, the Pioneer Valley Cuba Solidarity Committee, and No More Guantanamos.

We showed films about the problems facing us, like global warming and nuclear power, but we tried to show positive ones and local ones, too, sometimes involving students. In 2012 we showed a film about a Honduras factory that had not been paying the workers properly. They had been working under very poor conditions until the people got involved, and now it's a model factory run by the people who work there.

245

That film was made by students at Hampshire College and they came to show it. Then we showed a film about North Adams and what's happened to that factory town. Maynard Seider, the filmmaker who teaches sociology at Mass College of Liberal Arts in North Adams, came. We also showed *The Greening of Southie*, a film about a building in Roxbury that was filled with all kinds of toxins. The community took it over and now it's a green building remodeled with mostly local materials.

There are so many films, and they keep emerging. We didn't show any fiction: only documentaries. The same people didn't come every week. But forty or more people came most weeks. We never had nobody come. Even once when we had a big snowstorm, a blizzard, and we decided to cancel, some people got there. These films have been part of my finding my radical soul. I grow as truth reveals itself.

Now the Media Education Foundation is also handling films that they haven't made but they feel are important for people to see. And they're very busy. Every day UPS picks up huge bags of films that they're selling to universities and high schools all over the country. I think films are a very good way to change people's thinking and the culture.

A few years ago when I had a cancerous tumor in my duodenum operated on at Mass General Hospital in Boston, I was in the hospital for a couple of weeks. I think everyone thought I was going to die. So someone—I think it was Lisa Baskin—came up with the idea to name the community room for me. Amy Goodman came to Northampton to dedicate the room complete with a community reception. Affirming as the event turned out, I'm glad to say I'm still here.

Unfortunately, the Frances Crowe Community Room was sold to the Woodstar Café along with the rest of the first floor. We haven't shown films there since February of 2014. The Media Education Foundation gave us the screen, the projector, and chairs, and we are trying to find another place in town to show our films. I've shown films a few Saturday afternoons at the Forbes Library in Northampton and we are hoping to continue to show films. We have no money, so it is a challenge to figure out how to keep the initiative going. Showing films is so important and thought provoking. People say it is important to have discussions following films and that it is good to come together and listen to each other. We are trying to change the culture one documentary at a time by focusing on the issues of the day and talking about what we can do individually and together.

Northampton Committee
To Stop the Wars

Site Contents:

Home

Weekly Vigil

Film Series

Contacts

Contact Congress

Getting Out:
A Guide To
Military Discharges

Event Archive

Peace and Justice Film Series

For further information about the films, use this contact info.

Previous Films

Date	Film
Sep 6	**Fruitvale Station** **Forbes Library, 2:00 p.m.** Drama based on the story of Oscar Grant, who was killed by a Bay Area Rapid Transit police officer in 2009.
May 1	American Meltdown **Senior Center, 67 Conz Street, Thursday 1:30 p.m.** A fictional look at the terrorist takeover of an American nuclear plant
Mar 22	Nuclear Nation **Forbes Library Community Room, Saturday 1:00 p.m.** Their town leveled by the tsunami then contaminated by the meltdown, the former residents of Futaba, Japan struggle for environmental justice.
Mar 1	Dirty Wars **Forbes Library Community Room, Saturday 1:00 p.m.** Journalist Jeremy Scahill investigates the netherworld of U.S. covert operations, including the tragic Khataba raid, "kill lists", and warlord alliances.
Feb 15	The Crossing **Forbes Library Community Room, Saturday, 2:00 p.m.**
Feb 14	Students and Goliath **Last film in the Frances Crowe Community Room** Young activists at the 5 Colleges, aware that climate change is killing their birthright, fight the fossil fuel industry through divestment campaigns. Discussion with the film maker, Hampshire College student Alex Leff.
Feb 8	Under Rich Earth **Saturday 2:00 p.m.** Farmers in a remote region of Equador stand off against Canadian mining interests and the paramilitaries who support them.
Feb 7	High Power In India, the problems with nuclear power are compounded by those of colonialism - and darkened by the shadow of the mass destruction at Bhopal. Discussion with the film maker, Pradeep Indulkar.
Feb 1	The Age of Stupid **Saturday 2:00 p.m.** A documentarian in the year 2055 gathers (real) footage to answer the question of why humanity failed to avoid catastrophic climate change.
Jan 31	Brothers on the Line As the leaders who brought the United Auto Workers union to power, Walter Reuther and his brothers were central to the labor movement.
Jan 25	Quietly into Disaster **Saturday 2:00 p.m.** Through the actions of its citizens, Germany will

2014 film schedule found at www.northamptoncommittee.org

Frances settles in as usual to read

We need to reeducate our society so
that people realize that we cannot
sustain mainstream lifestyles based on
consumerism and greed. If we do not see
this light, we are an extinct species,
because power is very corrupting. The
bottom is falling out of this lifestyle.
One of the advantages of my longevity is
that I can begin to understand the flow
of the work. Howard Zinn was right when
he said that everything you do matters.
And that's my message, too.

PUTTING IT ALL TOGETHER

I didn't start out as a peace activist. It's an identity bestowed on me by others. There is nothing extraordinary about me. What I have done is something that anybody can do. I consider, work, and act. I like to think of my life as the development of my conscience. Being exposed to things is what is important. I feel that you live your life not so much as the way opens ahead of you but as the way closes in behind you. Therefore, you have to be aware of and pay attention to what is going on in the world.

The empire is crumbling and the emperors, who rule the global corporations are raging. I see Ukraine as a staging area for global corporations led by the United States to go in to Russia and get fossil fuels, including oil and gas, in order make a pipeline from the Arctic. The emperors know that, even with hydraulic fracturing, there is a finite amount of fossil fuel in the ground. The emperors are raging because they can't figure out how to make the planet more profitable for their own benefit.

Clearly, we invaded Afghanistan for control of the Caspian pipeline and obviously we invaded Iraq for oil. We allowed the looting of Iraq's museum treasures in 2003 in order to protect the oil, and we continue to put oil and commerce ahead of human lives throughout the middle east. As for Israel and Gaza, the United States decided Israel would be our land base in the Middle East to get fossil fuels in that region, and therefore, we support Israel regardless of what it does to the people of Gaza. I am afraid that Israel will exterminate them. The United States must stop sending money to Israel for military purposes and for persecuting the people of Gaza.

We need to reeducate our society so that people realize we cannot sustain a lifestyle based on consumerism, greed, and power, which so often results in corruption. The bottom is falling out of our lifestyle. If we do not see this light, we are an extinct species.

One of the advantages of my longevity is that I can begin to understand the flow of the work. Howard Zinn was right when he said that everything you do matters. And that's my message, too.

Back in the sixties volunteers were mostly married women whose chief commitment was to their family. They saw their social change work as part of their philosophy toward life. Many went back to school, many got jobs. It's really hard for a lot of people to go on year after year being a volunteer, being out there. Many felt that a job where the work is more routine would provide a sense of community for them. We haven't thought enough about ways to nourish our volunteers.

251

Some people started as volunteers and got married and found their work changed into a focus on the nuclear family. In many families, because of major changes in the economy, support from two incomes became the norm. There was little time for people to volunteer. As for civil disobedience, dedication to principles of nonviolence with a supportive community magnifies the experience. Doing civil resistance in an affinity group provides such a community. Living in a full-time resistance community like Jonah House or a Catholic Worker house transforms civil disobedience in to a witness for peace, justice, and truth. A full-time community offers support of all kinds. Doing civil disobedience under such circumstances transforms a person's life.

As an older woman, I have a certain amount of freedom that younger people don't have. When I first became involved in the peace movement, I was a full-time mother and homemaker. The more time went on and I was freed up, the more I seized the time to work on peace issues. For younger people, life is hard. They face a lot of difficult decisions—-about commitment and sexuality, marriage, family, finding a decent place to live, getting themselves established in productive work that will pay.

I'm always learning how to do things better from the way that young people see things and from their ideas on how to do things. It is important

Hattie and Frances look up something on Frances's iPad

to work intergenerationally. Older people have a lot to offer, with their experience of having lived through the war, the McCarthy period, etc. This society always looks for quick solutions, for the "new and improved." As an older person I see the importance of working consistently, of being in it for the long haul. But I do see the good things that are happening with support for civil resistance coming from the resistant community.

In the summer of 2008, the Catholic Worker movement celebrated its seventy-fifth anniversary at their national gathering in Worcester which was wonderful. Jim Douglass, the author of *JFK and the Unspeakable,* was one of the speakers. I was not feeling well, but I went anyway and it was just great to connect with people from around the country.

Locally, groups are working on issues that need to be addressed. In Northampton, should we enlarge the landfill dump? What is the future of Hospital Hill and downtown Northampton? What should be done with the land in meadows? How can Northampton feed this community in ten or twenty years? Groups focused on these issues are doing very good work. People are intent also in initiating action to reverse climate change and confront racism, prisons, and immigration. Opposition grows to a cross-state pipeline for hydraulically fractured natural gas.

There are groups like the Raging Grannies who come together and sing and protest. None of us has the whole answer, but we're exploring and trying to figure out what we need to do.

A few years ago when I was introduced to the concept of peak oil, I realized that our lifestyle demands war. The only answer is to downsize, to simplify. I'm starting to look at my ecological footprint. If everyone lived on the planet the way we've been living, I think it would take seven planets and we only have one. I try to eat locally by restricting my diet to food grown within twenty miles and by canning, freezing, and dehydrating.

Because I'm a vegetarian it's easier. I do buy grains and beans and lentils that come from a distance, but otherwise all of my produce I get locally. I have a garden in my front yard with an apple tree and lots of kale. One year my grandson Sean helped me can applesauce. But I could do a lot more. I'm shopping locally, not buying anything that comes to me by air, and not buying clothing from sweatshops. So I buy most of my clothing in used clothing stories like the Salvation Army where I am not only reusing clothes but also helping the organization. I find that I get more energy to go on to do the work when I take control of my life. When I'm doing these things, when I'm resisting, like when I risk arrest, there comes a tremendous surge of energy that takes me through.

I started walking every place in Northampton. I have a shopping cart that I pull along after myself, and I try not to take my car out of the

Frances at harvest time in her front-yard garden

garage at all. I sort of pledged to myself that I wouldn't use the car in Northampton. I also dropped my membership at the Y. Why should I go walk on their treadmills when I can walk doing my errands? I like getting out of that "steel coffin." I feel that it really humanizes me. I notice the neighbors, the people when I shop locally on Main Street. One of the best birthday presents I ever received was from my grandson Tomas. He asked his friends not to drive on my birthday. It spread and turned into a campaign. People in other countries heard about the campaign and decided to join "Don't Drive for Frances Crowe" for one day.

I think people need to stay in touch with the truth by listening to *Democracy Now!* and Free Speech Radio and reading the progressive presses like *The Progressive, The Nation,* and *Mother Jones.* Those are extremely good ways of keeping your conscience alive.

Finally I came to the point where I thought, "I'm working against all these things and I'm still paying for them." So I decided I could no longer pay taxes. My conscience wouldn't let me write that check to the IRS. I had always wanted to be a tax resister, but Tom said it would be very complicated and that the government would do an audit. But now I file a tax return and then redirect the tax money that I should send to the IRS to other places. A third of the money goes to public education; a third goes for aid to Iraqi and Afghani war victims; and a third goes to the peace movement in this country. And that feels good.

I couldn't do these things alone. I have a lot of support. My family is very cooperative and I'm part of a local tax resistance group. Most people lower their income so they don't have to pay taxes; they live below the taxable level. I know several people who live in someone else's house and take care of people so that they get room and board and manage. Another friend of mine Aaron Falbel, a wonderful tax resister, became an organic farmer and has only a bicycle for transportation. He works part time at the Sunderland Library, but he keeps his hours down below the taxable level. His wife is not a tax resister and they don't have children so they can manage. I wanted to continue my lifestyle somewhat and yet be able to witness.

I've also joined an international lawsuit against the IRS because there is a history in this country of Quakers and other people of conscience who don't believe in war not having to pay for war. Back in the early1800s there were farmers in upstate New York who refused to pay. They were put in jail but people went before the state legislature and argued their case. They were judged to be exempt. So a young man Daniel Jenkins from upstate New York, whom I've met, has prepared

Thank you for planning this celebration today & inviting me to speak.

I want to talk about how I see the situation we face today & what my response is –

Frances's public speaking notes on the back of used paper for her International Women's Day address in 2014 all the materials for a lawsuit against the government so that people of conscience won't have to pay. It's not just for Quakers, but for anyone who has a moral, ethical objection if they hold this objection with the same degree of intensity as they would hold a religious belief, somewhat like conscientious objectors.

The lawsuit actually went before the New York state tax court but was turned down and then the US Supreme Court refused to take it. Now he's found that he can take the suit to the UN through the Human Rights Commission. There is not much media coverage of this but I've joined this suit as one of the people to take it before the International Court. We have people from England and Germany on the case. About seventy people have signed on. We're looking for help from international law that would protect those who don't want to pay for war. We need some kind of international force to rein in our government. The US is too big and too powerful. It is hard to depend on the UN, though, because it is so controlled by the global corporations that it does not function well in helping out the common citizenry. But it's all we have. Perhaps the Human Rights Commission will act on it.

The biggest threat I see facing us as I live into my tenth decade is the end of life on this planet. I feel that the way we are living now cannot continue. We cannot maintain our lifestyle without finding alternative sources of energy and, individually and collectively, using fewer resources. There's a possibility that we will all go down because humans will be unable to live in the changed climate. Our planet cannot sustain our way of living now, and we have to make drastic changes. I don't know whether there's time, but I feel that we must try to reverse the effects of irresponsible use of resources.

I recently read Naomi Klein's book, *The Shock Doctrine*. I think that what we see happening now in our own economy is *The Shock Doctrine* coming home. When we look at what the corporate world has done to the rest of the globe, I feel that our society can't weather it.

And I really think that we have to stop the manufacture and distribution of nuclear weapons and to stop any possible war in Iran and the wars in Iraq and Afghanistan. We need to bring the troops home and let massive funding relief from our tax dollars go to pay for rebuilding Iraq and Afghanistan. And we need to dig in here and to rebuild our society by building community and local systems. Examples abound. There are people working on community gardens in Northampton. I feel that the answers have got to be found locally. I'm hopeful because of young people like my grandson Sean who gave a year of his life to AmeriCorps in

New Orleans after Katrina. He threw himself into that work and found it rewarding. That's the way humans were made to live their lives, not bottled up in the corporate empire.

Mary Pipher, the author of *Reviving Ophelia,* has written a book called *The Green Boat: Reviving Ourselves in Our Capsized Culture.* She writes about how we need to adjust to what the future is bringing. I think that I would be more positive than she is. I feel we are creating the new society in the shell of the old. I feel good. I'm building the community for the future.

One of the things she advises is to soften the blow of what is in store. She said we should invite some friends over to talk about the issues. But she said you should give them wine and have a little supper and that's exactly what I did one Saturday. It worked. At the Friends Meeting in Northampton I couldn't get anyone interested in the issue of food so I just said, "All right, I'm going to have a vegetarian potluck and we'll come together and we'll talk about right sharing of the world's resources as it is related to food, nutrition, and global warming." And six people came and we talked and it was really good.

These are people I didn't know very well, but we decided to do it again. I think we'll call ourselves a Witness for the Planet Committee. And we'll talk about what we can do in our personal lives. One of the things I do is eat vegetarian. I'm very well nourished with beans and nuts. It was Frances More Lappe who really convinced me that I should eat the beans and not give them to chickens. I found at Deals and Steals in Northampton I could get sardines from Maine in a can and so I've been buying sardines recently and getting my Omega–3 acids that way. I know the fishermen in Maine need the money. I find sardines and beets make a wonderful sandwich.

So that's kind of where I'm at now. It's not a pretty picture for the future. But it's been a good way to have led my life. I feel that I've led a meaningful life because I've had a passion for something that was very important. I've negotiated my way to get where I am. My family has always come first. If I have a decision of whether or not to do an action when the family needs me or on a holiday, I choose the family. But my family has always been very supportive. I've been able to negotiate and find my way through.

I don't really know what keeps me going—one thing is the people in the work. We keep each other hopeful, we refuse to give up. No one can do this work alone. We need a community so that we can check things out and get and give support and move ahead together. It's very important that people find a community they can work with. When I get really depressed, I go out and distribute fliers around town, show a film, write a newsletter, try to keep my sanity, and process the distress I feel.

I saw Charlie Clements in 2014 when we were both on the UMass-Boston Joyner Program on Violence to talk about war. Meeting him again after many years reminded me of how so many of our actions can come together and have an effect.

Charlie was a pilot who came out of the Air Force Academy in Colorado Springs and went to Vietnam as a transport pilot flying huge planes delivering people and material from one place to another. He had some questions in his mind about the war, but he thought if he wasn't bombing people and was just transporting soldiers, it was okay. When he was in San Francisco for a short training, every day he passed a vigil against the war in Vietnam as he went to lunch. He said, "They were standing there silently with their sign but it had an impact on me. I kept thinking I would never want to be a bomber pilot and was glad I was only a transport pilot." Then he began to realize that what he was doing was supporting the bombing and there wasn't much difference between being a bomber pilot and being a transport pilot. He tried to get a CO discharge because he refused to continue flying. He ended up getting a medical discharge. After he returned to the US and went to medical school, he worked in El Salvador during the contra war. A year later, he came back and wrote a book called *Witness to War.* One of the films we showed at the Friday film nights was about Charlie Clements. Produced by the AFSC, it was also called *Witness to War.* I hadn't seen him for a while but now he's the executive director of the Carr Center for Human Rights Policy at the Kennedy School of Government at Harvard and is teaching a course on human rights.

After the program at UMass, Charlie took several of us out to dinner. I said to him, "There's something I want to ask you. Westover is the largest training center for the National Guard. Troops are coming in on the weekends. I'm trying to organize vigils, and there are a few of us who leaflet. I was wondering if what we are doing is worthwhile. Can we ever reach anybody that way?"

He said, "Frances never for a moment doubt how effective you are being. My conscience was pricked by a group of vigilers." He said, "Vigil even if there's only one or two of you. You will be touching someone's conscience." Charlie's story exemplifies the power of witness and persistence.

I say to my grandchildren: find important work that needs to be done and figure out what part of that you want to do and get training for it, get prepared for it; planning and acting is where you find hope; let your lives speak for you. We all have a part to play. So don't feel because you can't change Wall Street or Washington that what you are doing isn't important. It's very important to resist, hold firm, and keep the spirit alive for the people who come after us. It's a long, long trip.

The way I've lived my life I have found extremely satisfying. It's been an exciting, fulfilling life. I have no regrets about my activities of community building, organizing, and resistance. I think that my only regret is that I didn't do more. You need to resist and take courage to move ahead as your conscience leads. You need to let your conscience crystallize and grow and peel off the layers and get to what is the core of yourself.

Rejoice in life.

And act.

Frances's living room table provides food for thought in the midst of the site for many an organizing meeting

Pioneer Valley Life
The Republican.

30 MAR. '13, SAT.

Section P
85 %

Activist
still
active
at
93

Frances Crowe is
shown in her
Northampton home.
Staff photo by
MICHAEL S. GORDON

2012 Pioneer Valley Life *supplement of* The Republican, *a
Springfield newspaper, recognizes Frances's activism with
Frances under the watchful eye of Northampton hero Sojourner Truth
as presented by Harriet Diamond*

REMEMBER

Once people believed in human sacrifice—

not any more.

Once people believed in slavery—

not any more.

Once people believed women were not as

intelligent as men—

not any more.

I hope you will be able to say

in your lifetime,

"Once people believed in war—

not any more."

—Frances Crowe

FINDING MY RADICAL SOUL *TIMELINE*

1913   Thomas J. Crowe born in Waterbury, Connecticut – November 29

1914   Frances's mother and father marry
         World War I begins – July 28

1918   Germany surrenders – November 11

1919   Frances born in Carthage, Missouri – March 15
         Treaty of Versailles ends World War I – June 28
         US declines to join League of Nations; League proceeds without the US and meets the
             first time – November 15

1920   League of Nations formally begins – January 10

1932   Franklin Delano Roosevelt elected president

1933   Dorothy Day starts the Catholic Worker movement and the newspaper
         The Catholic Worker - May

1934   Frederic and Irene Joliot-Curie discover induced radioactivity
         American Board of Radiology is formed

1937   Frances graduates from Carthage Senior High School

1939   Frances graduates from Stephens College and continues her education at Syracuse University
         Hitler invades Czechoslovakia and Poland
         Great Britain and France declare war on Germany

1940   Hitler invades France
         Selective Service Act establishes first peacetime conscription in US history –September 16

1941   Frances earns her BA from Syracuse University, starts work at Stephens College in the fall
         Tom Crowe earns his MD from Syracuse University Medical School
         Japanese bomb Pearl Harbor – December 7

1942   Frances takes a summer course in industrial supervision at Mount Holyoke College,
             Massachusetts
         Frances begins to work in New York City
         Tom joins the army as a physician

1945   Frances and Tom marry - May 16
         FDR dies. Harry S. Truman becomes president – April 12
         US drops atomic bomb on Hiroshima and Nagasaki – August 6 and August 9

1946   Caltha born in Rochester, New York – December 6

1948   Jarlath born in Rochester, New York – February 23

1951 Frances, Tom, and their children move to Northampton
   Tom Crowe becomes associated with Cooley Dickinson Hospital

1952 Young Tom born in Northampton – March 14
   Jarlath attends Clarke School
   Dwight D. Eisenhower elected president

1954 Frances's mother dies
   Frances, Tom, and their children move to Round Hill Road, Northampton

1957 National Committee for a Sane Nuclear Policy (SANE) founded

1960 John Fitzgerald Kennedy elected president
   Jarlath attends Roberts School
   Tom Crowe establishes Cooley Dickinson Hospital Radiotherapy Department

1961 Four hundred military advisers sent to Vietnam by JFK
   Physicians for Social Responsibility (PSR) founded
   JFK authorizes the Bay of Pigs invasion in Cuba – April 17
   Northampton chapter of Women's International League for Peace and Freedom (WILPF) founded

1962 Northampton WILPF sponsors activities advocating peace especially targeted to young people
    (Frances is on Program Committee)
   Russia moves missiles to Cuba (Cuban Missile crisis) - October
   Frances demonstrates against the launch of missile-carrying submarine at Electric Boat,
    Groton, Connecticut

1963 Southern Christian Leadership Conference led by Martin Luther King, Jr. directs campaign of
    nonviolent direct action against racial discrimination in Birmingham, Alabama
   Two hundred civil rights demonstrators are arrested in Birmingham
    Betty Friedan writes *The Feminine Mystique*
   Northampton WILPF sponsors high school institutes
   Martin Luther King gives "I Have a Dream" speech at the March on Washington for
    Jobs and Freedom – August 28
   President Kennedy signs Limited Test Ban Treaty (prohibiting atmospheric testing of
    nuclear weapons) with USSR – October 7
   President Kennedy assassinated. Lyndon Baines Johnson becomes president – November 22

1964 US passes Civil Rights Act – July 2
   Gulf of Tonkin Resolution gives LBJ permission to continue fighting in Vietnam – August 10
   Frances, Tom, and their children travel in Europe during July and August

1965 US passes Voting Rights Act – August 6
   Frances takes part in March on Washington for Peace in Vietnam – November 27

1966   Chinese Cultural Revolution begins under Mao Zedong, Chairman of the
            Communist Party in China– August
        Frances attends national meeting of WILPF and chairs Northampton branch of WILPF
        Northampton WILPF sponsors a panel on chemical and biological weapons
        Frances joins AFSC Outreach Committee
        Amherst Friends begins weekly peace vigil on Amherst Common

1967   Tom Crowe sets up x-ray department at Albert Schweitzer Hospital in Haiti; Frances and
            young Tom accompany him
        Frances takes draft counseling training with Central Committee for Conscientious
            Objectors in Philadelphia

1968   Communist Tet offensive begins in Vietnam – January 30
        Frances advertises a draft counseling/information session and
            begins draft counseling
        US soldiers kill civilians at MyLai in Vietnam – March 16
        Martin Luther King, Jr. assassinated. Riots follow his death – April 4
        Robert Fitzgerald Kennedy assassinated – June 5
        NonProliferation Treaty regarding nuclear weapons opened for signatures
        Riots at the Democratic National Convention, Chicago – August 26-28
        WILPF sponsors Don Luce's slide show, *Remember Vietnam;* a course in history of African
            Americans at Northampton High School; and Childhood Education for Peace
        Richard Milhous Nixon elected president
        Frances and Tom move to Langworthy Road, Northampton, when their children have grown
        Frances establishes American Friends Service Committee (AFSC) office in basement of
            Langworthy Road residence

1969   Public Service Company of New Hampshire (PSNH) announces plans to build
            Seabrook Nuclear Power Plant
        US institutes first lottery in twenty-seven years for draft into the military – December 1
        Jarlath attends National Technical Institute for the Deaf (NTID) from 1969 to 1975

1970   Massachusetts legislature first to pass resolution for withdrawal of troops from Vietnam
        Randy Kehler starts twenty-two-month prison term for draft violation
        Northampton WILPF chapter closes
        Helen Caldicott speaks about danger of nuclear power at Sage Hall, Smith College – April 22
        Soldiers from Ohio National Guard kill four students at Kent State University during
            demonstration against the Vietnam War – May 4
        US conducts campaign of bombing in Cambodia – May-June 30

1971   President Nixon signs a bill repealing Gulf of Tonkin resolution – January 13
        Barn at Woolman Hill burns down
        Young Tom graduates from East Hill School
        Tom Crowe becomes the first full-time radiotherapist at Cooley Dickinson Hospital
        Until-then secret *Pentagon Papers,* officially titled *United States-Vietnam relations from
        1945-1967:A Study Prepared by the Department of Defense, published* – June

1972   Nixon becomes first president to visit the People's Republic of China- February 17-28
          US signs Biological Weapons Convention with a hundred other nations
          Frances arrested for trespassing at Westover Air Force Base during protest of Vietnam War on
              International Women's Day with Women against the War
          Massachusetts legislature passes Chapter 766, Special Education Law
          Young Tom travels in Ireland and Europe
          Operatives of the Republican Party break into Democratic campaign headquarters in the
              Watergate Apartments in Washington, DC – June 17

1973   Military draft ends – January 27
          Last American troops leave Vietnam (official end of Vietnam War, but American embassy open
              until the fall of Saigon in 1975) – March 29
          Vermont Yankee goes on line
          Jarlath attends National Outdoor Leadership School (NOLS) - summer
          Frances joins Friends' delegation to China and Vietnam
          Congress passes War Powers Resolution to limit presidential power by requiring
              Congressional approval to commit US troops to prolonged armed conflict – November 7

1974   Sam Lovejoy topples nuclear-power-associated weather-testing tower on
              Montague Plains – February 22
          President Nixon resigns; Gerald Rudolph Ford becomes president – August 8
          Lovejoy's case is thrown out at trial because of a technicality – September
          Non-binding vote against a nuclear power plant in Montague passes in Wendell, Leverett, an
              Shutesbury town meetings but not Amherst
          Energy Reorganization Act replaces Atomic Energy Commission with the
              Nuclear Regulatory Commission
          Frances leads nonviolence training at Woolman Hill
          Young Tom attends Antioch College - 1974-1977

1975   Anti –nuclear activists occupy nuclear site in Whyl, Germany
          Caltha Crowe visits Red Star Commune in China

1976   Mao Zedong dies
          James Earl "Jimmy" Carter, Jr. elected president
          Non-binding referendum in Seabrook, New Hampshire, passes to ban transportation and
              storage of nuclear fuel
          Antinuclear Clamshell Alliance holds first annual fall conference
          Clamshell Alliance occupies Seabrook Station construction site for the first time – August 1

1977   Frances among 1,414 arrested at Seabrook and spends two weeks in
         Manchester Armory - May
       Tom Crowe retires as Chief of Radiology at Cooley-Dickinson
       Radiation Oncology Unit at Cooley-Dickinson opened and named in honor of Tom Crowe
       Daniel Ellsberg, David Dellinger and others found Mobilization for Survival
       Helen Caldicott and others help reinvigorate Physicians for Social Responsibility
       Leon Sullivan proposes the Sullivan principles, corporate codes of conduct for corporations
         doing business in South Africa during apartheid
       Hampshire College votes to divest from South Africa
       Frances shows anti apartheid film to UMass trustees and they vote to divest
       UMass first university in US to vote to divest from South Africa
       Randy Kehler and Betsy Corner, husband and wife war tax resisters, announce to the Internal
         Revenue Service that they have stopped paying federal income taxes calculated to be their
         amount supporting US defense

1978   Clamshell Allliance sponsors Alternative Energy Fair at Seabrook
       UN holds first special session on disarmament; thousands rally outside
       Woolman Hill School closes
       Frances takes part in demonstrations against Steigers and Kaye Coin store for
         carrying South African products
       Meldrim Thomson, governor of New Hampshire, loses reelection
       Frances officially joins Society of Friends

1979   Frances meets with Ralph Steiger about selling blouses made in South Africa
       Sandanistas overthrow Somoza in Nicaragua
       Nuclear accident at Three-Mile Island (Pennsylvania) occurring in one of two reactors and
         rated at five of seven on International Nuclear Event Scale – March 29
       Mass rally takes place against nuclear power in Washington DC
       The movie *China Syndrome* depicts nuclear reactor meltdown
       Frances, along with other anti-nuke activists, meets with President Carter to persuade him
         not to deploy Pershing II missiles in Europe
       President Carter agrees with NATO to introduce Pershing Cruise missiles in
         Western Europe by 1983
       Soviet Union invades Afghanistan starting nine-year war
       President Carter removesStrategic Arms Limitation Treaty (SALTII) from
         consideration by Congress
       Traprock Peace Center founded
       Margaret Thatcher elected Prime Minister in Great Britain
       Ground Zero founded and sponsors the Sister City campaign
       Repressive junta comes to power in El Salvador
       France sends effigy of herself to demonstration opposing Yankee Rowe nuclear reactor
       Northampton Mobilization for Survival ad "Women for Nuclear Free Future"
         signed by 504 women
       Vigil to promote nuclear disarmament returns to Amherst Common

1980   President Carter reinstates requirements to register with the Selective Service System
       Fifty-nine of sixty-two towns that included it on the ballot vote to endorse the
           nuclear weapons freeze
       Nuclear weapons freeze, proposed for the Democratic Platform, defeated 78-51
       Ronald Wilson Reagan elected president
       Frances, Randy Kehler, and others meet with forty arms-control advocates in New York
       Plowshares 8 hammers on Minuteman missiles and throws blood on records and tools
       Guerrillas unify to fight El Salvadoran government
       Archbishop Oscar Romero assassinated in El Salvador
       Three American nuns and a lay person killed in El Salvador
       Sanctuary Movement begins
       Patrick, Frances and Tom's grandson, born

1981   Montague nuclear reactor cancelled
       Massachusetts House and Senate endorse nuclear freeze
       Frances keynote speaker at National Strategy Conference for a Nuclear Weapons Freeze
       Randy Kehler elected one of two national coordinators of newly-created
           Nuclear Weapons Freeze Campaign
       Frances arrested supporting the Freeze during a sit-down on the White House driveway
       Frances receives Peace Mother Award "for eternal vigilance on behalf of people of Guatemala,
           Nicaragua, El Salvador, Chile, Korea, South African, Namibia"
       Frances receives New England Award for Excellence in Social Justice Actions

1982   Frances arrested after throwing blood on Trident missile submarine at April 7 launch in
           Groton, Connecticut
       More than 750,000 attend nuclear weapons freeze and disarmament rally in
           New York City - June
       Massachusetts Congressmen introduce Freeze resolution; it loses 204-202 in US House
       Massachusetts Representative Edward Boland's amendment in US Congress prohibits
           military aid to Nicaragua
       Michael Dukakis elected governor of Massachusetts

1994   Frances retires as head of the regional chapter of AFSC
        Karuna Center for Peacebuilding established
        Frances joins board of Karuna Center
        UMass announces it will no longer accept biological defensive anthrax contracts

1996   Frances receives degree of honorary doctorate of humane letters from UMass
        Democracy Now! goes on the air in New York City – February 19

1997   Frances's husband Tom dies at 83 – May 2
        Philip Berrigan and six others sentenced to two years in prison for their February 12
            Prince of Peace Plowshares witness on board a US Navy guided-missile destroyer at
            Portland, Maine, Bath Iron Works – October 28

1998   Frances arrested for trespass at Sanders facility of Lockheed-Martin in
            Nashua, New Hampshire during protest of weapons manufacture there; conviction results
            in five days in New Hampshire women's prison at Goffstown
        Frances arrested for trespass during action at Raytheon facility in Andover, Massachusetts in
            March; conviction results in sentence of community service – October
        Northampton Committee to Lift the Sanctions (later changed to Northampton Committee to
            Stop the Wars) founded

1999   Thousands protest World Trade Organization in Seattle

2000   George Walker Bush elected president

2001   Terrorists fly planes into World Trade Center in New York and the Pentagon in Washington, DC
            and attempt to attack a third target – September 11
        US invades Afghanistan – October 7

2002   Frances works with a friend to re-broadcast *Democracy Now!* from her
            backyard transmitter and antenna
        US withdraws from Anti-Ballistic Missile Treaty - June

2003   Northampton Committee to Stop the War's resolution to oppose pending US invasion of Iraq
            adopted by Northampton City Council – February
        US invades Iraq –March 19
        Frances demonstrates to block gates at Westover Air Force Base

2004   Valley Free Radio obtains license to operate/assigned WXOJ-LP by the FCC
        Frances shows *Bush's Brain,* the first film in the weekly media series held in the
            community room of the Media Education Foundation in Northampton – December 3

2005   WMUA, the UMass student radio station, begins broadcasting *Democracy Now!* – February
        Frances arrested for trespass along with others in Shut It Down Affinity Group presence to
            oppose the Vermont Yankee nuclear reactor in first of more than forty demonstrations
            through 2014 at the reactor and VY headquarters

2006   Valley Free Radio (103.3 FM WXOJ) goes live in Northampton – September 6

2007   Nuclear Free Future Coalition of Western Massachusetts (later Nuclear and Carbon Free
            Coalition of Western Massachusetts) founded
        Yankee Rowe nuclear power plant completely dismantled
        Frances receives Courage of Conscience Award from Peace Abbey in
            Sherborn, Massachusetts – May 4

2008   Barack Hussein Obama elected president

2009   Amy Goodman dedicates the Frances Crowe Community Room of the
            Media Education Foundation in honor of Frances-April 3
        Frances receives Joe A. Callaway Award for Civic Courage, presented by
            The Shafeek Nader Trust for Community Interest

2010   President Obama and Russian President Dmitry Medvedev sign an arms reduction
            agreement replacing the expired START I with the "New START Treaty" – April 10
        US Senate ratifies the "New Start Treaty" – December 22

2012   Large demonstration is held at Vermont Yankee on day after expiration of VY's original
            forty-year license; more than one hundred arrested for trespass - March 22

2013   Helen Caldicott visits Shut It Down Affinity Group in Northampton before talk sponsored by
            the then Nuclear Free Future Coalition of Western Massachusetts
        Entergy announces that Vermont Yankee will shut down in late 2014
        Dusty Miller publishes first Alice Ott mystery, *Danger in the Air*

2014   Amy Goodman interviews Frances at UMass on her ninety-fifth birthday – March 15
        Dusty Miller publishes second Alice Ott mystery, *Danger at the Gates*

–compiled by Mary-Ann DeVita Palmieri

A NOTE ABOUT METHOD

The following explains the process used for Frances's memoir. Haley's, my ISBN publishing company, has produced 125 books, including a series of oral histories with veterans from the North Quabbin, where I live and Haley's is situated. Haley's has published perhaps twenty biographies or memoirs. I realize that there are vast differences in approaches to memoir. Because I was a working journalist for years and also a teacher of journalism, Haley's methodology tends more toward the journalistic than toward the historiographic. We try to be scrupulous about fact-checking (when we can discern what is so-called fact), originality, credibility, and nuance. We also attempt to encourage authors toward comprehensive reportage along with, when the author seems up to it, explication and even reflection.

Haley's routinely applies a house style predicated on *Chicago 16.* We work with a copy editor and proofreader for all books and sometimes develop house style for a given book (when we published the biography of a composer of music, for example, or when we published the veterans' histories). We attempt, when it seems advisable, to hire a copy editor whose outlook may be congenial to the author's. Usually, we follow *Chicago's* advice and insulate the author from the copy editor and vice versa. Connie Harvard filled the bill to a tee, in my opinion, for Frances's memoir, and due to the unique process devised for this book, Connie routinely met with Frances and me. Typically (and this is why I started Haley's—because I love this work), I am the substantive editor, line editor, and (when called for) manuscript developer. In most cases, in collaboration with the publishing team, I design, lay out, and format the book. We endorse teams and collaboration here and assemble a fresh team for each book. We sometimes hire cover designers, photographers, visual artists, and other professionals. Although we produced books via offset printing through 2008, we have since used the print-on-demand arm of Ingram, which therefore gives us access to the vast possibilities of their distribution system. When we release a book, I publicize it in regional media. We have a generally good relationship with regional media.

When Haley's decided with Frances in 2011 that we would publish her memoir, my friend Mary-Ann DeVita Palmieri agreed to obtain recorded interviews with Frances. Mary-Ann has often copy-edited Haley's books and wrote the biography of the composer Carolyn Brown Senier in the Haley's publication *The Mattawa Song Cycle.* Mary-Ann has dependably supported the Shut It Down Affinity Group since 2005 at Vermont Yankee. Mary-Ann and I brainstormed potential areas for interviews with Frances. Guided by the brainstorm and using few prompts, Mary-Ann did seven recorded interviews with Frances from February through April 2012 and ten recorded interviews with Frances from February through June 2013. She transcribed them and used the transcription as a basis for the manuscript. Mary-Ann also relied on a typescript of an interview with Frances done by Sarah Hunter as a student project in 2008, a typescript of a series of video interviews done by Robbie Leppzer of Turning Tide Productions around 2012, a chapter in Frances's words from Tom Weiner's 2011 Leveller's Press book, *Called to Serve Vietnam*, and transcripts of interviews done by Frances's son Tom and grandson Sean, including a *StoryCorps* interview.

Mary-Ann created a 130-page draft entirely of Frances's words in December 2012 after the first set of interviews. I reviewed that draft and suggested possible areas for questions. Mary-Ann elaborated on the suggestions and conducted clarifying interviews with Frances. Concurrently, sometimes with a friend along to assist, Mary-Ann reviewed Frances's archives at Smith College and went to Mount Holyoke to review an archive pertaining to a World War II course that Frances took. I accompanied Mary-Ann to Frances's twice in order to take photos of the many posters in her home as well as other memorabilia from Frances's activism. Mary-Ann also investigated the quality of memoir and discussed memoir techniques and emphases with her friend Mira Bartok, a recent winner of the Book Critics Circle award for memoir.

After processing information from fresh answers as well as from time with the archives, Mary-Ann developed a second draft in November 2013 organized around the areas of Frances's interests. About the same time, Mary-Ann, Frances, and I lit on the title for the memoir, *Finding My Radical Soul*. We developed fund-raising (including a successful KickStarter), sponsorship, and pre-sale campaigns.

Seven people, including Frances, her daughter Caltha, and several of Frances's friends and associates (some who, like Frances, have served jail time for civil resistance) reviewed the November 2013 draft. I collated the results and revised them into a new draft manuscript in April 2014 and began meeting with Frances nearly every week for further interviews. At the same time, we developed the cover in consultation with Frances and the manuscript readers. Through interactions with the manuscript readers, we realized there were many omissions of events as well as many inaccuracies. As an experienced ghost writer, I translated information from my own interviews with Frances as well as information picked up from interviews with others and reading in primary sources. A great late find was a set of appointment calendars Frances kept from 1954-1969.

Frances reviewed every word as the manuscript evolved. The manuscript and subsequent layout went back and forth with her at least four times. Frances values this effort to transform her spoken words in to written words that she claims as her own. In August 2014, after Mary-Ann and I visited the UMass archives for information about the Northampton vigils, I re-revised the manuscript to 185 pages with no graphics. During the re-revision, Frances, Mary-Ann, and I collaborated around the theme of "finding Frances's radical soul" on wording for chapter transitions.

Frances, Mary-Ann, Connie, and Caltha reviewed the manuscript at every stage. Caltha clarified genealogical information and conferred with her brothers and other family members about facts and useful family insights. I collated the results and introduced the manuscript to a layout program. Connie, Mary-Ann, Frances, Caltha, and I were in frequent communication as we worked to bring this memoir to fruition. The layout includes photos, diagrams, images of posters, and a timeline created by Mary-Ann. Frances, Connie, Caltha, Mary-Ann, and I reviewed the entire layout until we believed it was ready for printing, when proofreaders Anneke Corbett and Susan B. Lantz did a review on a very tight turnaround.

Our basis for fact-checking was the simplest of journalistic approaches: corroboration by three sources, although sometimes corroboration of memory is impossible.

Despite the number of us at work on this memoir, each of us has committed herself to facilitating Frances's satisfaction with her words regardless of how they are generated. This is to explain that nothing lives for publication unless Frances approved it and accepted it as what she wants to say.

—*Marcia Gagliardi, publisher*
Haley's

ABOUT THE AUTHOR

Longtime pacifist Frances Crowe counseled more than fifteen hundred conscientious objectors during the Vietnam War. With her husband, physician Tom Crowe, Frances began resisting nuclear weapons the day the United States dropped the atomic bomb on Hiroshima. She is noted for her witness against war and weapons.

Tireless advocate for peace and justice and a Quaker, Frances heeds her conscience. A compelling influence in the Pioneer Valley of Massachusetts, Frances has encouraged others for more than six decades to discern the truth of their own consciences.

For many years the face of Western Massachusetts American Friends Service Committee, Frances has spearheaded countless campaigns to encourage truth in the communities of humankind.

Frances resides in Northampton. She has three adult children and five grandchildren. She spends her days gathering her food, cooking, exercising, and sustaining herself: reading, thinking, organizing, and acting. Always acting.

ABOUT THE FOREWORD AUTHOR

Amy Goodman is the host and executive producer of *Democracy Now!*, a national, daily, independent, award-winning news program airing on more than twelve hundred public television and radio stations worldwide. *Time Magazine* named *Democracy Now!* its "Pick of the Podcasts," along with NBC's *Meet the Press*.

Goodman is the first journalist to receive the Right Livelihood Award, widely known as the Alternative Nobel Prize for "developing an innovative model of truly independent grassroots political journalism that brings to millions of people the alternative voices that are often excluded by the mainstream media." She is the first co-recipient of the Park Center for Independent Media's Izzy Award, named for the great muckraking journalist I.F. Stone. *The Independent* of London called Amy Goodman and *Democracy Now!* "an inspiration." PULSE named her one of the 20 Top Global Media Figures of 2009.

Goodman's fifth book, *The Silenced Majority: Stories of Uprisings, Occupations, Resistance, and Hope*, written with Denis Moynihan, rose to Number 11 on *The New York Times* bestseller list. This timely follow-up to her fourth *New York Times* bestseller, *Breaking the Sound Barrier*, gives voice to the many ordinary people standing up to corporate and government power. She co-authored the first three bestsellers with her brother, journalist David Goodman: *Standing Up to the Madness: Ordinary Heroes in Extraordinary Times* (2008), *Static: Government Liars, Media Cheerleaders, and the People Who Fight Back* (2006) and *The Exception to the Rulers: Exposing Oily Politicians, War Profiteers, and the Media That Love Them* (2004). She writes a weekly column (also produced as an audio podcast) syndicated by King Features, for which she was recognized in 2007 with the James Aronson Award for Social Justice Reporting.

Goodman has received the American Women in Radio and Television Gracie Award; the Paley Center for Media's She's Made It Award; and the Puffin/Nation Prize for Creative Citizenship. Her reporting on East Timor and Nigeria has won numerous awards, including the George Polk Award, Robert F. Kennedy Prize for International Reporting, and the Alfred I. duPont-Columbia Award. She has also received awards from the Associated Press, United Press International, the Corporation for Public Broadcasting, and Project Censored. Goodman received the first ever Communication for Peace Award from the World Association for Christian Communication. She was also honored by the National Council of Teachers of English with the George Orwell Award for Distinguished Contribution to Honesty and Clarity in Public Language.

FRANCES'S ACKNOWLEDGMENTS

I am grateful to my family for their loving support. I am enormously proud of the kind of people they have become and of their commitment to justice and service. Thank you to my husband Tom; our children Caltha, Jarlath, and Tommy; and our grandchildren Patrick, Rosa, Simone, Sean, and Tomas.

Thank you for inspiration and nourishment to organizations such as American Friends Service Committee, Atlantic Life Community/Jonah House, Catholic Worker movement, Citizens Awareness Network, Fellowship of Reconciliation, Global Network Against Nuclear Power and Weapons in Space, National War Tax Resistance Coordinating Committee, New England Coalition, and Northampton Committee to End the Wars.

Also, Nuclear and Carbon Free Future Coalition of Western Massachusetts, *Nuclear Resister*, Nuclear Watch, Nuclear Weapons Freeze Campaign, Religious Society of Friends (Quakers), Safe and Green Campaign, SAGE, School of the Americas Watch, Shut It Down Affinity Group, War Resisters League, Witness for Peace, Women's Congress for Peace, Women's International League for Peace and Freedom, and The Women's Movement.

Thank you to individuals including Medea Benjamin, Philip Berrigan, Helen Caldicott, Noam Chomsky, John Dear, Bruce Gagnon, Joseph Gerson, Amy Goodman, Bishop Thomas Gumbleton, Chris Hedges, Trudy Huntington, Russell Johnson, Randy Kehler, Naomi Klein, Ralph Nader, Wally and Juanita Nelson, Hattie Nestel, John Pilger, Jonathan Schell, Josh Silver, John and Carrie Schuchardt, Paki Wieland, Plowshares Activists, and John Woolman.

Thank you to student interns in the AFSC office Nazir Ahmad, Ruth Benn, Frida Berrigan, John Bonifaz, Dierdre Cornell, Rachel King, and Denise Mock.

Thank you to American Friends Service Committee working groups including Michael Holyrode and Nancy Talanian on Southern Africa; Lois Ahrens,Jean Allen, Barbara Kelly, Julliette Rapaport, and Susan Thiola on Central American; and Andrea Ayvaszian and Ruth Benn on Disarmament.

Thank you to the Area Support Committee including David Kielson, Arky Markham, Wendy Saviano, and the many volunteers who helped.

Thank you to those along the way, including Beverly Duncan, Bella Halstad, Claudia Lefko, Jim Levey, E. Jefferson Murphy, and "Pat."

Thank you to Mary-Ann DeVita Palmieri, Marcia Gagliardi, and Connie Harvard for assistance in preparing my memoir for publication.

And a special acknowledgment to all the war victims, living and dead.

MARY-ANN'S ACKNOWLEDGMENTS

My thanks go to, first of all,

Frances for the life she has led and her willingness to share her story

Marcia Gagliardi who initiated this project and worked on it at every stage

Frances's family, especially her daughter, Caltha, who has read and reread the many drafts that we generated and her son Tom and grandson Sean who made available typescripts of interviews they did with their mother and grandmother

Tom Weiner who generously allowed me to use Frances' words from his book *Called to Serve: The Stories of the Men and Women Confronted by the Vietnam War Draft*

Robbie Leppzer who made available to me the typescript of interviews he has done with Frances in the making of a video on Vermont Yankee and whose videos of Seabrook actions and other local events proved invaluable in providing background

Sarah Hunter who gave me permission to use Frances's words from the typescript of an interview she did of Frances for an oral history she made as a student in 2008

Mike Kirby for forwarding to me information on "Take Off the Boards"

Dan Keller for clearing up some inaccuracies and for lending me videos his company made of local actions and events, especially *Lovejoy's Nuclear War*

Robert Surbrug, Jr. whose book *Beyond Vietnam: The Politics of Protest in Massachusetts, 1974-1990* provided invaluable information about that period

the staff at the Smith College archives who were very welcoming as I navigated the seventy-five plus boxes of Frances's materials and to Ellen Woodbury who accompanied me in an early visit

the staff at the Mount Holyoke archives who provided me access to specific information related to Frances's time at a post-World War II summer institute and to the staff at UMass archives where artifacts of the Northampton Committee to Stop the Wars are stored

my daughter Crissy and husband Tony who patiently read an early draft and gave me insightful feedback

MARCIA'S ACKNOWLEDGMENTS

Thanks to

Mary-Ann DeVita Palmieri for her focused and dedicated pursuit of recorded interviews with Frances, preparation of early manuscripts, conceptualization of Frances's memoir as it now appears, and dependable advice, consideration, and care

Connie Harvard for endless support at every turn and diligent, intelligent, and appropriate copy editing

Caltha Crowe for thoughtful review at every stage

Claudia Lefko and Joan Braderman for early design ideas

Susan B. Lantz and Anneke Corbett for graciously proofreading at the very last minute

Denis Moynihan and Amy Goodman for cordiality and professional support

Sponsors and donors for generous financial assistance

the Shut It Down Affinity Group for warmth, generosity, and care

Pat Hynes for encouragement and wisdom

Hattie Nestel for perspective, understanding, and always "being there"

Ann Gagliardi, Jane Gagliardi, and Susan Gagliardi for unflinching, pertinent, and valuable advice whenever I asked

and, of course, Frances for unfailing diligence, spirit, and inspiration

With thanks to generous individual donors

Sue Ablao
Anonymous
Ruth Benn
Suzanne Carlson
Anthony Chan
Claire Chang
Felice Cohen-Joppa
Roger Conant
Margo Culley
Dorthee (her full name)
John and Georgianna Foster
Jeanne Gallo
Carol Gilbert, OP
Kay Gleason
Andy Grant
Bruce and Ruth Hawkins
Jim Herbert
Ken and Jan Hoffman
Barbara Huntington
Lissa Kiernan
Sam Koplinka-Loehr
Patricia Larson
Susan Lantz
Linda LeTendre
George and Ann Levinger
Emily Lewis

Elizabeth McAlister
Bob McCormick
Joy McNulty
Anne Moore
Genny Morley
Hattie Nestel
Carolyn Toll Oppenheim
Linda Overing
Paula Green and Jim Perkins
Ardeth Platte, OP
Niki Rosen
Nelia Sargent
Craig Simpson
Dade Singapuri and Al Cohen
Kate Stevens
Don Stone
Alice Swift
Nicholas Thaw
Linda M. Thurston
James and Mary Todd
Ulrike von Moltke
Ellen Woodbury
David Zackon
Al Zook
Sarah W. Zorn

Organizational sponsors are listed on Pages iv and v

*Paul Shoul's photo captures Frances with a Claudia Lefko banner
that poses Frances's perennial challenging question*

CPSIA information can be obtained
at www.ICGtesting.com
Printed in the USA
BVOW07s0858230716

456563BV00007B/21/P